Science and Technology in Mass Communication

Concepts, Systems and Processes

Biswajeet Guha

KANISHKA PUBLISHERS, DISTRIBUTORS
NEW DELHI-110 002

KANISHKA PUBLISHERS, DISTRIBUTORS
4697/5-21A, Ansari Road, Daryaganj
New Delhi-110 002
Phones : 2327 0497, 2328 8285
Fax : 011-2328 8285
e-mail: kanishka_publishing@yahoo.co.in

First Published 2009

ISBN 978-81-8457-160-8

PRINTED IN INDIA

Published by Madan Sachdeva for Kanishka Publishers, Distributors, 4697/5-21A, Ansari Road, Daryaganj, New Delhi-110 002; Typeset by Sunshine Graphics, Delhi, and Printed at Rajdhani Printers, Delhi.

Preface

This publication provides readers with an introductory overview of basic concepts, tools and techniques applied in the subject areas of mass media, mass communication and journalism. The whole science and technology applicable in this area of study is covered with focus on various concepts, systems and processes. The book will serve the purpose of an introductory reference book on the subject covering such a wide spectrum. An introductory overview of photography is provided with focus on history, types and styles. Understanding the composition of camera and its movement is presented. The issue of digital versus film photography is debated. The documentary photography is elaborated with the help of a case study of "Skill set". Major areas in photography and film career are identified. Focus also lies on coding and encoding techniques of videography and video equipments. The subject areas of video display standards, videotapes, video connectors, MPEGs, ATSC standards, codecs and other systems. It also focuses on related resolution and application issues. Mobile TV and countries using ATSC systems are covered. This publication also covers the concepts, tools and techniques of cinematography, film editing and filmmaking. Other areas which have been highlighted in this publication include film, film production overview, film pre-production and film post-production. Introduction to film scoring, blocking, programme continuity, video-shooting, screenplay, etc. are made. Similarly, themes like basic filmmaking by high school drama departments, character animation, digital puppet animation, directing actors, slate management and keeping the crew happy are addressed in depth. The new subject areas of digital cinema and digital cinematography are also discussed in brief. A brief overview is also provided about both normal and digital telephony. With special focus on digital technology and process, the subject areas of broadcasting and digital video broadcasting are covered. Special highlight has been made that of ISDB, ISDB-S and ISDB-T. Various kinds of wireless communication systems have been covered with special attention given to wireless local loop, Wi-Fi, network security, bluetooth and GSM interworking profile. The areas of discussion also include enhanced digital cordless telecommunication systems and health impacts of wireless electronic devices. Last, but not the least, an overview is also provided to that of sound recording and reproduction, and digital audio broadcasting. An extensive bibliography has been provided to make this book a research oriented one after itself providing a strong basic conceptual understanding of the science and technology being applied in the modern areas of mass communication.

Biswajeet Guha

Contents

1

Photography: An Introductory Overview

INTRODUCTION

Photography is the process of recording pictures by means of capturing light on a light-sensitive medium, such as a film or electronic sensor. Light patterns reflected or emitted from objects expose a sensitive silver halide based chemical or electronic medium during a timed exposure, usually through a photographic lens in a device known as a camera that also stores the resulting information chemically or electronically. The word "photography" comes from the French *photographie* which is based on the Greek words φως *phos* ("light"), and γραφις *graphis* ("stylus", "paintbrush") or γραφη *graphê* ("representation by means of lines" or "drawing"), together meaning "drawing with light." Traditionally, the product of photography has been called a *photograph*, commonly shortened to photo.

Photographic Cameras/Instruments

The camera or camera obscura is the image-forming device, and photographic film or a silicon electronic image sensor is the sensing medium. The respective recording medium can be the film itself, or a digital electronic or magnetic memory. Photographers control the camera and lens to "expose" the light recording material (such as film) to the required amount of light to form a "latent image" (on film) or "raw fiie" (in digital cameras) which, after appropriate processing, is converted to a usable image. Modern digital cameras replace film with an electronic image sensor based on light-sensitive electronics such as charge-coupled device (CCD) or complementary metal-oxide-semiconductor (CMOS) technology. The resulting digital image is stored electronically, but can be reproduced on paper or film. The controls usually include but are not limited to the following:

Focus of the Lens

(a) *Aperture of the lens*—adjustment of the iris, measured as f-number, which controls the amount of light entering the lens. Aperture also has an effect on focus and depth of field, namely, the smaller the opening [aperture], the less light but the greater the depth of field—that is, the greater the range within which objects appear to be sharply focused.

(b) *Shutter speed*—adjustment of the speed (often expressed either as fractions of seconds or as an angle, with mechanical shutters) of the shutter to control the amount of time during which the imaging medium is exposed to light for each exposure. Shutter speed may be used to control the amount of light striking the image plane; 'faster' shutter speeds (that is, those of shorter duration) decrease both the amount of light and the amount of image blurring from subject motion or camera motion.

(c) *White balance*—on digital cameras, electronic compensation for the colour temperature associated with a given set of lighting conditions, ensuring that white light is registered as such on the imaging chip and therefore that the colours in the frame will appear natural. On mechanical, film-based cameras, this function is served by the operator's choice of film stock. In addition to using white balance to register natural colouration of the image, photographers may employ white balance to aesthetic end, for example white balancing to a blue object in order to obtain a warm colour temperature.

(d) *Metering*—measurement of exposure at a midtone so that highlights and shadows are exposed according to the photographer's wishes. Many modern cameras feature this ability, though it is traditionally accomplished with the use of a separate light metering device.

(e) *ISO speed*—traditionally used to set the film speed of the selected film on film cameras, ISO speeds are employed on modern digital cameras as an indication of the system's gain from light to numerical output and to control the automatic exposure system. A correct combination of ISO speed, aperture, and shutter speed leads to an image that is neither too dark nor too light.

(*f*) *Auto-focus point*—on some cameras, the selection of a point in the imaging frame upon which the auto-focus system will attempt to focus. Many Single-lens reflex cameras (SLR) feature multiple auto-focus points in the viewfinder.

Many other elements of the imaging device itself may have a pronounced effect on the quality and/or aesthetic effect of a given photograph; among them are:

(*i*) *Focal length and type of lens* (telephoto, macro, wide angle, fisheye, or zoom).
(*ii*) *Filters or scrims* placed between the subject and the light recording material, either in front of or behind the lens.
(*iii*) Inherent sensitivity of the medium to light intensity and colour/wavelengths.
(*iv*) The nature of the light recording material, for example its resolution as measured in pixels or grains of silver halide.

Photographic Exposure and Rendering

Camera controls are inter-related, the total amount of light reaching the film plane (the "exposure") changes with the duration of exposure, aperture of the lens, and focal length of the lens (which changes as the lens is zoomed). Changing any of these controls alters the exposure. Many cameras may be set to adjust most or all of these controls automatically. This automatic functionality is useful in many situations, and in most situations to occasional photographers. The duration of an exposure is referred to as shutter speed, often even in cameras that don't have a physical shutter, and is typically measured in fractions of a second. Aperture is expressed by an f-number or f-stop (derived from focal ratio), which is proportional to the ratio of the focal length to the diameter of the aperture. If the f-number is decreased by a factor of aperture, the aperture diameter is increased by the same factor, and its area is increased by a factor of 2. The f-stops that might be found on a typical lens include 2.8, 4, 5.6, 8, 11, 16, 22, 32, where going up "one stop" (using lower f-stop numbers) doubles the amount of light reaching the film, and stopping down one stop halves the amount of light.

Exposures can be achieved through various combinations of shutter speed and aperture. For example, f/8 at 8 ms (=1/125th of a second) and f/5.6 at 4 ms (=1/250th of a second) yield the same amount of light. The chosen combination has an impact on the final result. In addition to the subject or camera movement that might vary depending on the shutter speed, the aperture (and focal length of the lens) determine the depth of field, which refers to the range of distances from the lens that will be in focus. For example, using a long lens and a large aperture (f/2.8, for example), a subject's eyes might be in sharp focus, but not the tip of the nose. With a smaller aperture (f/22), or a shorter lens, both the subject's eyes and nose can be in focus. With very small apertures, such as pinholes, a wide range of distance can be brought into focus.

Image capture is only part of the image forming process. Regardless of material, some process must be employed to render the latent image captured by the camera into the final photographic work. This process consists of two steps, development, and printing.

During the printing process, modifications can be made to the print by several controls. Many of these controls are similar to controls during image capture, while some are exclusive to the printing process. Most controls have equivalent digital concepts, but some create different effects. For example, dodging and burning controls are different between digital and film processes. Other printing modifications include:

(*i*) Chemicals and process used during film development
(*ii*) Duration of exposure—equivalent to shutter speed
(*iii*) Printing aperture—equivalent to aperture, but has no effect on depth of field
(*iv*) Contrast
(*v*) Dodging—reduces exposure of certain print areas, resulting in lighter areas
(*vi*) Burning—increases exposure of certain areas, resulting in darker areas
(*vii*) Paper quality—glossy, matte, etc.
(*viii*) Paper size

Uses

Photography gained the interest of many scientists and artists from its inception. Scientists have used photography to record and study movements, such as Eadweard Muybridge's study of human and animal locomotion in 1887. Artists are equally interested by these aspects but also try to explore avenues other than the photo-mechanical representation of reality, such as the pictorialist movement. Military, police, and security forces use photography for surveillance, recognition and data storage. Photography is used to preserve memories of favourite times, to capture special moments, to tell stories, to send messages, and as a source of entertainment. Commercial advertising relies heavily on photography and has contributed greatly to its development.

HISTORY

Photography is the result of combining several technical discoveries. Long before the first photographs were made, Ibn al-Haytham (Alhazen) (965–1040) invented the camera obscura and pinhole camera, Albertus Magnus (1193–1280) discovered silver nitrate, and Georges Fabricius (1516–1571) discovered silver chloride. Daniel Barbaro described a diaphragm in 1568. Wilhelm Homberg described how light darkened some chemicals (photochemical effect) in 1694. The fiction book Giphantie (by the French Thiphaigne de La Roche, 1729-1774) described what can be interpreted as photography.

Photography as a usable process goes back to the 1820s with the development of chemical photography. The first permanent photograph was an image produced in 1826 by the French inventor Nicéphore Niépce. However, the picture took eight hours to expose, so he went about trying to find a new process. Working in conjunction with Louis Daguerre, they experimented with silver compounds based on a Johann Heinrich Schultz discovery in 1724 that a silver and chalk mixture darkens when exposed to light. Niépce died in 1833, but Daguerre continued the work, eventually culminating with the development of the Daguerreotype in 1839.

Meanwhile, Hercules Florence had already created a very similar process in 1832, naming it *Photographie*, and William Fox

Talbot had earlier discovered another means to fix a silver process image but had kept it secret. After reading about Daguerre's invention, Talbot refined his process so that it might be fast enough to take photographs of people. By 1840, Talbot had invented the calotype process, which creates negative images. John Herschel made many contributions to the new methods. He invented the cyanotype process, now familiar as the "blueprint." He was the first to use the terms "photography", "negative" and "positive." He discovered sodium thiosulphate solution to be a solvent of silver halides in 1819, and informed Talbot and Daguerre of his discovery in 1839 that it could be used to "fix" pictures and make them permanent. He made the first glass negative in late 1839. In 1851, Frederick Scott Archer published his findings in "The Chemist" on the wet plate Collodion process. This became the most widely used process between 1852 and the late 1880s when the dry plate was introduced. There are three subsets to the Collodion process; the Ambrotype (positive image on glass), the Ferrotype or Tintype (positive image on metal), and the negative which was printed on Albumen or Salt paper. Many advances in photographic glass plates and printing were made in through the nineteenth century. In 1884, George Eastman developed the technology of film to replace photographic plates, leading to the technology used by film cameras today.

TYPE

Black-and-White

All photography was originally monochrome, or *black-and-white*. Even after colour film was readily available, black-and-white photography continued to dominate for decades, due to its lower cost and its "classic" photographic look. It is important to note that some monochromatic pictures are not always pure blacks and whites but contain other hues depending on the process. The Cyanotype process produces an image of blue and white for example. Many photographers continue to produce some monochrome images. Some full colour digital images are processed using a variety of techniques to create black and whites, and some cameras have even been produced to exclusively shoot monochrome.

Colour

Colour photography was explored beginning in the mid 1800s. Early experiments in colour could not fix the photograph and prevent the colour from fading. The first permanent colour photo was taken in 1861 by the physicist James Clerk Maxwell.

One of the early methods of taking colour photos was to use three cameras. Each camera would have a colour filter in front of the lens. This technique provides the photographer with the three basic channels required to recreate a colour image in a darkroom or processing plant. Russian photographer Sergei Mikhailovich Prokudin-Gorskii developed another technique, with three colour plates taken in quick succession. Practical application of the technique was held back by the very limited colour response of early film; however, in the early 1900s, following the work of photo-chemists such as H.W. Vogel, emulsions with adequate sensitivity to green and red light at last became available. The first colour plate, Autochrome, invented by the French Lumière brothers, reached the market in 1907. It was based on a 'screen-plate' filter made of dyed dots of potato starch, and was the only colour film on the market until German Agfa introduced the similar Agfacolour in 1932. In 1935, American Kodak introduced the first modern ('integrated tri-pack') colour film, Kodachrome, based on three coloured emulsions. This was followed in 1936 by Agfa's Agfacolour Neue. Unlike the Kodachrome tri-pack process the colour couplers in Agfacolour Neue were integral with the emulsion layers, which greatly simplified the film processing. Most modern colour films, except Kodachrome, are based on the Agfacolour Neue technology. Instant colour film was introduced by Polaroid in 1963.

Colour photography may form images as a positive transparency, intended for use in a slide projector or as colour negatives, intended for use in creating positive colour enlargements on specially coated paper. The latter is now the most common form of film (non-digital) colour photography owing to the introduction of automated photoprinting equipment.

Digital

Traditional photography burdened photographers working at remote locations without easy access to processing facilities, and competition from television pressured photographers to deliver images to newspapers with greater speed. Photo journalists at remote locations often carried miniature photo labs and a means of transmitting images through telephone lines. In 1981, Sony unveiled the first consumer camera to use a charge-coupled device for imaging, eliminating the need for film: the Sony Mavica. While the Mavica saved images to disk, the images were displayed on television, and the camera was not fully digital. In 1990, Kodak unveiled the DCS 100, the first commercially available digital camera. Although its high cost precluded uses other than photojournalism and professional photography, commercial digital photography was born.

Digital imaging uses an electronic image sensor to record the image as a set of electronic data rather than as chemical changes on film. The primary difference between digital and chemical photography is that analog photography resists manipulation because it involves film, optics and photographic paper, while digital imaging is a highly manipulative medium. This difference allows for a degree of image post-processing that is comparatively difficult in film-based photography and permits different communicative potentials and applications. Digital imaging is rapidly replacing film photography in consumer and professional markets. Digital point-and-shoot cameras have become widespread consumer products, outselling film cameras, and including new features such as video and audio recording. Kodak announced in January 2004 that it would no longer produce reloadable 35 mm cameras after the end of that year. This was interpreted as a sign of the end of film photography. However, Kodak was at that time a minor player in the reloadable film cameras market. In January 2006, Nikon followed suit and announced that they will stop the production of all but two models of their film cameras: the low-end Nikon FM10, and the high-end Nikon F6. On May 25, 2006, Canon announced they will stop developing new film SLR cameras.

Because photography is popularly synonymous with truth ("The camera doesn't lie"), digital imaging has raised many ethical concerns. Many photojournalists have declared they will not crop their pictures, or are forbidden from combining elements of multiple photos to make "illustrations," passing them as real photographs. Many courts will not accept digital images as evidence because of their inherently manipulative nature. Today's technology has made picture editing relatively easy for even the novice photographer.

STYLE

Commercial

The commercial photographic world can be broken down to:

(*a*) *Advertising photography*: Photographs made to illustrate and usually sell a service or product. These images are generally done with an advertising agency, design firm or with an in-house corporate design team.

(*b*) *Fashion and glamour photography*: This type of photography usually incorporates models. Fashion photography emphasizes the clothes or product, glamour emphasizes the model. Glamour photography is popular in advertising and in men's magazines. Models in glamour photography may be nude, but this is not always the case.

(*c*) *Crime scene photography*: This type of photography consists of photographing scenes of crime such as robberies and murders. A black-and-white camera or an infrared camera may be used to capture specific details.

(*d*) Still life photography usually depicts inanimate subject matter, typically commonplace objects which may be either natural or man-made.

(*e*) Food photography can be used for editorial, packaging or advertising use. Food photography is similar to still life photography, but requires some special skills.

(*f*) *Editorial photography*: Photographs made to illustrate a story or idea within the context of a magazine. These are usually assigned by the magazine.

(*g*) *Photojournalism*: This can be considered a subset of editorial photography. Photographs made in this context are accepted as a documentation of a news story.

(*h*) *Portrait and wedding Photography*: photographs made and sold directly to the end user of the images.

(*i*) *Fine art photography*: Photographs made to fulfil a vision, and reproduced to be sold directly to the customer.

(*j*) *Landscape photography*: Photographs of different locations made to be sold to tourists as postcards.

(*k*) *Wildlife photography* that demonstrates life of the animals.

The market for photographic services demonstrates the

aphorism "one picture is worth a thousand words," which has an interesting basis in the history of photography. Magazines and newspapers, companies putting up websites, advertising agencies and other groups pay for photography.

Many people take photographs for self-fulfillment or for commercial purposes. Organizations with a budget and a need for photography have several options: they can assign a member of the organization or hire someone to shoot exactly what they want, run a public competition, or obtain rights to stock photographs either through traditional stock giants, such as Getty Images, Corbis, or through smaller microstock agencies, such as Fotolia.

As an Art Form

During the twentieth century, both fine art photography and documentary photography became accepted by the English-speaking art world and the gallery system. In the United States, a handful of photographers, including Alfred Stieglitz, Edward Steichen, John Szarkowski, and Edward Weston, spent their lives advocating for photography as a fine art. At first, fine art photographers tried to imitate painting styles. This movement is called Pictorialism, often using soft focus for a dreamy, 'romantic' look. In reaction to that, Weston, Ansel Adams, and others formed the f/64 Group to advocate 'straight photography', the photograph as a (sharply focused) thing in itself and not an imitation of something else.

The aesthetics of photography is a matter that continues to be discussed regularly, especially in artistic circles. Many artists argued that photography was the mechanical reproduction of an image. If photography is authentically art, then photography in the context of art would need redefinition, such as determining what component of a photograph makes it beautiful to the viewer. The controversy began with the earliest images "written with light"; Nicéphore Niépce, Louis Daguerre, and others among the very earliest photographers were met with acclaim, but some questioned if their work met the definitions and purposes of art.

Clive Bell in his classic essay Art states that only "significant form" can distinguish art from what is not art.

> "There must be some one quality without which a work of art cannot exist; possessing which, in the least degree, no work is

altogether worthless. What is this quality? What quality is shared by all objects that provoke our aesthetic emotions? What quality is common to Sta. Sophia and the windows at Chartres, Mexican sculpture, a Persian bowl, Chinese carpets, Giotto's frescoes at Padua, and the masterpieces of Poussin, Piero della Francesca, and Cezanne? Only one answer seems possible—significant form. In each, lines and colours combined in a particular way, certain forms and relations of forms, stir our aesthetic emotions."

Technical

The camera has a long and distinguished history as a means of recording phenomena from the first use by Daguerre and Fox-Talbot, such as astronomical events (eclipses for example) and small creatures when the camera was attached to the eyepiece of microscopes (in photomicroscopy). The camera also proved useful in recording crime scenes and the scenes of accidents, one of the first uses being at the scene of the Tay Rail Bridge disaster of 1879. The set of accident photographs was used in the subsequent court of inquiry so that witnesses could identify pieces of the wreckage, and the technique is now commonplace in courts of law.

Other Image Forming Techniques

Besides the camera, other methods of forming images with light are available. For instance, a photocopy or xerography machine forms permanent images but uses the transfer of static electrical charges rather than photographic film, hence the term electrophotography. Photograms are images produced by the shadows of objects cast on the photographic paper, without the use of a camera. Objects can also be placed directly on the glass of an image scanner to produce digital pictures.

CAMERA

A camera is a device used to capture images, either as still photographs or as sequences of moving images (movies or videos). The term comes from the Latin *camera obscura* for "dark chamber" for an early mechanism of projecting images where an entire room functioned as a real-time imaging system; the modern camera evolved from the camera obscura.

Cameras may work with the light of the visible spectrum or with other portions of the electromagnetic spectrum. A camera generally consists of an enclosed hollow with an opening (aperture) at one end for light to enter, and a recording or viewing surface for capturing the light at the other end. Most cameras have a lens positioned in front of the camera's opening to gather the incoming light and focus all or part of the image on the recording surface. The diameter of the aperture is often controlled by a diaphragm mechanism, but some cameras have a fixed-size aperture.

Exposure Control

The size of the aperture and the brightness of the scene control the amount of light that enters the camera during a period of time, and the shutter controls the length of time that the light hits the recording surface. Equivalent exposures can be made with a larger aperture and a faster shutter speed or a corresponding smaller aperture and with the shutter speed slowed down.

Focus

Due to the optical properties of photographic lenses, only objects within a certain range of distances from the camera will be reproduced clearly. The process of adjusting this range is known as changing the camera's focus. There are various ways of focusing a camera accurately. The simplest cameras have fixed focus and use a small aperture and wide-angle lens to ensure that everything within a certain range of distance from the lens, usually around 3 metres (10 ft) to infinity, is in reasonable focus. Fixed focus cameras are usually inexpensive types, such as single-use cameras. The camera can also have a limited focusing range or scale-focus that is indicated on the camera body. The user will guess or calculate the distance to the subject and adjust the focus accordingly. On some cameras this is indicated by symbols (head-and-shoulders; two people standing upright; one tree; mountains).

Rangefinder cameras allow the distance to objects to be measured by means of a coupled parallax unit on top of the camera, allowing the focus to be set with accuracy. Single-lens reflex cameras allow the photographer to determine the focus and composition visually using the objective lens and a moving mirror to project the image onto a ground glass or plastic micro-prism screen. Twin-lens reflex cameras use an objective lens and a focusing lens unit (usually identical to the objective lens) in a parallel body for composition and focusing. View cameras use a ground glass screen which is removed and replaced by either a photographic plate or a reusable holder containing sheet film before exposure. Modern cameras often offer autofocus systems to focus the camera automatically by a variety of methods.

Image Capture

Traditional cameras capture light onto photographic film or photographic plate. Video and digital cameras use electronics, usually a charge coupled device (CCD) or sometimes a CMOS sensor to capture images which can be transferred or stored in tape or computer memory inside the camera for later playback or processing.

Cameras that capture many images in sequence are known as movie cameras or as ciné cameras in Europe; those designed for single images are still cameras. However, these categories overlap, as still cameras are often used to capture moving images in special effects work and modern digital cameras are often able to trivially switch between still and motion recording modes. A video camera is a category of movie camera that captures images electronically (either using analogue or digital technology).

A Stereo camera can take photographs that appear "three-dimensional" by taking two different photographs that can be combined to create the illusion of depth in the composite image. Stereo cameras for making 3D prints or slides have two lenses side by side. Stereo cameras for making lenticular prints have 3, 4, 5, or even more lenses. Some film cameras feature date imprinting devices that can print a date on the negative itself.

History

The forerunner to the camera was the camera obscura. The camera obscura is an instrument consisting of a darkened chamber or box, into which light is admitted through a double convex lens, forming an image of external objects on a surface of paper or glass, etc., placed at the focus of the lens. The camera obscura was first invented by the Iraqi scientist Ibn al-Haytham (Alhazen) as described in his *Book of Optics* (1015-1021). English scientist Robert Boyle and his assistant Robert Hooke later developed a portable camera obscura in the 1660s.

The first camera that was small and portable enough to be practical for photography was built by Johann Zahn in 1685, though it would be almost 150 years before technology caught up to the point where this was practical. Early photographic cameras were essentially similar to Zahn's model, though usually with the addition of sliding boxes for focusing. Before each exposure, a sensitized plate would be inserted in front of the viewing screen to record the image. Jacques Daguerre's popular daguerreo type process utilized copper plates, while the calo type process invented by William Fox Talbot recorded images on paper.

The first permanent photograph was made in 1826 by Joseph Nicéphore Niépce using a sliding wooden box camera made by Charles and Vincent Chevalier in Paris. Niépce built on a discovery by Johann Heinrich Schultz (1724): a silver and chalk mixture darkens under exposure to light. However, while this was the birth of photography, the camera itself can be traced back much further. Before the invention of photography, there was no way to preserve the images produced by these cameras apart from manually tracing them. The development of the collodion wet plate process by Frederick Scott Archer in 1850 cut exposure times dramatically, but required photographers to prepare and develop their glass plates on the spot, usually in a mobile darkroom. Despite their complexity, the wet-plate ambrotype and tintype processes were in widespread use in the latter half of the 19th century. Wet plate cameras were little different from previous designs, though there were some models, such as the sophisticated Dubroni of 1864, where the sensitizing and developing of the plates could be carried out inside the camera itself rather than in a separate darkroom. Other cameras were fitted with multiple lenses for making cartes de visite. It was during the wet plate era that the use of bellows for focusing became widespread.

The first colour photograph was made by James Clerk Maxwell, with the help of Thomas Sutton, in 1861.

Image Gallery

Contax S—the world's first pentaprism SLR

Asahiflex IIa of 1955

Kodak Retina IIIC of 1957

Nikon F of 1959—the first 35 mm system camera

Voigtländer Vitoret of 1962

Silvestri Flexicam

Opened up Cine Kodak, used 35 mm movie film

Voigtländer Brillant twin-lens reflex camera

1921 Kodak

1952 Voigtländer Vito

Overview

Camera basics will introduce you to different types of cameras, explain the different parts of a camera, show you how to use a camera, and a give you a glossary of camera terms. Beyond just taking photographs, photographers need to know about the legal issues. While the legal issues vary greatly depending on circumstances and location, there is some basic information that everyone should know.

The camera is just the beginning of the equipment used in photography. Here you will find information on lenses, flashes, tripods, and camera cases. There are advantages and disadvantages with both film and digital photography. These pages will give you information on the differences of each and help you decide which is right for you. Taking pictures is what photography is all about. Here we have gathered together detailed information on taking better pictures, avoiding common mistakes like blurry images, and a glossary of photographic terms. There are certain holidays, events, and types of photography that have specific needs. These pages explain the challenges of these events and how to take great images in each circumstance.

Well, you have taken a bunch of photos, now what? There are actually nearly unlimited options for displaying your memories. From frames to mounted images to photo room dividers and many more options, let us show you the possibilities.

What do you do with your photographs after you have taken them? You develop them and get them printed of course! Tired of looking longingly at the backgrounds and props in the local photographer's studio? Wishing you could make some of those cute photo gifts they offer? You have found the right place to learn how to do it yourself and have a lot of fun in the process. We have all seen them, the shoeboxes stacked in the closet, each one filled with random photographs that will probably never see the light of day. And in this digital age our computers are facing a future of becoming virtual shoeboxes. Never fear, there are easy ways to organize your photographs...and reclaim your closet or computer in the process.

Photography has a much longer history than you may think and it is full of innovation and discovery. These pages will guide you through the journey that has led to our current photographic world.

- **24 mm APS Cameras** represent a film camera format focused on ease of use and picture printing options.
- **35 mm Cameras** are one of the most widely used film camera formats.
- **CDs, CD-ROMs, and DVDs** are small, polymer discs on which sound, images, and data are imprinted.
- **Digital** means describes any technological device that stores and/or uses information in the form of ones and zeros.
- **Digital camera** means a camera that records images in digital form and stores them as pixels. Digital camera developing is the process of professionally printing digital pictures on high-quality photographic paper.
- **A film** is plastic base coated with emulsion that records visible light as a chemical record.
- **Flash and xD-picture cards** are compact, lightweight memory source that stores large amounts of data and allows fast access.
- **Floppy Disks** are a common magnetic storage format used to transfer digital information between computers and store small amounts of data.
- **Magnetic tapes** are plastic strip coated with iron particles that records large amounts of sound, images, and data.
- **Motion picture film** are similar to standard film, but records and displays images in rapid sequence to create moving pictures.
- **One-time-use cameras** are a basic, affordable, plastic-body camera used to take one roll of pictures before processing and recycling.

- **Point-and-shoot cameras** are a basic, easy-to-use-camera. Just point, click, and go.
- **USB Drives** are lipstick-sized storage for large amounts of information. Also runs software applications.
- **VHS and SVHS videocassettes** are common magnetic tape recording format for movies, TV and video.
- **Zip disks** are a storage disk with vastly increased capacity over the floppy disk.

UNDERSTANDING THE COMPOSITION AND CAMERA MOVEMENT

Composition

Composition exists in a context. That context is the frame, which is itself an element of picture composition. In 1894 Thomas Edison introduced the Kinetoscope motion picture format, with an aspect ratio (ratio of picture width to height) of four units wide to three units high, or 1.33 to 1. For the next fifty years most film used the 1.33 aspect ratio. Sixteen millimeter, eight and "super eight" millimeter film formats and NTSC, PAL, and SECAM television standards all share the 1.33 ratio.

From an optical standpoint, the most efficient rectangular format would be square, since it would use as much of the lens area as possible. So why don't we have square pictures?

Artists and mathematicians from the ancient Greeks and Egyptians have focused on the "golden rectangle" as the perfect shape. The aspect ratio of the golden rectangle is 1.618. One might presume (although I have found no evidence so far) that the 1.33 aspect ratio is a compromise between the most efficient ratio and the most esthetically pleasing.

Over the years a number of standard sizes with different aspect ratios became popular. The 8 × 10 photograph (1.25), the 4 × 6 photograph (1.5), and the 35 mm slide (1.5) are a few examples. Film evolved, too. Cinerama (2.5-3.0), Cinemascope (2.55), and Panavision (1.78-2.4) are a few standards among many. High definition television has an aspect ratio of 16 by 9, or 1.78. The shape of the frame is the first consideration in composition.

Ideally, every shot in a television programme should be composed as carefully as a still photograph. While this is not often possible, some general rules of composition should be kept in mind.

The face of the typical television screen has been surrounded by a frame called a shadow mask, which hides about five per cent of the picture. The composition of the same image will be different with and without the shadow mask. The presence of the shadow mask has always caused a problem for films transferred to video because they were generally composed to be shown "edge to edge." Now the same problem occurs when images are composed using a digital (LCD) monitor without taking the shadow mask into consideration.

The red border around the frame represents the shadow mask. It is unlikely the viewer will see anything in this area. The gold and green areas combined are referred to as the safe action area. Anything that takes place here is likely to be visible to the viewer. The green area is known as the safe title area. It is virtually certain that any text in the green area will be visible to the viewer.

Notice the difference in "head room" in the pictures below this text. If you are using a camera with a monitor that shows the entire picture, be sure to allow for the shadow mask when you are composing your shots. Some viewfinders have "safe area" masks or lines to help you.

Unless your subject is perfectly symmetrical, the screen should never be divided exactly in half by strong horizontal or vertical lines. Instead, it should be divided approximately into thirds. For example, the horizon (if you are shooting a corn field) should be either a third of the way from the bottom of the screen or a third of the way from the top. With the exception of titles, composition should not be perfectly symmetrical, but should rather balance positive and negative (filled and empty) space.

Intelligent use of composition can be used to draw the viewer's eye to important parts of the picture. When framing people, there are several additional concerns. By placing someone too high or too low in the frame, the individual can be made to seem taller or shorter than he actually is. The tendency is to place people too low. When the screen is filled with a face, the critical part of the face includes the eyes, mouth, and chin. The picture should be framed to include those, allowing hair or ears to fall outside the frame. When shooting a profile (side view) of a person, it is important to allow empty space in the direction the subject is looking. This extra space is called "nose room." Nose room applies not only to people, but to anyone or anything pointing or moving. There should be relatively more empty space in the direction of the pointing or movement.

The kind of framing a writer or director wants is usually described in terms of wide, medium, or close-up. A wide shot includes the entire subject and important objects in the immediate surroundings. It is used to show where he is in his environment. If it is used at the beginning of a scene it is often called an "establishing" shot. A medium shot shows most of the subject, including all parts of the subject that are important to understanding what the subject is doing. A medium shot of a person sitting still might show his body from the waist up, letting hands and the lower half of his body fall outside the frame. A medium shot of a person dancing or performing Tai Chi, on the other hand, would have to include his arms and hands, since these are generally important to understanding what he is doing. A close-up is used to isolate the most important part of the subject. For a speaker, this is generally the head. For an entire football team, a close-up might be a shot of the quarterback only.

An extreme close-up focuses on one important detail of the subject, perhaps the mouth alone, or just the eyes, if the subject is a person. The object is to focus on important detail either to increase the drama or impact on a situation or to allow the viewer to see necessary picture information more clearly. In shooting a group of people, we have a few special terms. A "one shot" is a medium shot of a single person. A "two shot," would still be a medium shot, but the "subject" is made up of two people and the shot is framed tightly around those two. We also use terms such as "head shot," "head and shoulders shot," and "waist-up shot."

Camera Movement

In the age of hand-held camcorders it must seem odd that there is an elaborate vocabulary describing how a camera can be moved. If you can do it, the industry has a technical term for it. The two camera movements you use routinely are the "pan" and "tilt." A pan is a turning of the camera to the left or right. A tilt involves tilting the camera up or down. The stand for a heavy studio television or film camera is called a "pedestal." That is why the term for raising the camera is "pedestal up," and the term for lowering the camera is "pedestal down." These terms have nothing to do with adjustments to the "pedestal," or setup of the black level of the picture, which is an electronic adjustment, not a camera movement.

In moving a camera from side to side you "truck right" or "truck left." To move the camera closer to the subject, you "dolly in." To move it farther away you "dolly out." Of course, whenever the camera-to-subject distance changes, the focus must be adjusted.

Purists will point out that dolly shots (in or out) are fundamentally different in effect from zooming in or out. They are right. But professionals will go to extreme lengths to get a smooth dolly shot, to the point of laying special tracks to roll the dolly on. People with more modest means have mounted cameras on bicycles, shopping carts and, of course, cars to get their dolly shots.

Finally, in situations where important parts of a scene are not the same distance from the camera, it is possible to change the emphasis of a shot from one part of the scene to another by changing focus alone. The instruction to do this is "rack" focus "in" or "out" for a particular object in a scene. "Rack focus into the cup on the table," would be an example. Such instructions are rarely used and are generally given for artistic effect.

DEBATING THE ISSUE OF DIGITAL *VS.* FILM PHOTOGRAPHY

While photographers debate over which of the two formats, digital or film, is superior, each format has advantages.

Quality

Spatial Resolution

There are many measures that can be used to assess the quality of still photographs. The most discussed of these is spatial resolution, i.e. the number of separate points in the photograph. This is measured by how many picture cells make up the photo, usually counted in the millions and hence called "megapixels." The comparison of resolution between film and digital photography is complex. Measuring the resolution of both film and digital photographs depends on numerous issues. For film, this issue depends on the size of film used (35 mm, Medium format or Large format), the speed of the film used and the quality of lenses in the camera. Additionally, since film is an analogue medium, it does not have pixels so its resolution measured in pixels can only be an estimate.

Similarly, digital cameras rarely perform to their stated megapixel count. Other factors are important in digital camera resolution such as the actual number of pixels used to store the image, the effect of the Bayer pattern or other sensor filters on the digital sensor, and the image processing algorithm used to interpolate sensor pixels to image pixels. In addition, digital sensors are generally arranged in a rectangular pattern, making images susceptible to moire pattern artifacts, whereas film is immune to such effects due to the random orientation of grains.

Estimates of the resolution of a photograph taken with a 35 mm film camera vary. It is possible for more resolution to be recorded if, for example, a finer grain film and/or developer are used or less resolution to be recorded with poor quality optics or low light levels. The digital megapixel equivalent of film is highly variable and roughly depends on film speed. Slow, fine-grained 35 mm B&W films with speeds of ISO 50 to 100 have estimated megapixel equivalents of 20 to 30 megapixels. Colour films (both negative and slide types) are estimated between 8 and 12 megapixels. This would place film cameras (as of 2008) well over almost all point and shoot digital cameras. However, different films with the same ISO speeds can have different linear resolutions, so a direct comparison to digital is not easy. Resolution for 35 mm film drops drastically with higher ISO ratings, particularly above ISO 400.

While 35 mm is the standard format for consumer cameras, many professional film cameras use Medium format or Large format (generally sheet) films which, due to the size of the film used, can boast resolution many times greater than the current top-of-the-range digital cameras. For example, it is estimated that a medium format film photograph can record around 50 megapixels, while large format films can record around 200 megapixels (4 × 5 inch) which would equate to around 800 megapixels on the largest common film format, 8 × 10 inches. However, the estimate above does not take into account lens sharpness.

So 4 × 5 inch sheet of may be able to capture 200 megapixels of information as shown above. In actual use however, it is rare to be able to impart that type of resolution to film, since even the best large format lenses rarely resolve more than 70 lines/mm, which puts 4 × 5 inch film at a respectable maximum of around 180 megapixels for a 40″ × 50″ print at 300 dpi.

When deciding between film and digital and between different types of camera you want to use for a given project, it is necessary to take into account the medium which will be used for display, and the viewing distance. For instance, if a photograph will only be viewed on a television or computer display (which can resolve only about .3 megapixels and 1-2 megapixels, respectively, as of 2008. HD sets of 1080p are around 1.8mp), then the resolution provided by a low-end digital cameras may be sufficient. For standard 4 × 6 inch prints, it is debatable whether there will be any perceived quality difference between digital and film when it comes to resolution. However, colour film will generally have the ability to reproduce a much wider range of colours than digital sensors smaller than 3 megapixels. The difference is visible on most modern computer monitors and on traditional chemically processed prints, but may not be noticeable on output media with limited colour pallets such as lower end desktop inkjet prints and even large media such as billboards. Comparisons can depend on the gamut of the output media, which can influence the perception of resolution. An output media with a smaller gamut will need to use more dpi to reproduce a given colour.

Noise Levels

It should be noted that a special case exists for long exposure photography—Currently available technology contributes random noise to the images taken by digital cameras, produced by thermal noise and manufacturing defects. Some digital cameras apply noise reduction to long exposure photographs to counteract this. For very long exposures it is necessary to operate the detector at low temperatures to avoid noise impacting the final image. Film grain is not affected by exposure time, although the apparent speed of the film does change with longer exposures, a phenomenon known as reciprocity failure.

Dynamic Range

As of early 2008, many current DSLRs offer a dynamic range that is as wide or wider than film such as the Canon 5D, 30D, 40D,

Nikon D40, D40x, D80, D200), and Sony A700. CCDs such as Fuji's Super CCD, which combines photosites of different sizes, have also addressed this problem with a gain of a much as 3 stops of range, but this has been at the expense of decreased actual resolution.

Effects of Sensor Size

Most digital cameras, even most digital SLRs, have sensors that are smaller than a standard frame of 35 mm film. These smaller sensors have a number of effects on the captured image and the use of the camera:

1. Increased depth of field.
2. Decreased light sensitivity and increased pixel noise.
3. For digital SLRs, cropping of the field of view when using lenses designed for 35 mm camera.
4. Lenses can be smaller, since they only need to project light onto a smaller image area.
5. Increased degree of enlargement.

The depth of field of a camera/lens combination increases as the film/sensor size decreases. This is arguably an advantage for compact digital cameras since they are intended for taking snapshots. It means that more of the scene will be in focus than with a larger sensor, and the autofocus system does not need to be as accurate to capture an acceptable image. However, art photography often makes use of a limited depth of field to create special effects, such as isolating a subject from the background. When using a digital camera with a small sensor, the photographer would have to use a larger aperture on the lens to achieve similar amounts of "bokeh."

Light sensitivity and pixel noise are both related to pixel size, which is in turn related to sensor size and resolution. As the resolution of sensors increase, the size of the individual pixels has to decrease. This smaller pixel size means that each one collects less light and the resulting signal is amplified more to produce the final value. This amplification also includes an amount of noise in the signal. With a smaller signal, the signal-to-noise ratio decreases. Not only is more noise present in the image (relatively speaking), but the relatively higher noise floor means that less useful information can be extracted from the darker parts of the image.

Most digital SLRs use lens mounts originally designed for film cameras, commonly 35 mm. If the camera has a smaller sensor than the intended film frame, the field of view of the lens is cropped. This crop factor is often called a "focal length multiplier" since the effect can be simplified to that of multiplying the focal length of the lens. For lenses that are not "digital specific" (designed for a smaller sensor despite using the 35 mm-compatible lens mount) this has the slight beneficial side effect of only using the center part of the lens, where the image quality is normally best; the "soft edges" are cropped off.

Only a few of the most expensive digital SLRs have so-called "full-frame" sensors—a sensor the same size as a 35 mm film frame (36 × 24 mm). These larger sensors eliminate the issues of depth of field and crop factor when compared to 35 mm film cameras.

With compact digital cameras the sensors are tiny compared to DSLRs. This means that prints are extreme enlargements of the original image, and that the lens has to perform outstandingly in order to provide enough resolution to match the tiny pixels on the sensor. However, many modern compact camera lenses, even 12x "super-zoom" designs, achieve the needed sharpness. The use of a small sensor also has the effect of increasing depth of field to the extent of making images very "flat" looking because backgrounds cannot be blurred except for subjects very close to the camera.

Convenience and Flexibility

This has been one of the major drivers of the widespread adoption of digital cameras. Before the advent of digital cameras, once a photograph was taken, the roll of film would need to be finished and sent off to a lab to be developed. Only once the film was returned, it possible to see the photograph. However, most digital cameras incorporate an LCD screen which allows the photograph to be viewed immediately after it has been taken. This allows the photographer to delete undesired or unnecessary photographs, and offers an immediate opportunity to re-take. When a user desires prints, it is only necessary to print the good photographs.

Another major advantage of digital technology is that photographs can be conveniently moved to a personal computer for modification. Many professional-grade digital cameras are capable of storing pictures in a *Camera RAW* format which stores the output from the sensor directly rather than processing it immediately to an image. When edited in suitable software, such as Adobe Photoshop or dcraw, the photographer can manipulate certain parameters of the taken photograph (such as contrast, sharpness or colour balance) before it is "developed" into a final image. Less sophisticated users may choose to simply "touch up" the actual content of the recorded image; software with which to do this is often provided with consumer-grade cameras.

Price

The two formats (film and digital) have different cost emphases. With digital photography, cameras tend to be significantly more expensive than film ones, comparing like for like. This is offset by the fact that taking photographs is effectively cost-free.

With film photography, good-quality cameras tend to be less complicated and, therefore, less expensive, but at the expense of on-going film and processing costs. In particular, film cameras offer no chance to review photographs immediately after they are shot, and all photos taken must be processed before knowing anything about the quality of the final photograph.

However, there are additional costs associated with digital photography. Digital cameras make heavy use of batteries, some of which are proprietary and expensive. Whilst rechargeable, they degrade over time and must be periodically replaced. Although there is no film in digital cameras, they must store the images on memory cards or microdrives, which also have limited life. Additionally, some provision for long-term storage of the digital image must be made. This may be either an optical disc produced by a shop or photofinisher, or on the photographer's computer system.

With many photographers switching to digital, many film cameras (and associated equipment like lenses) are now available on the second-hand market (especially online auction sites like eBay) at often very reduced prices. This has allowed people on a budget to own a quality film camera when they might not have been able to afford the digital equivalent. Or alternatively, they are able to purchase more equipment (e.g. lenses, filters, etc.) than they could have with a digital camera.

The price differential between the two formats is often dictated by the intent of the photographer and the purpose of the work.

Robustness

Dust on the image plane is a constant issue for photographers. DSLR cameras are especially prone to dust problems because the sensor is reused for every shot, where a film SLR will effectively have a new "sensor" slid into place for every shot. A fresh, dust free film frame comes at risk of debris such as dust or sand in the camera scratching the film. A single grain of sand can damage a whole roll of film. Also as film SLRs age, they can develop burs in their rollers. With a digital SLRs dust is difficult to avoid, but easy rectify if one has a computer with photo editing software available. Some digital SLRs have systems that remove dust from the sensor by vibrating or knocking the sensor. Some cameras do this in conjunction with software that remembers where dust is located on the sensor and removes dust-affected pixels from images.

One huge advantage to compact point and shoot digital cameras is that they are exclusively available with fixed lenses, so dust is not an issue for them. This is not true of point an shoot film cameras, which are often only light tight and not environmentally sealed.

Archiving

When choosing between film and digital formats, one may need to consider the suitability of each as an archival medium.

Films and prints processed and stored in ideal conditions have demonstrated an ability to remain substantially unchanged for more than 100 years. Gold or platinum toned prints probably have a lifespan limited only by the lifespan of the base material, probably many hundreds of years.

The archival potential of digital photographs is less well understood since digital media have existed for only the last 50 years. There exist three problems which must be overcome for archival usage: physical stability of the recording medium, future readability of the storage medium and future readability of the file formats used for storage.

Many digital media are not capable of storing data for prolonged periods of time. For example, magnetic disks and tapes may lose their data after twenty years, flash memory cards even less. Good quality optical media may be the most durable storage media for digital data. It is important to consider the future readability of storage media. Assuming the storage media can continue to hold data for prolonged periods of time, the short lifespan of digital technologies often causes the drives to read media to become unavailable. For example, the first 5¼ inch Floppy disks were first made available in 1976. However, the drives to read them are already extremely rare just 30 years later.

It must also be considered whether there still exists software which can decode the data. For example, many modern digital cameras save photographs in JPEG format. This format has existed for only around 15 years. Whether it will still be readable in a century is unknown, although the huge number of JPEG files currently being produced will surely influence this issue.

Most professional cameras can save in a RAW image format, the future of which is much more uncertain. Some of these formats contain proprietary data which is encrypted or protected by patents, and could be abandoned by their makers at any time for simple economic reasons. This could make it difficult to read these 'raw' files in the future, unless the camera makers were to release information on the file formats. However, digital archives have several methods of overcoming such obstacles. In order to counteract the file format problems, many organizations prefer to choose an open and popular file format. Doing so increases the chance that software will exist to decode the file in the future. Additionally many organizations take an active approach to archiving rather than relying on formats being readable decades later. This takes advantage of the ability to make perfect copies of digital media. So, for example, rather than leaving data on a format which may potentially become unreadable or unsupported, the information can typically be copied to newer media without loss of quality. This is only possible with digital media. And, of course, the digital images can always be printed out and saved like traditional photographs although there are few, if any, commercial services available producing true silver halide prints from digital sources. All dye based prints, as noted above, have only limited permanence (with the exception of Cibachrome).

Integrity

Film produces a first generation image, which contains only the information admitted through the aperture of the camera. Film "sees" in colour, in a specific spectral band such as orthochromatic, or in broad panchromatic sensitivity. Differences in development technique can produce subtle changes in the finished negative or positive, but once this process is complete it is considered permanent.

Film images are very difficult to fabricate, thus in law enforcement and in cases where the authenticity of an image is important (passport or visa photographs), film provides greater security over digital, which has the disadvantage that photographs can be conveniently moved to a personal computer for modification.

Converting Film to Digital

Film photographs may be digitized in a process known as scanning. They may then be manipulated as digital photographs.

There are currently three ways to scan or convert a film image to digital format. The first is through a reflective image scanner. In expensive flatbed scanners, depending upon the model used, can scan a paper-sized image from 8" × 14" to ledger size, 11" × 17". An expensive and very high resolution drum scanner can also be used to scan reflective and transparent images.

The second method is to use a dedicated film scanner, such as the Nikon Coolscan (pictured) which can scan 35 mm transparencies and negatives. Other film scanners can scan 120 film, typically up to 6 × 7 cm or 6 × 9 cm.

The third method is to take a digital photograph of the source image. One can mount a digital camera on a copy stand (or an old enlarger with its projection head removed) and photograph the source image. It is also possible to use a slide projector to project the image from a transparency and then take a digital photograph of the projection.

ELABORATING UPON DOCUMENTARY PHOTOGRAPHY

Documentary photography usually refers to a type of professional photojournalism, but it may also be an amateur or student pursuit.

The photographer attempts to produce truthful, objective, and usually candid photography of a particular subject, most often pictures of people. The pictures usually depict a certain perspective of the photographer. Usually such photographs are meant for publication, but are sometimes only for exhibition in an art gallery or other public forum. Sometimes an organization or company will commission documentary photography of its activities, but the pictures will only be for its private archives.

Press Photographers

Photojournalists who adhere to generally accepted ethical practices such as those proposed by organizations like the National Press Photographers Association generally strive to make documentary photos instead of posed photos because of the innate power of the candid, unguarded moment in depicting genuine news events. The challenge for that type of photographer is to make pictures of sensitive scenes and moments without changing them by the presence of a camera.

Posing People for an Accurate Record

If the aim is simply to document something—costume for instance—then sometimes posing people is the best way to make the required clear documentary picture. For instance, the posed "straight up" style of picture pioneered by *iD* magazine—these were of punks and New Wave youth found on English streets and simply asked to stand against any nearby blank wall. The resulting pictures—the subjects facing the camera and seen from "top to toe"—are a vivid historical documentary photography archive, and have established the posed "straight up" as a valid style of documentary picture-making. One photographer who was exceptional in his efforts to pose and photograph individuals in their natural environment is found with the works of Milton Rogovin.

Amateur Photographers

Sometimes amateurs unintentionally make documentary pictures that are later found to be of great historical value, since they are good images of subjects that have since disappeared forever and which no-one else bothered to record. The work of Jacques Henri Lartigue would be one notable example.

Well-known Documentary Photographers

U.S. Documentary Photographers

(*i*) Jacob Riis
(*ii*) Lewis Hine
(*iii*) Berenice Abbott
(*iv*) Steve McCurry
(*v*) Walker Evans
(*vi*) Dorothea Lange
(*vii*) Mary Ellen Mark
(*viii*) W. Eugene Smith
(*ix*) Lee Friedlander
(*x*) Robert Frank
(*xi*) Gary Winogrand
(*xii*) Eugene Richards
(*xiii*) Eugene Atget

European Documentary Photographers

(*i*) Henri Cartier-Bresson
(*ii*) Bill Brandt
(*iii*) August Sander
(*iv*) Eugene Atget
(*v*) Gertrude Blom

Describing Commercials

Commercials are amongst the most highly skilled and effective pieces of film-making anywhere. They aim to have a significant impact through sound and vision on the emotions and thinking of the viewer, and to be pleasurable to watch over and over again.

Commercials should be wonderful pieces of film-making. They should be effective. They are usually made with very high budgets, the best of them spending more per second on screen time than even the biggest Hollywood movies. They also employ the best and the brightest writing and film-making talent. They also are usually shot on film, whether 35 mm or Super 16 mm, one of the few remaining guaranteed training grounds on film. Many people who aspire to working on feature films begin on Commercials, if they are lucky. Many also do move onto feature films in the UK and abroad. Commercials people live the filmmakers' dream. They are very well paid for concentrated periods of intense work.

Skills and Training

People from all kinds of educational and cultural backgrounds work in commercials. Once in the sector, people do tend to work for one or a few agencies, but they can move around, and the majority find work through contacts and word of mouth.

Jobs

There are three main areas of work in the commercials sector, and there are different types of people, skills, training routes and career paths for each.

Media Speak

Learn the langauge of the industry with our guide to Commercials and other media terms.

Runners

Commercials are sometimes described as 'mini feature films' and working in this area can be a valuable training ground for people who want to go on to work in films.

Money

The Broadcast "Rich List", published annually, shows that a small minority of people still make a vast amount of money out of the Commercials industry. Inevitably it is the owners of Agencies, or Senior Executives who earn the most.

First Jobs

Establishing credibility, and being useful, is essential for anyone hoping to gain relevant work experience or work in the Commercials sector.

Workforce

Commercials is one of the smaller sectors in the industry, representing only 3 per cent of those employed in audio-visual production and distribution.

SKILLSET: A CASE STUDY

Skillset is the Sector Skills Council for the Audio-Visual and Publishing Industries. Jointly funded by industry and government, our job is to make sure that the UK audio-visual industries have the right people, with the right skills, in the right place, at the right time, so that our industries remain competitive. We conduct consultation work with industry, publish research and strategic documents, run funding schemes and project work, and provide information about the challenges that face the industry and what we need to do to overcome them. We also provide impartial media careers advice for aspiring new entrants and established industry professionals, online, face to face and over the phone. Whether you are a freelancer looking for training information, a student seeking careers advice or a public agency partner, we aim to provide you with easy access to the information you may require.

This area of the website has information on our role, corporate information, such as annual reports, useful news and an events area. You will also be able to find contact details for Skillset staff, details of our Board and Patrons and information on how we are structured and deliver our role. If there is anything about Skillset that you feel is missing and would like to see included in this area. Skillset is the Sector Skills Council for the Audio-Visual and Publishing Industries and works to raise skills levels in every sector of industry within its remit. Skillset is the industry body which supports skills and training for people and businesses to ensure the UK audio-visual and publishing industries maintain their world class position. Skillset don't deliver training, provide job listings or fund productions: here is what we can and cannot offer you. Skillset works with key industry partners as well as experts in particular fields to progress its work. To ensure the close involvement of industry in our work, we use a number of distinct formal groups. Diversity is a key focus within the audio-visual industries as certain groups are under represented within the workforce. Skillset supports diversity in all its activities.

IDENTIFYING MAJOR AREAS IN PHOTOGRAPHY AND FILM CAREER

(a) Photography and Film Career Descriptions

- About Photography Careers

- Archivists
- Art Careers
- Art, Design and Media Careers
- Audio and Video Recording Technicians
- Audio and Visual Equipment Technicians
- Audio-Visual Technician
- Broadcast Journalists—Military
- Broadcast Media Careers
- Broadcast Technicians
- Business Managers for Artists
- Camera Equipment Repairers
- Camera Operator
- Careers in Moving Images
- Careers in Photography
- Cinematographers
- Directors—Stage, Film, TV, Radio
- Director—TV
- Dot Etchers
- Editorial Photographer
- Film and Theater Career View
- Film and TV Producer's Assistant
- Film and Video Editors
- Film Editing
- Film Editors
- Film Laboratory Technicians
- Film Star
- Film Studies
- Film Studies—What can I do with
- Film/Video Camera Operators
- Graphic Arts Careers
- Grips
- Mapping Technicians
- Media/Print Careers
- Medical Photographer
- Motion Picture and Video Industry
- Motion Picture Photographers
- Motion Picture Projectionist
- Movie and Stage Grips
- Movie Projectionist
- Multimedia Artists and Animators

- Performing Arts Careers
- Photo Engravers
- Photo Imaging Careers
- Photogrammetry Career
- Photographers
- Photographic Developers and Printers
- Photographic Equipment Technicians
- Photographic Process Workers
- Photographic Processor
- Photographic Restorers
- Photographic Specialists—Military
- Photojournalism
- Photojournalism Career
- Photojournalist
- Producer's Assistant—Film and TV
- Producers and Directors
- Producers FAQ
- Professional Photographers
- Programme Directors
- Public Relations Specialist
- Scientific Photographers
- Special Effects Technician
- Visual Arts Career Overview
- Visual Arts Careers

(b) Photography and Film Related Sites

Photography Directories

- Art Links and Resources
- Art and Photography
- Crime Scene and Evidence Photography
- Camera Works—Washington Post
- Focus on Photography—Fodors
- Graphic Arts Links and Resources
- Industrial Light and Magic
- Photo District News Online
- Photography—LII
- Photography—Voice of the Shuttle
- Photography in the Digital Era—Online Book

- Photography Directory—Yahoo
- Photography Magazines
- Photography—Wikipedia
- Photojournalist WebQuest
- Pinhole Photography

Camera

- Camera Basics
- Camera Brands
- Camera Calculators—Martindale's Reference Desk
- Camera Manufacturers
- Camera Optics
- Camera Overview—Wikipedia
- Depth of Field Calculators
- Hasselblad
- How Cameras Work
- How Long a Lens Do You Need
- Leica Camera
- Online Depth of Field Calculator
- Photo Companies and Equipment Links

Digital Photography

- Creating Digital Images
- Creating Digital Resources for the Visual Arts
- Digital Animation
- Digital Camera and Photography Reviews
- Digital Camera Resource Page
- Digital Camera Reviews—CNet
- Digital Cameras and Photography—A Complete Guide
- Digital Cameras HQ
- Digital Cameras, Imaging and Photography
- Digital Cameras Introduction
- Digital Image Glossary and Acronyms
- Digital Images—Creating, Using, Delivering, Managing
- Digital Learning Center—Kodak
- Digital Photography as Legal Evidence
- Digital Photography Photocourse—Online Textbook
- Digital Photography Resources—Say Cheese
- Digital Photography Short Courses

- Digital Tools for Artists
- Guide to DVD—Dolby Laboratories
- How Digital Cameras Work
- Kodak Digital Camera How to Learn Digital Photography
- Selecting Image File Formats

Photographers

- Documentary Educational Resources
- Edward S. Curtis—North American Indian
- Masters of Photography
- National Geographic
- National Press Photographers Association
- Newseum—Pulitzer Prize Photographs
- Photographer Legends
- Photojournalism—A Record of War Web Lesson
- Pictures of the Year
- Professional Photographic Procedures
- Starting Your Own Business
- Time Magazine—The Year in Pictures

Photography and Film Tutorials

- Animation 101—ThinkQuest
- CAD—Introductory Guide
- Camera Project—Make a Pinhole
- Caring for Your Collections
- Caring for Your Photographs
- Crime Scene Photography
- Digital Film Movie Maker
- Digital Image
- Film Making—So You Wanna Make a Low Budget Film
- How Films are Made
- How Movie Distribution Works—How Stuff Works
- How to Make and Use a Pin Hole Camera
- How Video Electronics Work
- Learn Equipment, Guides and How To's
- Licensing Still Images
- Photograph FAQ
- Photographic Processes
- Photography 101

- Photography Tutorials
- Photography Tutorials—Silverlight
- Preservation of Archival Materials
- Registering Your Copyright Guide
- Science of Photography
- Science of Photography
- Studio Lighting Tutorials
- Tips for Better Pictures NY Institute of Photography
- Tutorial Directories and Links
- What is Light

Film Festivals

- Cannes Film Festival
- Documentary Film Festivals
- Film Festivals.com
- Independent Film Market
- Locate a Film Commission and Production Guides
- Sundance Film Festival
- Tribecca Film Festival
- USA Film Festivals

Media Directories

- Images—Digital Librarian
- Internet Movie Database
- Major Media in the USA
- Media Studies—Voice of the Shuttle
- MPEG.org
- Movies Directory—Digital Librarian
- Movies—Ref Desk
- Movie Related Magazines
- Radio and Television Stations and Networks
- Who Owns the Media

Copyright and Intellectual Property

- Basic Facts about Trademarks
- Copyright and Intellectual Property
- Copyright Basics
- Copyright Commandments
- Copyright Legislation

- Copyright Resources—NPPA
- Digital Millennium Copyright Act—PDF
- How to Register Your Photographs
- Licensing and the Value of Copyright
- Fair Use
- US Copyright Office

Industry Overview and News

- Arts and Entertainment Magazines
- Media and Marketing News and Analysis
- Photography Magazines
- Television and Radio Related Magazines
- Who Owns What—What the Media Companies Own

Images and Photographs

- Classroom Clip Art
- Finding Images Online
- Image Collections
- Image Site Search—TASI
- Images—Digital Librarian
- Image Searcher—Virtual Learning Resource
- Internet Movie Archive
- Life Magazine Classic Pictures
- Links to Image Search Engines and Images
- National Geographic Photography
- Pic4Learning
- Pictures and Photography
- Scientific Photography
- Smithsonian Images
- Visual Effects Headquarters

Film and Film Making Tutorials

- Animation—Animated Films
- Cinematography.com
- Cyber Film School Moviemaking Website
- Entertainment Ratings
- Film and Television—Infosurf
- Film and Video Tutorials—Ron Dexter
- Film Glossaries

- Filmmaking 101—Filmmaking Steps
- Filmmaking General Resources
- Filmmaker's Bill of Rights—Legal Safeguards
- Filmmaker's FAQ
- Film Preservation Basics
- Film Sound Theory
- Film Sound.org
- Fundamentals of Screen Literacy
- How Movies Work
- How Televisions Work
- How Video Electronics Work
- Industrial Light—How Stuff Works
- Movie Genres
- No Budget Filmmaking Guide
- Online Film Production Guide—PA
- Screenwriting—Breaking into
- Teaching Action Photography
- Technical Manuals for Cinematographers
- Television Glossaries
- Television Production Manual
- Tutorial Directories and Links
- Voluntary Movie Rating System

Photography and Film History

- 100 Years of Film Sizes
- A Primer on Processes
- Adventures in Cybersound
- Albumen Photography
- American Film Institute—Top 100 Movies
- AIC—Conservation of Historic and Artistic Works
- American Museum of the Moving Image
- American Museum of Photography
- Animated Films Origins—Library of Congress
- Camera History—Images of Old Camera
- Cannon Camera's History
- Classic Movie Theaters—Cinema Treasures
- Colour Television Camera Development
- Daguerrotype
- Daguerreotype Portraits—Library of Congress
- Director's Guild of America

- Discovery of Cinematography History
- Early Cinema
- Early Cinema Pioneers
- Early Colour Picture Processes
- Eastman Legacy
- Edison Motion Picture and Sound Recordings
- Film History by Decade
- Film Sound History
- Great Photographs Online
- History of Film
- History of Film—Wikipedia
- History of Kodak
- History of Photography
- History of Photography and Photographers
- History of Photography Timeline
- History of Printing Processes
- History of the American West in Photographs-LOC
- Inventing Entertainment—LOC Motion Pictures and Sound
- Invention of Photography
- Inventors and Inventions
- Japanese Photo History
- Library of American Broadcasting
- Masters of Photography
- Panoramic Photographs -1851- 1991 Library of Congress
- Photography Timeline
- Prints and Photography—History
- Types of Cameras—History
- Vintage Film, Cameras and Projectors—Collecting
- UCLA Film and Television Archive
- Who Invented Television

Safety

- Arts Crafts and Theater Safety
- Electric and Magnetic Fields Health Risks
- Chemical and Darkroom Safety
- Chemicals in the Lab Safety
- Occupational and Industrial Safety Resources
- Occupational Dermatoses
- Pocket Guide to Chemical Hazards

- Recycling Electronics—PDF
- Safety Zone Newsletter
- Self Inspection Checklist

Photography, Film and Design Schools

- Photography and Film Schools and Programmes

Certification

- PPA Certification

Organizations, Guilds, Associations

- Academy of Motion Picture Arts and Sciences
- Academy of Television Arts
- American Cinema Editors
- American Society of Cinematographers
- American Film Institute
- American Society of Media Photographers
- American Society of Picture Professionals
- Association of Electronic Journalists
- Association of Film Commissioners International
- British Association of Picture Libraries and Agencies
- Dauguerreian Society
- Director's Guild of America
- Film Foundation—Protection and Preservation of Film Industry
- Film in PA
- International Image Association
- Motion Picture Association
- Moving Image Society
- National Film Preservation Society
- National Press Photographers Association
- Picture Agency Council of America
- Professional Women Photographers Online
- Radio Television News Directors Association
- Society of Motion Picture and Television Engineers
- Society of Camera Operators
- Short Film Group
- Technical Advisory Service for Images
- The Film Foundation

- The Producer's Guild of America
- Unions—IATSE
- Visual Arts Data Center
- Visual Effects Society
- Visual Resource Association

Lesson Plans

- A Beginner's Guide to Digital Photography
- Adobe Digital Kids
- Arts Edge
- Cameras and Careers
- Captions—A Picture is Worth a Thousand Words
- Cinematography Lessons
- Cyber Muse—Integrating Art into Your Lessons
- Digital Photography Workshop
- EDSITEment—Art and Culture Lesson Plans
- Education at the Getty—Art Lesson Plans
- Effective Photojournalism
- High School Journalism Lesson Plans
- Incredible Art Department—Photography
- Internet Photo Essay Project
- Introducing the Camera
- Photography and Graphic Arts Curriculum/Learning Modules
- Photography History Lesson
- Photography in Your Science Fair Project
- Photography Lesson Plans—Kodak
- Photography Project
- Photojournalism—A Record of War Web Lesson
- Photojournalism—Creating Layout
- Pinehole Camera Activity—PDF
- Pinhole Inquiry Activity
- Screen Writing Lessons
- Student Curriculum in Photography
- Vocational and Career Related Lesson Plans
- Web English Teacher—Photography
- You Oughta Be in Pictures—Making Videos
- Youth Media Teacher's Guide

2

Videography and Video Equipment: Focus on Coding and Encoding Techniques

VIDEOGRAPHY

Videography refers to the process of capturing moving images on electronic media (e.g., videotape, hard disk, or solid state storage, streaming media). The term includes methods of electronic production and post production. It is the equivalent of cinematography, but with images recorded on electronic media instead of film stock. The word combines "video" from Latin, meaning "I see" or "I apprehend", with the Greek terminal ending "graphy", meaning "to write." Its contemporary sense is rooted in an article titled "Videography: What Does It All Mean?" (*American Cinematographer*, October 1972). The advent of digital imaging in the late 20th century began to blur the distinction between videography and cinematography. The videography market has grown to include distribution as well as production. With this growth has come market segmentation, based on the application: event video, corporate video, broadcast video, etc.

The advent of the Internet has created a global environment where videography covers many more fields than just shooting video with a camera. Included under the videography umbrella are digital animation (such as Flash), gaming, web streaming, video blogging, still slideshows, remote sensing, spatial imaging, medical imaging, and in general the production of most bitmap- and vector-based assets. As the field progresses videographers may produce their assets entirely on a computer without ever involving an imaging device, using software-driven solutions. Moreover, the very concept of sociality and privacy are being reformed by the proliferation of cell-phone video cameras, which are spreading at an exceptional rate in industrialized societies. A videographer may be the person actually operating the camera or he or she may be the person in-charge of the visual design of a production (the latter being the equivalent of a cinematographer). Videography also refers to the compiling of an artist's music videos or video releases (compare with "filmography" or "discography").

VIDEO

Video is the technology of electronically capturing, recording, processing, storing, transmitting, and reconstructing a sequence of still images representing scenes in motion.

History

Video technology was first developed for cathode ray tube television systems, but several new technologies for video display devices have since been invented. Standards for television sets and computer monitors have tended to evolve independently, but advances in computer performance and digital television broadcasting and recording are producing some convergence. Computers can now display television and film-style video clips and streaming media, encouraged by increased processor speed, storage capacity, and broadband access to the Internet. General-purpose computing hardware can now be used to capture, store, edit, and transmit television and movie content, as opposed to older dedicated analog technologies.

Description of Video

The term *video* (from Latin: "I see") commonly refers to several storage formats for moving eye pictures: digital video formats, including DVD, QuickTime, and MPEG-4; and analog videotapes, including VHS and Betamax. Video can be recorded and transmitted in various physical media: in magnetic tape when recorded as PAL or NTSC electric signals by video cameras, or in MPEG-4 or DV digital media when recorded by digital cameras.

Quality of video essentially depends on the capturing method and storage used. Digital television (DTV) is a relatively recent format with higher quality than earlier television formats and has become a standard for television video. 3D-video, digital video in three dimensions, premiered at the end of 20th century. Six or eight cameras with realtime depth measurement are typically used to capture 3D-video streams. The format of 3D-video is fixed in MPEG-4 Part 16 Animation Framework eXtension (AFX). In the , Australia, The Netherlands, Finland, Hungary and New Zealand, the term video is often used informally to refer to both Videocassette recorders and video cassettes; the meaning is normally clear from the context.

Characteristics of Video Streams

Number of Frames Per Second

Frame rate, the number of still pictures per unit of time of video, ranges from six or eight frames per second (*frame/s*) for old mechanical cameras to 120 or more frames per second for new professional cameras. PAL (Europe, Asia, Australia, etc.) and SECAM (France, Russia, parts of Africa etc.) standards specify 25 frame/s, while NTSC (USA, Canada, Japan, etc.) specifies 29.97 frame/s. Film is shot at the slower frame rate of 24 frame/s, which complicates slightly the process of transferring a cinematic motion picture to video. The minimum frame rate to achieve the illusion of a moving image is about fifteen frames per second.

Interlacing

Video can be interlaced or progressive. Interlacing was invented as a way to achieve good visual quality within the limitations of a narrow bandwidth. The *horizontal scan lines* of each interlaced frame are numbered consecutively and partitioned into two *fields*: the *odd field* (upper field) consisting of the odd-numbered lines and the *even field* (lower field) consisting of the even-numbered lines. NTSC, PAL and SECAM are interlaced formats. Abbreviated video resolution specifications often include an *i* to indicate interlacing. For example, PAL video format is often specified as *576i50*, where *576* indicates the vertical line resolution, *i* indicates interlacing, and *50* indicates 50 fields (half-frames) per second. In *progressive scan* systems, each refresh period updates all of the scan lines. The result is a higher perceived resolution and a lack of various artifacts that can make parts of a stationary picture appear to be moving or flashing. A procedure known as deinterlacing can be used for converting an interlaced stream, such as analog, DVD, or satellite, to be processed by progressive scan devices, such as TFT TV-sets, projectors, and plasma panels. Deinterlacing cannot, however, produce a video quality that is equivalent to true progressive scan source material.

Display Resolution

The size of a video image is measured in pixels for digital video, or horizontal scan lines and vertical lines of resolution for analog video. In the digital domain (e.g. DVD) standard-definition television (SDTV) is specified as *720/704/640×480i60* for NTSC and *768/720×576i50* for PAL or SECAM resolution. However, in the analog domain, the number of visible scanlines remains constant (486 NTSC/576 PAL) while the horizontal measurement varies with the quality of the signal: approximately 320 pixels per scanline for VCR quality, 400 pixels for TV broadcasts, and 720 pixels for DVD sources. Aspect ratio is preserved because of non-square "pixels." New high-definition televisions (HDTV) are capable of resolutions up to *1920×1080p60*, i.e. 1920 pixels per scan line by 1080 scan lines, progressive, at 60 frames per second. Video resolution for 3D-video is measured in voxels (*volume picture element*, representing a value in three dimensional space). For example 512×512×512 voxels resolution, now used for simple 3D-video, can be displayed even on some PDAs.

Aspect Ratio

Aspect ratio describes the dimensions of video screens and video picture elements. All popular video formats are rectilinear, and so can be described by a ratio between width and height. The screen aspect ratio of a traditional television screen is 4:3, or about 1.33:1. High definition televisions use an aspect ratio of 16:9, or about 1.78:1. The aspect ratio of a full 35 mm film frame with soundtrack (also known as the Academy ratio) is 1.375:1.

Ratios where the height is taller than the width are uncommon in general everyday use, but do have application in computer systems where the screen may be better suited for a vertical layout. The most common tall aspect ratio of 3:4 is referred to as *portrait mode* and is created by physically rotating the display device 90 degrees from the normal position. Other tall aspect ratios such as 9:16 are technically possible but rarely used.

Pixels on computer monitors are usually square, but pixels used in digital video often have non-square aspect ratios, such as those used in the PAL and NTSC variants of the CCIR 601 digital video standard, and the corresponding anamorphic widescreen formats. Therefore, an NTSC DV image which is 720 pixels by 480 pixels is displayed with the aspect ratio of 4:3 (which is the traditional television standard) if the pixels are thin and displayed with the aspect ratio of 16:9 (which is the anamorphic widescreen format) if the pixels are fat.

Colour Space and Bits Per Pixel

Colour model name describes the video colour representation. *YIQ* was used in NTSC television. It corresponds closely to the *YUV* scheme used in NTSC and PAL television and the *YDbDr* scheme used by SECAM television.

The number of distinct colours that can be represented by a pixel depends on the number of *bits per pixel* (bpp). A common way to reduce the number of bits per pixel in digital video is by chroma subsampling (e.g. 4:4:4, 4:2:2, 4:2:0, 4:1:1).

Video Quality

Video quality can be measured with formal metrics like PSNR or with subjective video quality using expert observation.

The subjective video quality of a video processing system may be evaluated as follows:

(*i*) Choose the video sequences (the *SRC*) to use for testing.
(*ii*) Choose the settings of the system to evaluate (the *HRC*).
(*iii*) Choose a test method for how to present video sequences to experts and to collect their ratings.
(*iv*) Invite a sufficient number of experts, preferably not fewer than 15.
(*v*) Carry out testing.
(*vi*) Calculate the average marks for each *HRC* based on the experts' ratings.

Many subjective video quality methods are described in the ITU-T recommendation BT.500. One of the standardized method is the *Double Stimulus Impairment Scale* (DSIS). In DSIS, each expert views an *unimpaired* reference video followed by an *impaired* version of the same video. The expert then rates the *impaired* video using a scale ranging from "impairments are imperceptible" to "impairments are very annoying".

Video Compression Method (Digital only)

A wide variety of methods are used to compress video streams. Video data contains spatial and temporal redundancy, making uncompressed video streams extremely inefficient. Broadly speaking, spatial redundancy is reduced by registering differences between parts of a single frame; this task is known as *intraframe compression* and is closely related to image compression. Likewise, temporal redundancy can be reduced by registering differences between frames; this task is known as *interframe compression,* including motion compensation and other techniques. The most common modern standards are MPEG-2, used for DVD and satellite television, and MPEG-4, used for home video.

Bit Rate (Digital only)

Bit rate is a measure of the rate of information content in a video stream. It is quantified using the bit per second (bit/s or bps) unit or Megabits per second (Mbit/s). A higher bit rate allows better video quality. For example VideoCD, with a bit rate of about 1 Mbit/s, is lower quality than DVD, with a bit rate of about 5 Mbit/s. HDTV has a still higher quality, with a bit rate of about 20 Mbit/s.

Variable bit rate (VBR) is a strategy to maximize the visual video quality and minimize the bit rate. On fast motion scenes, a variable bit rate uses more bits than it does on slow motion scenes of similar duration yet achieves a consistent visual quality. For real-time and non-buffered video streaming when the available bandwidth is fixed, e.g. in videoconferencing delivered on channels of fixed bandwidth, a constant bit rate (CBR) must be used.

Stereoscopic Video

Stereoscopic video can be created using several different methods:

- *Two channels*—A right channel for the right eye and a left channel for the left eye. Both channels may be viewed simultaneously by using light-polarizing filters 90 degrees off-axis from each other on two video projectors. These separately polarized channels are viewed wearing eyeglasses with matching polarization filters.
- One channel with two overlayed colour coded layers. This left and right layer technique is occasionally used for network broadcast, or recent "anaglyph" releases of 3D movies on DVD. Simple Red/Cyan plastic glasses provide the means to view the images discretely to form a stereoscopic view of the content.
- One channel with alternating left/right frames for each eye, using LCD shutter glasses which read the frame sync from the VGA Display Data Channel to alternately cover each eye, so the appropriate eye sees the correct frame. This method is most common in computer virtual reality applications such as in a Cave Automatic Virtual Environment, but reduces the effective video frame rate to one-half of normal (for example, from 120Hz to 60Hz).

New HD DVD and Blu-ray Discs will greatly improve the sharpness and detail of the two-colour 3D effect in colour coded stereo programmes. The first commercially available HD players were expected to debut at the 2006 NAB Show in Las Vegas in April.

Video Formats

There are different layers of video transmission and storage, each with its own set of formats to choose from.

For transmission, there is a physical connector and signal protocol ("video connection standard" below). A given physical link can carry certain "display standards" which specify a particular refresh rate, display resolution, and colour space. There are a number of analog and digital tape formats, though digital video files can also be stored on a computer file system which have their own formats. In addition to the physical format used by the storage or transmission medium, the stream of ones and zeros that is sent must be in a particular digital video "encoding", of which a number are available.

VIDEO DISPLAY STANDARDS

Digital Television

New formats for digital television broadcasts use the MPEG-2 video codec and include:

1. ATSC—USA, Canada, etc.; a DVB video standard,
2. Digital Video Broadcasting (DVB)—European,
3. Integrated Services Digital Broadcasting (ISDB)—Japanese; also a DVB video standard.

Analogue Television

Analogue television broadcast standards include:

1. Field-sequential colour system—USA, Russia; obsolete.
2. Multiplexed Analogue Components (MAC)—Europe, obsolete.
3. Multiple sub-nyquist sampling Encoding (MUSE)—Japan, analogue HDTV.
4. NTSC—USA, Canada, Japan, etc.
5. PAL—Europe, Asia, Australia, etc.
   (*i*) PAL-M—PAL variation. Brazil.
   (*ii*) PALplus—PAL extension, Europe only.
6. RS-343 (military).
7. SECAM—France, ex-USSR, Central Africa.

An analogue video format consists of more information than the visible content of the frame. Preceding and following the image are lines and pixels containing synchronization information or a time delay. This surrounding margin is known as a blanking interval or blanking region; the horizontal and vertical front porch and back porch are the building blocks of the blanking interval.

Many countries are planning a digital switchover to cease using these analogue formats via terrestrial television broadcast. However, analogue television sets expecting these older standards as input will be able to display digital signals if coupled with a converter box.

Computer Displays

Computer display standard for a list of standards used for computer monitors and comparison with those used for television.

Recording Formats before Video Tape

Kinescope

Analogue Tape Formats

(*i*) 1″ Type B video tape (Bosch)
(*ii*) 1″ Type C videotape (Ampex and Sony)
(*iii*) 2″ Quadruplex videotape (Ampex)
(*iv*) Ampex
(*v*) Betacam
(*vi*) Betacam SP
(*vii*) Betamax (Sony)
(*viii*) Philips videotape recorder EL3400 1″ helical scan ca.1963
(*ix*) S-VHS (JVC)
(*x*) U-matic (Sony)
(*xi*) VCR, VCR-LP, SVR
(*xii*) VERA (BBC experimental format ca. 1958)
(*xiii*) VHS (JVC)
(*xiv*) VHS-C (JVC)
(*xv*) Video 2000 (Philips)
(*xvi*) Video8
(*xvii*) Video Hi8

Digital Tape Formats

(*i*) Betacam IMX (Sony)
(*ii*) D-VHS (JVC)
(*iii*) D-Theater
(*iv*) D1 (Sony)
(*v*) D2 (Sony)
(*vi*) D3
(*vii*) D5 HD
(*viii*) Digital Betacam (Sony)
(*ix*) Digital8 (Sony)
(*x*) DV
(*xi*) HDV
(*xii*) ProHD (JVC)
(*xiii*) MiniDV
(*xiv*) MicroMV

Optical Disc Storage Formats

(*i*) Blu-Ray Disc (Sony)

(*ii*) DVD (was Super Density Disc, DVD Forum)
(*iii*) Enhanced Versatile Disc (EVD, Chinese government-sponsored)
(*iv*) HD DVD (NEC and Toshiba)
(*v*) HD-VMD
(*vi*) Laserdisc (old, MCA and Philips)
(*vii*) UMD (Sony)
(*viii*) CBHD (Chinese government-sponsored)

Digital Encoding Formats

(*i*) CCIR 601 (ITU-T)
(*ii*) H.261 (ITU-T)
(*iii*) H.263 (ITU-T)
(*iv*) H.264/MPEG-4 AVC (ITU-T + ISO)
(*v*) M-JPEG (ISO)
(*vi*) MPEG-1 (ISO)
(*vii*) MPEG-2 (ITU-T + ISO)
(*viii*) MPEG-4 (ISO)
(*ix*) Ogg-Theora
(*x*) VC-1 (SMPTE)

VIDEOTAPE

Videotape is a means of recording images and sound onto magnetic tape as opposed to movie film. In most cases, a helical scan video head rotates against the moving tape to record the data in two dimensions, because video signals have a very high bandwidth, and static heads would require extremely high tape speeds. Video-tape is used in both video tape recorders [(*VTRs* or, more common, video cassette recorders (VCRs)] and video cameras. Tape is a linear method of storing information, and since nearly all video recordings made nowadays are digital, it is expected to gradually lose importance as non-linear/random access methods of storing digital video data are becoming more common.

Early Formats

The electronics division of entertainer Bing Crosby's production company, Bing Crosby Enterprises (BCE), gave the world's first demonstration of a videotape recording in Los Angeles on November 11, 1951. Developed by John T. Mullin and Wayne R. Johnson since 1950, the device gave what were described as "blurred and indistinct" images, using a modified Ampex 200 tape recorder and standard quarter-inch (0.6 cm) audio tape moving at 360 inches (9.1 m) per second. A year later, an improved version, using one-inch (2.6 cm) magnetic tape, was shown to the press, who reportedly expressed amazement at the quality of the images, although they had a "persistent grainy quality that looked like a worn motion picture." Overall, the picture quality was still considered inferior to the best kinescope recordings on film. Bing Crosby Enterprises hoped to have a commercial version available in 1954, but none came forth. BCE demonstrated a colour model in February 1955, using a longitudinal recording on half-inch (1.3 cm) tape, essentially similar to what RCA had demonstrated in 1953. CBS, RCA's competitor, was about to order BCE machines when Ampex introduced the superior Quadruplex system.

RCA demonstrated the magnetic tape recording of both black-and-white and colour programmes at its Princeton laboratories on December 1, 1953. The high-speed longitudinal tape system, called Simplex, in development since 1951, could record and play back only a few minutes of a programme. The colour system used half-inch (1.3 cm) tape to record five tracks—one each for red, blue, green, synchronization, and audio. The black-and-white system used quarter-inch (1.9 cm) tape with two tracks, one for picture and one for sound. Both systems ran at 360 inches (9.1 m) per second. RCA-owned NBC first used it on the *The Jonathan Winters Show* on October 23, 1956, when a pre-recorded song sequence by Dorothy Collins in colour was included in the otherwise live programme.

The BBC experimented from 1952 to 1958 with a high-speed linear videotape system called VERA, but this was ultimately unfeasible. It utilized 1/2 inch (1.27 cm) tape travelling at 200 inches (5.08 m) per second.

Broadcast Video

Quad

The first practical professional videotape machines were the

Quadruplex machines introduced by Ampex in the United States on April 14, 1956. Quad employed a transverse (scanning the tape across its width) four-head system on a two-inch (5.08 cm) tape, and linear heads for the soundtrack. CBS first used the Ampex Mark IV at its Television City studios in Hollywood on November 30, 1956 to play a delayed broadcast of *Douglas Edwards and the News* from New York to the Pacific Time Zone.

Although Quad became the industry standard for 20 years, it had drawbacks such as an inability to freeze pictures, no picture search, and in early machines, a tape could only reliably be played back using the same set of hand-made tape heads, which wore out very quickly. Despite these problems, Quad could produce excellent images. Unfortunately, very few early videotapes still exist. The high cost of early videotapes meant that most broadcasters erased and reused them, and (in the United States) regarded videotape as simply a better and more cost-effective means of time-delaying broadcasts than the previous kinescope technology, which recorded television pictures onto photographic film. It was the four time zones of the continental United States which had made the system very desirable in the first place. However, some early broadcast videotapes have survived, including *The Edsel Show*, broadcast live in 1957, and 1958's , the oldest colour videotape of an entertainment programme known to exist (the oldest colour videotape is the May 1958 dedication of the WRC-TV studios in Washington, DC). In 1976, NBC's 50th anniversary special included an excerpt from a 1957 colour special starring Donald O'Connor; despite some obvious technical problems, the colour tape was remarkably good. Subsequent videotape systems have used helical scan, where the video heads record diagonal tracks (of complete fields) on to the tape.

Type C and Type B

The next format to gain widespread usage was the 1" (2.54 cm) Type C format from 1976 onward. It introduced features such as shuttling and still framing, but the sound and picture reproduction attainable on the format were of just slightly lower quality than Quad (although 1" Type C's quality was still quite high). However, unlike Quad, 1" Type C machines required much less maintenance, took up less space, and consumed much less electrical power.

In Europe a similar tape format was developed, called Type B. Type B machines (also known as BCN) used the same 1" tape as Type C but they lacked C's shuttle and slow-motion options. The picture quality was slightly better, though. Type B was the broadcast norm in continental Europe for most of the 1980s.

Cassette Formats

In 1969, Sony introduced a prototype for the first widespread video cassette, the 3/4" (1.905 cm) composite U-matic system, which Sony introduced commercially in September 1971 after working out industry standards with other manufacturers. Sony later refined it to *Broadcast Video U-matic* or BVU.

Sony continued its hold on the professional market with its ever-expanding 1/2" (1.27 cm) component video Betacam family (introduced in 1982), which, in its digital variants, is still among the professional market leaders.

Panasonic had some limited success with its MII system, but never could compare to Betacam in terms of market share.

The next step was the digital revolution. Among the first digital video formats Sony's D-1, which featured uncompressed digital component recording. Because D-1 was extremely expensive, the composite D-2 and D-3 (by Sony and Panasonic, respectively) were introduced soon after. Ampex introduced the first compressed component recording with its DCT series in 1992. Panasonic trumped D-1 with its D-5 format, which was uncompressed as well, but much more affordable.

DV standard debuted in 1996 and has become widely used both in its native form and in more robust forms such as Sony's DVCAM and Panasonic's DVCPRO as an acquisition and editing format. However, due to concerns by the entertainment industry about the format's lack of copy protection, only the smaller MiniDV cassettes used with camcorders became commonplace, with the full-sized DV cassettes restricted entirely to professional applications.

For camcorders, Sony adapted the Betacam system with its Digital Betacam format, later following it up with the more low-cost Betacam SX and MPEG IMX formats, and the semi- professional DV-based DVCAM system. Panasonic used its DV variant DVCPRO for all professional cameras, with the higher end format DVCPRO50 being a direct descendant. JVC developed the competing D9/Digital-

S format, which compresses video data in a way similar to DVCPRO but uses a cassette similar to S-VHS media.

High Definition

The introduction of HDTV production necessitated a medium for storing high-resolution video information. In 1997, Sony bumped its Betacam series up to HD with the HDCAM standard and its higher-end cousin HDCAM SR. Panasonic's competing format for cameras was based on DVCPRO and called DVCPRO HD. For VTR and archive use, Panasonic expanded the D-5 specification to store compressed HD streams and called it D-5 HD.

Home Video

VCRs

The first consumer videocassette recorders were launched in 1971 (based around U-matic technology), but it was not until Sony's Betamax (1975) and JVC's VHS (1976) were launched that videotape moved into the mass market, resulting in what came to be known as the "videotape format war", which VHS finally won.

VHS has been the leading consumer VCR format since then, though its follow-ups S-VHS, W-VHS and D-VHS never caught up in popularity. In prerecorded video market VHS has been all but displaced with DVD, but until recently consumers could not make home recordings onto DVD disks. This last barrier to DVD domination has been broken with the recent advent of inexpensive DVD recorders and digital video recorders (DVR). Several retail chains in the United States and in Europe planned to stop selling VHS equipment in 2004, 2005, and 2006. Despite these plans, VHS recorders and tapes are still being sold in 2008 in major stores worldwide.

Comcorders

Early consumer camcorders used full-size VHS or Betamax cassettes. Later models switched to more compact formats, designed explicitly for camcorder use, like VHS-C and Video8. VHS-C was a downsized version of VHS, using the same recording method and the same tape, but in a smaller cassette. It was possible to play VHS-C tapes in a regular VHS tape recorder by using an adaptor. After Super VHS had appeared, a corresponding compact version, Super VHS-C, was released as well.

Video8 was an indirect descendant of Betamax, using narrower tape and smaller cassette. Because of intricate U-shaped tape loading and narrower tape it was not possible to develop an adapter from Video8 to Betamax. Video8 was later replaced with Hi8, which provided better resolution and high quality sound recording, and was similar to Super VHS-C.

In 1995 the MiniDV digital video format was introduced. It utilized DV encoding scheme and smaller cassettes compared to Video8/Hi8 with different magnetic formulation. The format provided near-broadcast quality video and sophisticated nonlinear editing capability on consumer equipment.

In 1999 Sony backported DV recording scheme to 8 mm systems, creating Digital8. By using the same cassettes as Hi8, many Digital8 camcorders were able to play analog Video8/Hi8 recordings, preserving compatibility with already recorded analog tapes. As of 2008 Digital8 camcorders have been removed from the equipment offered by Sony.

Sony introduced another camcorder cassette format called MicroMV, but consumer interest was low due to the proprietary nature of the format and limited support for anything but low-end Windows video editors, and Sony shipped the last MicroMV unit in 2005.

Presently, MiniDV and its high definition cousin, HDV, are the two most popular consumer tape-based formats. The formats use different encoding methods, but the same cassette type.

Since 2001, when MicroMV was presented, no new tape-based formats have been introduced.

Future of Tape

The latest trend in consumer camcorders shows the switch from tape-based to tapeless solutions, like built-in HDDs, optical disks and solid-state media.

Professional solutions still widely rely on tapes, but tapeless formats like DVCPRO P2 and XDCAM are gaining broader acceptance, especially for initial acquisition.

LIST OF VIDEO CONNECTORS

This is a list of physical video connectors and related video signal standards.

By Signal Standard

Signal standard name	Year introduced	Connector	Analog or digital	Max resolution (X-pix × Y-pix @ Hz)	Used for	Notes
Composie video	1956?	1 RCA, BNC, Antenna socket, or Mini-VGA	Analog	728 × 576 @ 25 PAL	Consumer electronics, including VCR and LaserDisc, 1980s-1990s video game consoles like the Nintendo Entertainment System, 1970-1980s home computers like the Commodore VIC-20, some laptop computers	
S-Video	1979?	1 Mini-DIN 4 pin, 1 Mini-VGA, 2 BNC, 2 RCA connector	Analog	728 × 576 @ 25 PAL	S-VHS, some laptop computers, analog broadcast video, 1980-1990s home computers including the Commodore C64, C128 and the Atari 8-bit family	The 4 pin mini-DIN that is most common in consumer products today debuted in JVC's 1987 S-VHS.
SCART	1977	SCART 21-pin	Analog	728 × 576 @ 25 PAL	European Union "unified" A/V interface, Commodore Amiga and various video games	Unified interface for composite video, composite synch RGB, audio and S-video
CGA	1981	DE-9	Digital	640 × 200 @ 60	Pre-i80386 x86 machines	
MDA	1981	DE-9	Digital	720 × 350 @ 50		
HGC	1982	DE-9	Digital	720 × 348 @ 50		
EGA	1984	DE-9	Digital	640 × 350 @ 60		

(Contd.)

(*Contd.*)

Signal standard name	*Year introduced*	*Connector*	*Analog or digital*	*Max resolution (X-pix × Y-pix @ Hz)*	*Used for*	*Notes*
Amiga video	1985	DB23	Both, GenLock	1280 × 400/512 @ 60/50	Commodore Amiga	Similar to SCART, but also includes a digital RGBI signal, genlock clock, composite sync and +12/+5VDC power
VGA	1987	VGA connector variants include DE-15/HD-15 (canonical), DE-9, and Mini-VGA. Also carried by Mini-DVI	Analog	2048 × 1536 @ 85 (2560 × 1600 @ 60 in theory)	Introduced with IBM × 86 machines, but became a universal analog display interface. VESA Display Data Channel was later added to allow monitors to identify themselves to graphic cards, and graphic cards to modify monitor settings.	Successor analog protocols include SVGA, XGA, etc. DVI is a more modern digital alternative.
Mac-II/ Quadra	1987	DA15F	Analog	1152 × 870 @ 75	Macintosh	Mac-DA15F and Sun-13W3 were similar in capability to VGA. Some Sun machines used 4 or 5 BNC connectors to transfer video signal.
13W3	1990?	DB13W3	Analog	1152 × 900 @ 76	SUN computer systems	
OpenLDI	1998	MDR36	LVDS Digital			
Component video	199x?	3 RCA or BNC	Analog	1920×1080 @ 60	Consumer electronics	
D-Terminal	199x?	Apple-AAUI	Analog	1920×1080 @ 60	Japanese consumer electronics	Uses component video and resolution selection via voltage levels.

(*Contd.*)

(Contd.)

Signal standard name	*Year introduced*	*Connector*	*Analog or digital*	*Max resolution (X-pix × Y-pix @ Hz)*	*Used for*	*Notes*
Digital Visual Interface (DVI)	1999	DVI, Mini-DVI, Micro-DVI	Both	2560 × 1600 @ 60	Recent video cards	Almost a ubiquitous computer display link. Uncompressed video only. High-bandwidth Digital Content Protection (HDCP) encryption optional.
ADC	2000	Apple-ADC	Both	2560 × 1600 @ 60	Apple computers	Proprietary connector with DVI signals.
High-Definition Multimedia Interface (HDMI)	2003	HDMI Type A/C	Digital	2560 × 1600 @ 75	Many A/V systems and video cards (including motherboards with IGP)	High-bandwidth Digital Content Protection (HDCP) encryption is mandatory.
Display Port	2007	20-pin (external) 32-pin (internal)	Digital	2560 × 1600 @ 75	DELL monitors upcoming: ATI RV670 based graphics cards and NVIDIA G92 graphics cards (both as OEM optional implementations)	DisplayPort introduced the 128bit-AES to replace HDCP. DisplayPort version 1.1 added support for HDCP.
Serial Digital Interface		BNC	Digital	From 143 Mbit/s to 2.970 Gbit/s, depending on variant. 480i, 576i, 480p, 576p, 720p, 1080i, 1080p.	Broadcast video. Variants include SD-SDI, HD-SDI, Dual Link HD-SDI, 3G-SDI.	

Physical Connectors

Class or connector name	*Used for*	*Notes*
RF Connectors (analog radio frequency signals). Generally use coaxial cable types such as RG-6 and RG-59.		
TV aerial plug, (a.k.a. PAL connector in Europe)	Most video devices in the world connected directly to a roof antenna. Used by early home computers and game consoles to connect them to TVs because the lack of any other connector.	No longer used for antennas in the United States, where it has been replaced by the more reliable F-connector.
BNC (Bayonet Niell-Concelman)	Alternative to RCA for professional video electronics. Protocols: Serial Digital Interface (SDI) and HD-SDI.	75 Ω for video signal on, for example, RG59 e RG6. 50 Ω for data link, like Ethernet on RG58. 93 Ω on RG62.
C connector (Concelman connector)		
GR connector (General Radio connector)		
F connector	Used for U.S. domestic television installations	
N connector (Neill connector)		
Threaded Neill-Concelman connector (TNC)		
UHF connector (e.g. PL-259/SO-239)		
D-Subminiature family		
VGA connector (DE-15 is a common variant.)	Became a nearly ubiquitous analog computer display connector after first being introduced with IBM × 86 machines. Older VGA	Being replaced by DVI from 1990 onwards.

(Contd.)

(*Contd.*)

Class or connector name	*Used for*	*Notes*
	connectors were DE-9 (9-pin). The modern DE-15 connector can carry VESA Display Data Channel to allow the monitor to communicate with the graphics card, and optionally vice versa.	
DB13W3	Analog computer video, colour and monochrome. Sun Microsystems, Silicon Graphics, IBM RISC, Intergraph and some Apple Computer computer workstations.	Obsolete; replaced by VGA and DVI. Same connector was used by 3Com for a redundant PSU on the 3300 switch family.
Digital Visual Interface (DVI). 5 variants are: DVI-I single link, DVI-I dual link, DVI-D single, DVI-D double, and DVI-A.	Almost ubiquitous for modern computer video cards.	
Mini-DVI	VGA, DVI, television. Apple Computer alternative to Mini-VGA.	
Micro-DVI	DVI-D dual link	
DMS-59	DVI dual link	
Apple Display Connector	Combines DVI, USB, and power.	
High-Definition Multimedia Interface (HDMI)	High definition digital video devices (HDMI protocol)	Electrically compatible with DVI-D and DVD-I, using a simple adapter.
DIN/mini-DIN		
Mini-DIN 4-pin	S-Video	
Various Mini-DIN configurations	Various systems and protocols	
Others		
RCA connector	Widely used in consumer electronics for audio and video.	A single connector must be used for each signal.

(*Contd.*)

(*Contd.*)

Class or connector name	*Used for*	*Notes*
SCART	Consumer electronics, mostly in Europe. Carries stereophonic audio (analog), along with either composite video or RGB video. Some devices support S-Video but the use of S-Video is not standardized and use the same pins as composite video and RGB.	
D-Terminal	Popular in Japan for analog high definition video. Available sizes are D1 through D5.	Replacing RCA connectors.
Mini-VGA (used for laptops)	Used for laptops, especially from Apple Computer and some from Sony.	
AV Multi	Combines composite video, S-Video, RGB, component video, and stereophonic sound (two analog channels).	
34-pin MicroCross Molex connector	VESA Enhanced Video Connector and VESA Plug and Display (a.k.a. M1-DA) both used this connector with slightly different pin assignments. These schemes combined VGA or digital video, audio, Fire Wire, and USB signals into a single connector.	Defunct, obsoleted by DFP and later DVI
Digital Flat Panel	Used with the PanelLink digital video protocol.	Obsoleted by DVI
Unified Display Interface		Proposed to replace both DVI and HDMI. Deprecated by Intel in favor of DisplayPort.
DisplayPort	DisplayPort is also the name of the protocol, which is proposed to replace DVI for computer monitors, and consumer electronics (such as home theatre systems).	

MPEG-2

MPEG-2 is a standard for "the generic coding of moving pictures and associated audio information". It describes a combination of lossy video compression and lossy audio compression (audio data compression) methods which permit storage and transmission of movies using currently available storage media and transmission bandwidth.

Main Characteristics

MPEG-2 is widely used as the format of digital television signals that are broadcast by terrestrial (over-the-air), cable, and direct broadcast satellite TV systems. It also specifies the format of movies and other programmes that are distributed on DVD and similar disks. As such, TV stations, TV receivers, DVD players, and other equipment are often designed to this standard. MPEG-2 was the second of several standards developed by the Moving Pictures Expert Group (MPEG) and is an international standard (ISO/IEC 13818). Parts 1 and 2 of MPEG-2 were developed in a joint collaborative team with ITU-T, and they have a respective catalog number in the ITU-T Recommendation Series.

While MPEG-2 is the core of most digital television and DVD formats, it does not completely specify them. Regional institutions can adapt it to their needs by restricting and augmenting aspects of the standard.

MPEG-2 includes a Systems section, Part 1, that defines two distinct, but related, container formats. One is the Transport Stream, designed to carry digital video and audio over possibly lossy media, such as broadcasting, examples of which include ATSC, DVB and SBTVD. MPEG-2 Systems also defines Programme Stream, a container format designed for reasonably reliable media such as optical disks, DVDs and SVCDs. MPEG-2/System is formally known as ISO/IEC 13818-1 and as ITU-T Rec. H.222.0.

The Video section, Part 2 of MPEG-2, is similar to the previous MPEG-1 standard, but also provides support for interlaced video, the format used by analog broadcast TV systems. MPEG-2 video is not optimized for low bit-rates, especially less than 1 Mbit/s at standard definition resolutions. However, it outperforms MPEG-1 at 3 Mbit/s and above. All standards-compliant MPEG-2 Video decoders are fully capable of playing back MPEG-1 Video streams. MPEG-2/Video is formally known as ISO/IEC 13818-2 and as ITU-T Rec. H.262.

With some enhancements, MPEG-2 Video and Systems are also used in some HDTV transmission systems.

The MPEG-2 Audio section, defined in Part 3 of the standard, enhances MPEG-1's audio by allowing the coding of audio programmes with more than two channels. This method is backwards-compatible, allowing MPEG-1 audio decoders to decode the two main stereo components of the presentation.

Part 7 of the MPEG-2 standard specifies a rather different, non-backwards-compatible audio format. Part 7 is referred to as MPEG-2 AAC. While AAC is more efficient than the previous MPEG audio standards, it is much more complex to implement and somewhat more powerful hardware is needed for encoding and decoding. Advanced Audio is also defined in Part 3 of the MPEG-4 standard.

History

MPEG-2 evolved out of the shortcomings of MPEG-1

MPEG 1's known weaknesses:

(*a*) A lower resolution, slightly sub-optimal for modern televisions,
(*b*) A less efficient audio compression system,
(*c*) Lack of flexibility (fewer variations of acceptable packet types),
(*d*) Many access control issues (many MPEG-1 encryption systems were broken), and
(*e*) Unsuitable for HDTV.

Video Coding (Simplified)

An HDTV camera generates a raw video stream of up to 233,280,000 bytes per second. This stream must be compressed if digital TV is to fit in the bandwidth of available TV channels and if movies are to fit on DVDs. Fortunately, video compression is practical because the data in pictures is often redundant in space and time. For example, the sky can be blue across the top of a picture and that blue sky can persist for frame after frame. Also, because of the way the eye works, it is possible to delete some data from video pictures with almost no noticeable degradation in image quality.

TV cameras used in broadcasting usually generate 25 pictures a second (in Europe) or 29.97 pictures a second (in North America). Digital television requires that these pictures be digitized so that they can be processed by computer hardware. Each picture element (a pixel) is then represented by one luma number and two chrominance numbers. These describe the brightness and the colour of the pixel. Thus, each digitized picture is initially represented by three rectangular arrays of numbers.

A common (and old) trick to reduce the amount of data is to separate the picture into two fields: the "top field," which is the odd numbered rows, and the "bottom field," which is the even numbered rows. The two fields are displayed alternately. This format is called interlaced video; two successive fields are called a frame. The typical frame rate is then 25 or 29.97 frames per second. If the video is not interlaced, then it is called progressive video and each picture is a frame. MPEG-2 supports both options.

Another common practice to reduce the data rate is to "thin out" or subsample the two chrominance planes. In effect, the remaining chrominance values represent the nearby values that are deleted. Thinning works because the eye better resolves brightness details than chrominance details. The 4:2:2 chrominance format indicates that half the chrominance values have been deleted. The 4:2:0 chrominance format indicates that three quarters of the chrominance values have been deleted. If no chrominance values have been deleted, the chrominance format is 4:4:4. MPEG-2 allows all three options.

MPEG-2 specifies that the raw frames be compressed into three kinds of frames: intra-coded frames (I-Frame), predictive-coded frames (P-frames), and bidirectionally-predictive-coded frames (B-frames).

An I-Frame is a compressed version of a single uncompressed (raw) frame. It takes advantage of spatial redundancy and of the inability of the eye to detect certain changes in the image. Unlike P-frames and B-frames, I-frames do not depend on data in the preceding or the following frames. Briefly, the raw frame is divided into 8 pixel by 8 pixel blocks. The data in each block is transformed by a discrete cosine transform. The result is an 8 by 8 matrix of coefficients. The transform converts spatial variations into frequency variations, but it does not change the information in the block; the original block can be recreated exactly by applying the inverse cosine transform. The advantage of doing this is that the image can now be simplified by quantizing the coefficients. Many of the coefficients, usually the higher frequency components, will then be zero. The penalty of this step is the loss of some subtle distinctions in brightness and colour. If one applies the inverse transform to the matrix after it is quantized, one gets an image that looks very similar to the original image but that is not quite as nuanced. Next, the quantized coefficient matrix is itself compressed. Typically, one corner of the quantized matrix is filled with zeros. By starting in the opposite corner of the matrix, then zigzagging through the matrix to combine the coefficients into a string, then substituting run-length codes for consecutive zeros in that string, and then applying Huffman coding to that result, one reduces the matrix to a smaller array of numbers. It is this array that is broadcast or that is put on DVDs. In the receiver or the player, the whole process is reversed, enabling the receiver to reconstruct, to a close approximation, the original frame.

Typically, every 15th frame or so is made into an I-frame. P-frames and B-frames might follow an I-frame like this, IBBPBBPBBPBB(I), to form a Group of Pictures (GOP); however, the standard is flexible about this.

Macroblocks

P-frames provide more compression than I-frames because they take advantage of the data in the previous I-frame or P-frame. I-frames and P-frames are called reference frames. To generate a P-frame, the previous reference frame is reconstructed, just as it would be in a TV receiver or DVD player. The frame being compressed is divided into 16 pixel by 16 pixel macroblocks. Then, for each of those macroblocks, the reconstructed reference frame is searched to find that 16 by 16 macroblock that best matches the macroblock being compressed. The offset is encoded as a "motion vector." Frequently, the offset is zero. But, if something in the picture is moving, the offset might be something like 23 pixels to the right and 4 pixels up. The match between the two macroblocks will often not be perfect. To correct for this, the encoder computes the strings of coefficient values as described above for both macroblocks and, then, subtracts one from the other. This "residual" is appended to the motion vector and the result sent to the receiver or stored on the DVD for each macroblock being compressed. Sometimes no suitable match is found. Then, the macroblock is treated like an I-frame macroblock.

The processing of B-frames is similar to that of P-frames except that B-frames use the picture in the following reference frame as well as the picture in the preceding reference frame. As a result, B-frames usually provide more compression than P-frames. B-frames are never reference frames.

While the above generally describes MPEG-2 video compression, there are many details that are not discussed including details involving fields, chrominance formats, responses to scene changes, special codes that label the parts of the bitstream, and other pieces of information.

Audio Encoding

MPEG-2 also introduces new audio encoding methods. These are:

(*a*) Low bitrate encoding with halved sampling rate (MPEG-1 Layer 1/2/3 LSF),
(*b*) Multichannel encoding with up to 5.1 channels, and
(*c*) MPEG-2 AAC.

Video Profiles and Levels

MPEG-2 video supports wide range of applications from mobile to high quality HD editing. For many applications, it is unrealistic and too expensive to support the entire standard. To allow such applications to support only subsets of it, the standard defines profile and level. The profile defines the subset of features such as compression algorithm, chroma format, etc. The level defines the subset of quantitative capabilities such as maximum bit rate, maximum frame size, etc.

A MPEG application then specifies the capabilities in terms of profile and level. For example, a DVD player may say it supports up to main profile and main level (often written as MP@ML). It means the player can play back any MPEG stream encoded as MP@ML or less.

Table 2.1 and Table 2.2 summarizes the limitations of each profile and level. There are many other constraints not listed here.

Table 2.1: MPEG-2 Profiles

Abbr.	*Name*	*Picture Coding Types*	*Chroma Format*	*Aspect Ratios*	*Scalable modes*
SP	Simple profile	I, P	4:2:0	Square pixels, 4:3, or 16:9	None
MP	Main profile	I, P, B	4:2:0	Square pixels, 4:3, or 16:9	None
SNR	SNR Scalable profile	I, P, B	4:2:0	Square pixels, 4:3, or 16:9	SNR (signal-to-noise ratio) scalable
Spatial	Spatially Scalable profile	I, P, B	4:2:0	Square pixels, 4:3, or 16:9	SNR- or spatial-scalable
HP	High profile	I, P, B	4:2:2 or 4:2:0	Square pixels, 4:3, or 16:9	SNR- or spatial-scalable

Exempting scalability (a rarely used feature where one MPEG-2 stream augments another), the following are some of the constraints on levels (*see* Table 2.2).

Table 2.2: MPEG-2 Levels

Abbr.	*Name*	*Frame rates (Hz)*	*Max horizontal resolution*	*Max vertical resolution*	*Max luminance samples per second (approximately height × width × framerate)*	*Max bit rate in Main profile (Mbit/s)*
LL	Low Level	23.976, 24, 25, 29.97, 30	352	288	3,041,280	4
ML	Main Level	23.976, 24, 25, 29.97, 30	720	576	10,368,000, except in High profile, where constraint is 14,475,600 for 4:2:0 and 11,059,200 for 4:2:2	15

(Contd.)

(Contd.)

H-14	High 1440	23.976, 24, 25, 29.97, 30, 50, 59.94, 60	1440	1152	47,001,600, except that in High profile with 4:2:0, constraint is 62,668,800	60
HL	High Level	23.976, 24, 25, 29.97, 30, 50, 59.94, 60	1920	1152	62,668,800, except that in High profile with 4:2:0, constraint is 83,558,400	80

APPLICATIONS

DVD

The DVD standard uses MPEG-2 video, but imposes some restrictions:

1. *Allowed Resolutions:*

   (*a*) 720 × 480, 704 × 480, 352 × 480, 352 × 240 pixel (NTSC)
   (*b*) 720 × 576, 704 × 576, 352 × 576, 352 × 288 pixel (PAL)

2. *Allowed Aspect ratios* (Display AR):

   (*a*) 4:3
   (*b*) 16:9
   (*c*) (1.85:1 and 2.35:1, among others, are often listed as valid DVD aspect ratios, but are actually just a 16:9 image with the top and bottom of the frame masked in black).

3. *Allowed Frame rates:*

   (*a*) 29.97 frame/s (NTSC),
   (*b*) 25 frame/s (PAL).

   Note: By using a pattern of REPEAT_FIRST_FIELD flags on the headers of encoded pictures, pictures can be displayed for either two or three fields and almost any picture display rate (minimum 2/3 of the frame rate) can be achieved. This is most often used to display 23.976 (approximately film rate) video on NTSC.

4. *Audio + video bitrate:*

   (*a*) Video peak 9.8 Mbit/s

(*b*) Total peak 10.08 Mbit/s
(*c*) Minimum 300 kbit/s

5. YUV 4:2:0
6. Additional subtitles possible
7. Closed captioning (NTSC only)
8. *Audio:*

(*a*) Linear Pulse Code Modulation (LPCM): 48 kHz or 96 kHz; 16- or 24-bit; up to six channels (not all combinations possible due to bitrate constraints).
(*b*) MPEG Layer 2 (MP2): 48 kHz, up to 5.1 channels (required in PAL players only).
(*c*) Dolby Digital (DD, also known as AC-3): 48 kHz, 32-448 kbit/s, up to 5.1 channels.
(*d*) Digital Theater Systems (DTS): 754 kbit/s or 1510 kbit/s (not required for DVD player compliance).
(*e*) NTSC DVDs must contain at least one LPCM or Dolby Digital audio track.
(*f*) PAL DVDs must contain at least one MPEG Layer 2, LPCM, or Dolby Digital audio track.
(*g*) Players are not required to play back audio with more than two channels, but must be able to downmix multichannel audio to two channels.

9. *GOP structure:*

(*a*) Sequence header must be present at the beginning of every GOP
(*b*) Maximum frames per GOP: 18 (NTSC)/15 (PAL), i.e. 0.6 seconds both
(*c*) Closed GOP required for multi-angle DVDs.

DVB

Application-specific restrictions on MPEG-2 video in the DVB standard:

Allowed resolutions for SDTV:

1. 720, 640, 544, 480 or 352 × 480 pixel, 24/1.001, 24, 30/1.001 or 30 frame/s

2. 352 × 240 pixel, 24/1.001, 24, 30/1.001 or 30 frame/s
3. 720, 704, 544, 480 or 352 × 576 pixel, 25 frame/s
4. 352 × 288 pixel, 25 frame/s.

For HDTV

1. 720 × 576 × 50 frame/s progressive (576p50)
2. 1280 × 720 × 25 or 50 frame/s progressive (720p50)
3. 1440 or 1920 × 1080 × 25 frame/s progressive (1080p25 film mode)
4. 1440 or 1920 × 1080 × 25 frame/s interlace (1080i25)
5. 1920 × 1080 × 50 frame/s progressive (1080p50) possible future H.264/AVC format.

ATSC and ISDB-T

The ATSC A/53 standard, used in the United States, uses MPEG-2 video at the Main Profile @ High Level, with additional restrictions:

1. The maximum bitrate of the MPEG-2 video stream is exactly 19.4 Mbit/s for broadcast television, and exactly 38.8 Mbit/s for the "high-data-rate" mode (e.g., cable television). (The practical limit is somewhat lower, since the MPEG-2 video stream must fit inside a transport stream, with overhead, sent out at 19.3927... Mbit/s for broadcast.)
2. The amount of MPEG-2 stream buffer required at the decoder (the vbv_buffer_size_value) must be less than or equal to 999,424 bytes.
3. In most cases, the transmitter can't start sending a coded image until within a half-second of when it is to be decoded (vbv_delay less than or equal to 45000 90-kHz clock increments).
4. The stream must include colorimetry information (gamma curve, the precise RGB colours used, and the relationship between RGB and the coded YCbCr).
5. The video must be 4:2:0 (chrominance resolution must be 1/2 of luma horizontal resolution and 1/2 of luma vertical resolution).

Allowed video resolutions, aspect ratios, and frame/field rates:

1. 1920 × 1080 pixel (16:9, with square pixels), at 30p, 29.97p, 24p, 23.98p, 30i, or 29.97i.
2. 1280 × 720 pixel (16:9, with square pixels), at 60p, 59.94p, 30p, 29.97p, 24p, or 23.98p.
3. 704 × 480 pixel (either 4:3 or 16:9—either way, with non-square pixels), at 60p, 59.94p, 30p, 29.97p, 24p, 23.98p, 30i, or 29.97i.
4. 640 × 480 pixel (4:3, with square pixels), at 60p, 59.94p, 30p, 29.97p, 24p, 23.98p, 30i, or 29.97i.

Note that although the ATSC A/53 standard limits transmission to these 18 formats (and their 1000/1001-rate slowed-down versions), the U.S. Federal Communications Commission declined to mandate that television stations obey this part of the ATSC's standard. In theory, television stations in the U.S. are free to choose any resolution, aspect ratio, and frame/field rate, within the limits of Main Profile @ High Level. Many stations do go outside the bounds of the ATSC specification by using other resolutions—for example, 720 × 480.

Also note that the ATSC specification and MPEG-2 allow the use of progressive frames, even within an interlaced video sequence. For example, NBC stations transmit a 1080i30 video sequence—meaning the formal output of the MPEG-2 decoding process is sixty 540-line fields per second. But for prime-time television shows, those 60 fields can be coded with 24 progressive frames. Some NBC stations do this, meaning they actually transmit an 1080p24 video stream (a sequence of 24 progressive frames per second) with metadata instructing the decoder to interlace them (and repeat them in 3:2 pulldown) before display.

Thus, it would be incorrect to say that the ATSC standard doesn't contain 1080p video, or that broadcast HDTV doesn't use 1080p video. The ATSC specification allows 1080p30 and 1080p24 sequences—just not 1080p60 sequences. They aren't used in practice, because broadcasters want to be able to switch between 60 Hz (news, soap operas) and 24 Hz (prime-time) content without ending the MPEG-2 sequence. However, the ATSC specification also allows broadcasters to transmit progressive frames within an interlaced sequence, and some broadcasters actually do this in practice. Their transmissions could fairly be described as 1080p24, since they contain 24 progressively-coded frames per second. (This is the same mechanism used by HD-DVD to code 1080p24 content—progressive frames within an interlaced sequence.)

Note: The 1080-line formats are encoded with 1920 × 1088 pixel luma matrices and 960 × 540 chroma matrices, but the last 8 lines are discarded by the MPEG-2 decoding and display process.

MPEG-2 audio was a contender for the ATSC standard during the DTV "Grand Alliance" shootout, but lost out to Dolby AC-3.

Note: All the text about Mpeg2 in ATSC is also valid for ISDB-T, except that in the main TS is aggregated a second programme for mobile devices compressed in Mpeg-4 H.264 AVC for video and AAC-LC for audio, mainly known as 1Seg.

ISO/IEC 13818

Part 1: Systems—describes synchronization and multiplexing of video and audio. Also known as ITU-T Rec. H.222.0.

Part 2: Video—compression codec for interlaced and non-interlaced video signals. Also known as ITU-T Rec. H.262.

Part 3: Audio—compression codec for perceptual coding of audio signals. A multichannel-enabled extension of MPEG-1 audio.

Part 4: Describes procedures for testing compliance.

Part 5: Describes systems for software simulation.

Part 6: Describes extensions for DSM-CC (Digital Storage Media Command and Control).

Part 7: Advanced Audio Coding (AAC).

Part 9: Extension for real time interfaces.

Part 10: Conformance extensions for DSM-CC.

(Part 8: 10-bit video extension. Primary application was studio video. Part 8 has been withdrawn due to lack of interest by industry.)

Patent Holders

Approximately 640 patents worldwide make up the "essential" patents surrounding MPEG-2. These are held by over 20 corporations and one university. Where software patentability is upheld, the use of MPEG-2 requires the payment of licensing fees to the patent holders via the MPEG Licensing Association. The patent pool is managed and administered by MPEG Licensing Authority, a private organization. Other patents are licensed by Audio MPEG, Inc. The development of the standard itself took less time than the patent negotiations.

Patents

- Alcatel-Lucent:
  - US 4,833,543 Expired
  - US 4,970,590—System and device for package multiplexing in transmission of many data flows generated by a sole algorithm—Filed: December 21, 1989 Granted: November 13, 1990
  - US 5,453,790—Video decoder having asynchronous operation with respect to a video display—Filed: March 26, 1993 Granted: September 26, 1995
- British Telecommunications plc:
  - US 5,291,284—Predictive coding and decoding with error drift reduction—Filed: July 23, 1991 Granted: March 1, 1994
- Canon Inc.
  - US 4,982,270—Video data transmitting system—Filed: February 3, 1989 Granted: January 1, 1991
- CIF LICENSING, LLC
  - US 5,068,724—Adaptive motion compensation for digital television—Filed: June 15, 1990 Granted: November 26, 1991
  - US 5,091,782—Apparatus and method for adaptively compressing successive blocks of digital video—Filed: April 9, 1990 Granted: February 25, 1992
  - US 5,093,720—Motion compensation for interlaced digital television signals—Filed: August 20, 1990 Granted: March 3, 1992
- Columbia University
  - US Re 35,093—Systems and methods for coding even fields of interlaced video sequences—Filed:

December 9, 1994 Granted: November 21, 1995 Reissue of 05193004 Filed: Dec., 1990 Granted: Mar., 1993

- France Telecom (CNET)
  - US 4,796,087 Expired
- Fujitsu
  - US 5,235,618—Video signal coding apparatus, coding method used in the video signal coding apparatus and video signal coding transmission system having the video signal coding apparatus—Filed: November 6, 1990 Granted: August 10, 1993
- General Electric Capital Corporation
  - US 4,706,260 Expired
  - US 4,813,056 Expired
- General Instrument Corp. (now the broadband division of Motorola)
  - US 4,394,774 Expired
  - US 4,698,672 Expired
- GE Technology Development, Inc.
  - US 5,426,464—Field elimination apparatus for a video compression/decompression system—Filed: October 18, 1994 Granted: June 20, 1995
  - US 5,486,864—Differential time code method and apparatus as for a compressed video signal—Filed: May 13, 1993 Granted: January 23, 1996
  - US 5,491,516—Field elimination apparatus for a video compression/decompression system—Filed: January 14, 1993 Granted: February 13, 1996
  - US 5,600,376—Field elimination apparatus for a video compression/decompression system—Filed: March 20, 1995 Granted: February 4, 1997
  - US 5,796,743—Data word indicator in a system for assembling transport data packets—Filed: November 30, 1993 Granted: August 18, 1998

- Hitachi, Ltd.
- KDDI Corporation (KDDI)
- LG Electronics Inc.
    - US Re 37,057—Apparatus and method for converting an HDTV signal to a non-HDTV signal—Filed: May 18, 1998 Granted: February 20, 2001 Reissue of 05519446 Filed: Nov., 1994 Granted: May, 1996
    - US Re 37,568—Inverse Quantizer—Filed: March 31, 1999 Granted: March 5, 2002 Reissue of 05617094 Filed: Nov., 1993 Granted: April, 1997
- Matsushita
    - US Re 35,910—Moving image signal encoding apparatus and decoding apparatus—Filed: May 12, 1994 Granted: September 29, 1998 Reissue of 05113255 Filed: May., 1990 Granted: May, 1992
    - US Re 36,015—Apparatus and method for processing groups of fields in a video data compression system—Filed: October 2, 1995 Granted: December 29, 1998 Reissue of 05293229 Filed: March, 1992 Granted: March, 1994
    - US Re 36,507—Apparatus and method for processing groups of fields in a video data compression system to encode a single frame as an I-field and a P-field—Filed: October 21, 1997 Granted: January 18, 2000 Reissue of 05293229 Filed: March, 1992 Granted: March, 1994
    - US Re 39,276—Method for determining motion compensation—Filed: April 27, 2000 Granted: September 12, 2006
    - Reissue of 05745182 Filed: July, 1994 Granted: April, 1998
    - US Re 39,278—Method for determining motion compensation—Filed: April 13, 2001 Granted: September 12, 2006 Reissue of 05745182 Filed: July, 1994 Granted: April, 1998
    - US Re 39,280—Method for determining motion compensation—Filed: May 30, 2001 Granted: September 12, 2006 Reissue of 05745182 Filed: July, 1994 Granted: April, 1998

- US 5,223,949—Coding means for a signal processing system—Filed: April 17, 1992 Granted: June 29, 1993
- US 5,412,430—Image coding method and image coding apparatus—Filed: May 4, 1994 Granted: May 2, 1995
- US 5,784,107—Method and apparatus for picture coding and method and apparatus for picture decoding—Filed: January 23, 1996 Granted: July 21, 1998

❖ Mitsubishi

- US 4,954,892—Buffer controlled picture signal encoding and decoding system—Filed: October 4, 1989 Granted: September 4, 1990
- US 5,072,295—Adaptive quantization coder/decoder with limiter circuitry—Filed: August 20, 1990 Granted: December 10, 1991 46—Method and apparatus for nonsequential multimedia data interchange in a data processing system—Filed: April 10, 1991 Granted: December 7, 1993
- US 5,949,489—Image signal coding system—Filed: July 31, 1998 Granted: September 7, 1999
- US 5,963,258—Image signal coding system—Filed: July 31, 1998 Granted: October 5, 1999
- US 5,970,175—Image signal coding system—Filed: October 26, 1998 Granted: October 19, 1999
- US 5,990,960—Image signal coding system—Filed: December 9, 1998 Granted: November 23, 1999
- US 6,002,439—Image signal coding system—Filed: May 27, 1999 Granted: December 14, 1999
- US 6,097,759—Image signal coding system—Filed: November 22, 1999 Granted: August 1, 2000
- US 6,188,794—Image signal coding system—Filed: May 20, 1999 Granted: February 13, 2001
- US 6,307,973—Image signal coding system—Filed: December 4, 2000 Granted: October 23, 2001

❖ Nippon Telegraph and Telephone Corporation (NTT)
❖ NXP
❖ Philips

- US 4,849,812 Expired
- US 4,901,075 Expired
- US 5,021,879—System for transmitting video pictures—Filed: September 24, 1990 Granted: June 4, 1991
- US 5,027,206—High-definition television systems—Filed: September 13, 1989 Granted: June 25, 1991
- US 5,128,758—Method and apparatus for digitally processing a high definition television augmentation signal—Filed: June 2, 1989 Granted: July 7, 1992
- US 5,179,442—Method and apparatus for digitally processing a high definition television augmentation signal—Filed: November 26, 1990 Granted: January 12, 1993
- US 5,333,135—Identification of a data stream transmitted as a sequence of packets—Filed: February 1, 1993 Granted: July 26, 1994
- US 5,606,539—Method and apparatus for encoding and decoding an audio and/or video signal, and a record carrier for use with such apparatus—Filed: August 31, 1994 Granted: February 25, 1997
- US 5,608,697—Record carrier containing an audio and/or video signal which has been encoded and includes a decoder delay time parameter indicating a time delay for one or more portions of the signal—Filed: March 18, 1996 Granted: March 4, 1997
- US 5,740,310—Method of maintaining display continuity from a CD with slow-motion or freeze capability—Filed: June 28, 1994 Granted: April 14, 1998
- US 5,844,867—Methods and apparatus for encoding and decoding an audio and/or video signal, and a record carrier used therewith or produced therefrom—Filed: September 9, 1996 Granted: December 1, 1998

❖ Robert Bosch GmbH

❖ Samsung

- US 5,461,421—Encoding and decoding method and

apparatus thereof—Filed: November 29, 1993 Granted: October 24, 1995
- US 5,467,086—Apparatus and method of coding/decoding video data—Filed: June 18, 1993 Granted: November 14, 1995
- US 5,654,706—System for variable length decoding digital transmission data which has been compressed by selecting a scanning pattern—Filed: December 18, 1996 Granted: August 5, 1997
- US 6,680,975—Signal encoding and decoding system and method—Filed: November 2, 2000 Granted: January 20, 2004
- US 7,292,657—Signal compressing signal—Filed: July 3, 2003 Granted: November 6, 2007

❖ Sanyo Electric Co. Ltd.

❖ Scientific Atlanta

- US 5,418,782—Methods and apparatus for providing virtual service selection in a multi-service communications system—Filed: January 6, 1994 Granted: May 23, 1995
- US 5,420,866—Methods for providing conditional access information to decoders in a packet-based multiplexed communications system—Filed: March 29, 1994 Granted: May 30, 1995
- US 5,457,701—Method for indicating packet errors in a packet-based multi-hop communications system—Filed: January 6, 1994 Granted: October 10, 1995

❖ Sharp

❖ Sony

- US 4,864,393—Motion vector estimation in television images—Filed: May 31, 1988 Granted: September 5, 1989 Expired
- US Re 37,222—Video signal transmitting system—Filed: July 19, 1994 Granted: June 12, 2001 Reissue of 05132792 Filed: Oct., 1990 Granted: July, 1992
- US 5,191,436—Method for recording coded motion picture data—Filed: April 30, 1991 Granted: March 2, 1993

- US 5,291,486—Data multiplexing apparatus and multiplexed data demultiplexing apparatus—Filed: August 7, 1992 Granted: March 1, 1994
- US 5,298,991—Variable length coding apparatus and method for motion vector—Filed: July 24, 1992 Granted: March 29, 1994
- US 5,343,248—Moving image compressing and recording medium and moving image data encoder and decoder—Filed: July 16, 1992 Granted: August 30, 1994
- US 5,428,396—Variable length coding/decoding method for motion vectors—Filed: December 27, 1993 Granted: June 27, 1995
- US 5,461,420—Apparatus for coding and decoding a digital video signal derived from a motion picture film source—Filed: September 17, 1993 Granted: October 24, 1995
- US 5,481,553—Methods and apparatus for preventing rounding errors when transform coefficients representing a motion picture signal are inversely transformed—Filed: February 28, 1994 Granted: January 2, 1996
- US 5,510,840—Methods and devices for encoding and decoding frame signals and recording medium therefore—Filed: May 15, 1995 Granted: April 23, 1996
- US 5,539,466—Efficient coding apparatus for picture signal and decoding apparatus therefore—Filed: September 26, 1994 Granted: July 23, 1996
- US 5,543,847—Picture coding and decoding method for random accessing—Filed: December 13, 1993 Granted: August 6, 1996
- US 5,559,557—Motion video coding with adaptive precision for DC component coefficient quantization and variable length coding—Filed: September 28, 1993 Granted: September 24, 1996
- US 5,663,763—Picture signal encoding method and apparatus and picture signal decoding method and apparatus—Filed: October 18, 1993 Granted: September 2, 1997
- US 5,666,461—High efficiency encoding and

decoding of picture signals and recording medium containing same—Filed: May 30, 1995 Granted: September 9, 1997

- US 5,701,164—Macroblock coding including difference between motion vectors—Filed: December 19, 1996 Granted: December 23, 1997
- US 5,946,042—Macroblock coding including difference between motion vectors—Filed: July 2, 1997 Granted: August 31, 1999
- US 5,982,437—Coding method and system, and decoding method and system—Filed: October 15, 1993 Granted: November 9, 1999
- US 6,040,863—Method of coding and decoding motion vector and apparatus therefore, and method of coding and decoding picture signal and apparatus therefore—Filed: December 18, 1998 Granted: March 21, 2000
- US 6,160,849—Selectable field and frame based predictive video coding—Filed: May 30, 1995 Granted: December 12, 2000

❖ Thomson Licensing S.A.

- US 4,800,432 Expired
- US 4,969,055 Expired
- US 5,289,276—Method and apparatus for conveying compressed video data over a noisy communication channel—Filed: June 19, 1992 Granted: February 22, 1994
- US 5,365,272—Method for formatting compressed video data into transport cells—Filed: July 2, 1993 Granted: November 15, 1994
- US 5,381,181—Clock recovery apparatus as for a compressed video signal—Filed: May 13, 1993 Granted: January 10, 1995
- US 5,422,676—System for coding an image representative signal—Filed: October 22, 1993 Granted: June 6, 1995
- US 5,442,400—Error concealment apparatus for MPEG-like video data—Filed: April 29, 1993 Granted: August 15, 1995

- US 5,459,789—Packet TV programme component detector—Filed: April 22, 1994 Granted: October 17, 1995
- US 5,483,287—Method for forming transport cells for conveying compressed video data—Filed: August 3, 1994 Granted: January 9, 1996
- US 5,565,923—Apparatus for formatting a digital signal to include multiple time stamps for system synchronization—Filed: August 22, 1995 Granted: October 15, 1996
- US 5,784,110—Data processor for assembling transport data packets—Filed: May 23, 1996 Granted: July 21, 1998
- US 7,020,204—Adaptive method of encoding and decoding a series of pictures by transformation, and devices for implementing this method—Filed: February 8, 2002 Granted: March 28, 2006.

❖ Toshiba

- US 5,317,397—Predictive coding using spatial-temporal filtering and plural motion vectors—Filed: May 29, 1992 Granted: May 31, 1994
- US 5,424,779—Video coding apparatus—Filed: November 24, 1993 Granted: June 13, 1995
- US 5,467,136—Video decoder for determining a motion vector from a scaled vector and a difference vector—Filed: February 17, 1994 Granted: November 14, 1995
- US 5,742,344—Motion compensated video decoding method and system for decoding a coded video signal using spatial and temporal filtering—Filed: April 3, 1996 Granted: April 21, 1998
- US 5,986,713—Video coding apparatus using inter-field prediction—Filed: June 11, 1998 Granted: November 16, 1999

❖ Victor Company of Japan, Limited (JVC).

- US Re 34,965—Interframe predictive encoding system with encoded and transmitted prediction error—Filed: January 14, 1993 Granted: June 13, 1995 Reissue of 04985768 Filed: Jan., 1990 Granted: Jan., 1991

- US Re 35,158—Apparatus for adaptive interframe predictive encoding of video signal—Filed: December 28, 1992 Granted: February 20, 1996 Reissue of 04982285 Filed: Apr., 1990 Granted: Jan., 1991
- US Re 36,822—Moving image signal coding apparatus and coded signal decoding apparatus—Filed: October 2, 1998 Granted: August 15, 2000 Reissue of 05748784 Filed: Jan., 1996 Granted: May, 1998
- US 5,103,307—Interframe predictive coding/decoding system for varying interval between independent frames—Filed: January 18, 1991 Granted: April 7, 1992
- US 5,175,618—Compression method for interlace moving image signals—Filed: October 30, 1991 Granted: December 29, 1992

Non-MPEG-LA Patents

- Alcatel-Lucent:
    - US 5,341,457—Perceptual coding of audio signals—Filed: August 20, 1993 Granted: August 23, 1994
    - US RE39,080—Rate loop processor for perceptual encoder/decoder—Filed: August 13, 2002 Granted: April 25, 2006 Reissue of 05627938 Filed: September, 1994 Granted: May, 1997
- Audio MPEG, Inc.
    - US 4,972,484—Method of transmitting or storing masked sub-band coded audio signals—Filed: July 21, 1988 Granted: November 20, 1990
    - US 5,214,678—Digital transmission system using sub-band coding of a digital signal—Filed: May 31, 1990 Granted: May 25, 1993
    - US 5,323,396—Digital transmission system, transmitter and receiver for use in the transmission

system—Filed: December 21, 1992 Granted: June 21, 1994

- US 5,539,829—Sub-band coded digital transmission system using some composite signals—Filed: June 7, 1995 Granted: July 23, 1996
- US 5,606,618—Sub-band coded digital transmission system using some composite signals—Filed: December 27, 1993 Granted: February 25, 1997
- US 5,530,655—Digital sub-band transmission system with transmission of an additional signal—Filed: June 6, 1995 Granted: June 25, 1996
- US 5,777,992—Decoder for decoding and encoded digital signal and a receiver comprising the decoder—Filed: June 7, 1995 Granted: July 7, 1998
- US 6,289,308—Encoded wideband digital transmission signal and record carrier recorded with such a signal—Filed: March 8, 2000 Granted: September 11, 2001
- US 5,481,643—Transmitter, receiver and record carrier for transmitting/receiving at least a first and a second signal component—Filed: April 24, 1995 Granted: January 2, 1996
- US 5,544,247—Transmission and reception of a first and a second main signal component—Filed: October 25, 1994 Granted: August 6, 1996
- US 5,610,985—Digital 3-channel transmission of left and right stereo signals and a center signal—Filed: January 21, 1994 Granted: March 11, 1997
- US 5,740,317—Process for finding the overall monitoring threshold during a bit-rate-reducing source coding—Filed: August 30, 1995 Granted: April 14, 1998
- US 5,878,080—N-channel transmission, compatible with 2-channel transmission and 1-channel transmission—Filed: February 7, 1997 Granted: March 2, 1999
- US 5,960,037—Encoding of a plurality of information signals—Filed: April 9, 1997 Granted: September 28, 1999

- US 5,991,715—Perceptual audio signal sub-band coding using value classes for successive scale factor differences—Filed: August 31, 1995 Granted: November 23, 1999
- US 6,023,490—Encoding apparatus for encoding a plurality of information signals—Filed: April 9, 1997 Granted: February 8, 2000

❖ Thomson:

- US 4,821,260 Expired
- US 4,942,607 Expired
- US 5,214,742—Method for transmitting a signal—Filed: October 1, 1990 Granted: May 25, 1993
- US 5,227,990—Process for transmitting and receiving a signal—Filed: January 17, 1992 Granted: July 13, 1993
- US 5,384,811—Method for the transmission of a signal—Filed: August 24, 1992 Granted: January 24, 1995
- US 5,736,943—Method for determining the type of coding to be selected for coding at least two signals—Filed: May 31, 1996 Granted: April 7, 1998
- US 5,455,833—Process for the detecting of errors in the transmission of frequency-coded digital signals—Filed: April 26, 1993 Granted: October 3, 1995
- US 5,559,834—Method of reducing crosstalk in processing of acoustic or optical signals—Filed: April 15, 1994 Granted: September 24, 1996
- US 5,321,729—Method for transmitting a signal—Filed: April 26, 1993 Granted: June 14, 1994
- US 5,706,309—Process for transmitting and/or storing digital signals of multiple channels—Filed: May 2, 1995 Granted: January 6, 1998
- US 5,701,346—Method of coding a plurality of audio signals—Filed: September 12, 1996 Granted: December 23, 1997
- US 5,742,735—Digital adaptive transformation coding method—Filed: August 25, 1994 Granted: April 21, 1998
- US 5,812,672—Method for reducing data in the transmission and/or storage of digital signals of

several dependent channels—Filed: December 15, 1994 Granted: September 22, 1998

- US 5,579,430—Digital encoding process—Filed: January 26, 1995 Granted: November 26, 1996
- US 6,185,539—Process of low sampling rate digital encoding of audio signals—Filed: May 26, 1998 Granted: February 6, 2001
- US 6,009,399—Method and apparatus for encoding digital signals employing bit allocation using combinations of different threshold models to achieve desired bit rates—Filed: April 16, 1997 Granted: December 28, 1999
- US 5,924,060—Digital coding process for transmission or storage of acoustical signals by transforming of scanning values into spectral coefficients—Filed: March 20, 1997 Granted: July 13, 1999
- US 5,703,999—Process for reducing data in the transmission and/or storage of digital signals from several interdependent channels—Filed: November 18, 1996 Granted: December 30, 1997

According to the MPEG-LA Licensing Agreement MPEG-LA, any use of MPEG-2 technology is subject to royalties.

- Encoders are subject to a royalty of $2.50 per unit.
- Decoders are subject to a royalty of $2.50 per unit.
- Royalty-based sales of encoders and decoders are subject to different rules and $2.50 per unit.
- Also, any packaged medium (DVDs/Data Streams) is subject to licence fees according to length of recording/broadcast.

In the case of free software such as VLC media player (which uses the ffmpeg library) and in which the software is not sold, the end-user bears the royalty.

ATSC STANDARDS

ATSC Standards document a digital television format that will have replaced the analog NTSC television system by February 17,

2009 in the United States, and August 31, 2011 in Canada. It was developed by the Advanced Television Systems Committee.

The high definition television standards defined by the ATSC produce wide screen 16:9 images up to 1920×1080 pixels in size—more than six times the display resolution of the earlier standard. However, a host of different image sizes are also supported, so that up to six standard-definition "virtual channels" can be broadcast on a single 6 MHz TV channel.

ATSC also boasts "theater quality" audio because it uses the Dolby Digital AC-3 format to provide 5.1-channel surround sound. Numerous auxiliary datacasting services can also be provided.

Broadcasters who use ATSC and want to retain an analog signal must broadcast on two separate channels, as the ATSC system requires the use of an entire channel. Virtual channels allow channel numbers to be remapped from their physical RF channel to any other number 1 to 99, so that ATSC stations can either be associated with the related NTSC channel numbers, or all stations on a network can use the same number. There is also a standard for distributed transmission (DTx) which allows for booster stations.

ATSC standards are marked A/x (x is the standard number) and can be downloaded freely from ATSC website.

Many aspects of ATSC are patented, including elements of the MPEG video coding, the AC-3 audio coding, and the 8VSB modulation. As with other systems, ATSC depends on numerous interwoven standards, e.g. the EIA-708 standard for digital closed captioning, leading to variations in implementation.

RESOLUTION

The ATSC system supports a number of different display resolutions, *aspect ratios*, and *frame rates*. The formats are listed here by resolution, form of scanning (*progressive* or *interlaced*), and number of frames (or fields) per second. Table 2.3 includes formats from both A/53 Part 4 (MPEG-2 Video System Characteristics) and A/63 (Standard for Coding 25/50 Hz Video).

The different resolutions can operate in *progressive scan* or *interlaced* mode, although the highest 1080-line system cannot display progressive images at the rate of 59.94 or 60 frames per second. (Such technology was seen as too advanced at the time, plus the image quality was deemed to be too poor considering the

Table 2.3: Resolution

Resolution *Vertical*	*Horizontal*	*Aspect ratio*	*Pixel aspect ratio*	*Form of scanning*	*Framerate (Hz)*
288	352	4:3 or 16:9	non-square	progressive	25
				interlaced	29.97 (59.94 fields/s)
					30 (60 fields/s)
					23.976
	640	4:3	Square		24
				progressive	29.97
					30
					59.94
					60
480					29.97 (59.94 fields/s)
				interlaced	30 (60 fields/s)
	704	4:3 or 16:9	non-square		23.976
				progressive	24
					29.97
					30
					59.94
					60
	352	4:3 or 16:9	non-square	interlaced	25 (50 fields/s)
				progressive	25
	480	4:3 or 16:9	non-square	interlaced	25 (50 fields/s)
576				progressive	25
	544	4:3 or 16:9	non-square	interlaced	25 (50 fields/s)
				progressive	25
	720	4:3 or 16:9	non-square	interlaced	25 (50 fields/s)
				progressive	25
					50
720	1280	16:9	Square	progressive	23.976
					24
					25
					29.97
					30
					50
					59.94
					60
				interlaced	25 (50 fields/s)
					29.97 (59.94 fields/s)
					30 (60 fields/s)
1080	1920	16:9	Square		23.976
					24
				progressive	25
					29.97
					30

amount of data that can be transmitted.) A terrestrial (over-the-air) transmission carries 19.39 *megabits* of data per second, compared to a maximum possible bitrate of 10.08 Mbit/s allowed in the *DVD* standard.

"EDTV" displays can reproduce progressive scan content and frequently have a 16:9 wide screen format. Such resolutions are 720×480 in NTSC or 720×576 in PAL, allowing 60 progressive frames per second in NTSC or 50 in PAL.

There are three basic display sizes for ATSC. Basic and enhanced NTSC and PAL image sizes are at the bottom level at 480 or 576 lines. Medium-sized images have 720 scanlines and are 1280 pixels wide. The top tier has 1080 lines 1920 pixels wide. 1080-line video is actually encoded with 1920×1088 pixel frames, but the last eight lines are discarded prior to display. This is due to a restriction of the MPEG-2 video format, which requires the number of coded luma samples (i.e., pixels) to be divisible by 16.

CODECS

For transport, ATSC uses the *MPEG-2* systems specification, known as *transport stream,* to encapsulate data, subject to certain constraints. ATSC uses 188-byte MPEG transport stream packets to carry data. Before decoding of audio and video takes place, the receiver must *demodulate* and apply *error correction* to the signal. Then, the transport stream may be *demultiplexed* into its constituent streams.

MPEG—2 video is used as the *video codec,* also with certain constraints.

For more details on this topic, see MPEG-2#ATSC_and_ISDB-T.

Dolby Digital AC-3 is used as the *audio codec,* though it was officially standardized as A/52 by the ATSC. It allows the transport of up to five channels of sound with a sixth channel for *low-frequency effects* (the so-called "5.1" configuration). In contrast, Japanese *ISDB* HDTV broadcasts use MPEG's *Advanced Audio Coding* (AAC) as the audio codec, which also allows 5.1 audio output.

MODULATION AND TRANSMISSION

ATSC signals are designed to use the same 6 MHz *bandwidth* as *NTSC* television channels (the interference requirements of A/53

DTV standards with adjacent NTSC or other DTV channels are very strict). Once the video and audio signals have been compressed and multiplexed, the transport stream can be *modulated* in different ways depending on the method of transmission.

- Terrestrial (local) broadcasters use *8VSB* modulation that can transfer at a maximum rate of 19.39 *Mbit/s*, sufficient to carry several video and audio programmes and *metadata*.
- *Cable television* stations can generally operate at a higher *signal-to-noise ratio* and can use *16VSB* or *256-QAM* to achieve a throughput of 38.78 Mbit/s, using the same 6 MHz channel.

In recent years, cable operators have become accustomed to compressing standard-resolution video for *digital cable* systems, making it harder to find duplicate 6 MHz channels for local broadcasters on uncompressed "basic" cable.

Currently, the *Federal Communications Commission* requires cable operators in the United States to carry the analog or digital transmission of a terrestrial broadcaster (but not both), when so requested by the broadcaster (the "*must-carry* rule"). The *Canadian Radio-television and Telecommunications Commission* in Canada has similar rules in force with respect to carrying ATSC signals.

However, cable operators in the US (and to a lesser extent Canada) can determine their own method of modulation for their plants.

- Consequently, most North American cable operators have added *256-QAM* to the *16VSB* standard originally used.
- Cable operators have still been slow to add ATSC channels to their lineups for legal, regulatory, and plant & equipment related reasons.
- 256 QAM is a cable standard, not an ATSC standard; however, over time it is expected to be included in the ATSC standard.

There is also a standard for transmitting ATSC via satellite; however, this is only used by *TV networks*. Very few teleports outside the US support the ATSC satellite transmission standard, but teleport support for the standard is improving.

- The ATSC satellite transmission system is not used for *direct broadcast satellite* systems, which in North America have long used a system similar to *DVB-S*.

OTHER SYSTEMS

Digital terrestrial television broadcasting systems. A majority of the world's nations have chosen to adopt the *DVB* standard, as can be seen on the *status list on the DVB Project website*.

ATSC coexists with the *DVB-T* standard, and with *ISDB-T* being implemented in Japan. (ISDB modulation also serves as a basis of the *SBTVD-T* standard in *Brazil*.) A similar standard called *ADTB* was developed for use as part of *China*'s new *DMB-T/H* dual standard. While China has officially chosen a dual standard, there is no requirement that a receiver work with both standards and there is no support for the ADTB modulation from broadcasters or equipment and receiver manufacturers. *Taiwan* has chosen *DVB-T COFDM* as its official modulation.

Because of potential use outside of existing NTSC areas, the ATSC system includes the capability to carry *PAL* and *SECAM* formatted video (576 displayable lines, 50 fields or 25 frames per second) along with NTSC (486 displayable lines, 60 x 1000/1001 fields or 30 x 1000/1001 frames per second) and *film* (24 frames per second).

Comparison

While the ATSC system has been criticized as being complicated and expensive to implement and use, both broadcasting and receiving equipment are now comparable in cost with that of DVB.

The ATSC signal is more susceptible to changes in *radio propagation* conditions than *DVB-T*. If ATSC were able to dynamically change its error correction modes, code rates, interleaver mode, and randomizer, the signal could be more robust even if the modulation itself did not change. It also lacks true *hierarchical modulation*, which allows the SDTV part of an HDTV signal to be received even in fringe areas where *signal strength* is low. For this reason, an additional modulation mode, enhanced-VSB (*E-VSB*) has been introduced, allowing for a similar benefit.

In spite of ATSC's fixed transmission mode, it is still a robust signal under various conditions. 8VSB was chosen over *COFDM* in part because many areas of North America are *rural* and have a much lower *population density*, thereby requiring larger *transmitters* and resulting in large fringe areas. In these areas, 8VSB was shown to perform better than other systems.

COFDM is used in both DVB-T and ISDB-T, and for *1seg*, as well as *DVB-H* and *HD Radio* in the United States. In *metropolitan areas*, where the great and increasing majority of North Americans live, COFDM is said to be better at handling *multipath*. While ATSC is also incapable of true *single-frequency network* (SFN) operation, the distributed transmission mode, using on-channel repeaters, has been shown to improve reception under similar conditions. Thus, it may not require more *spectrum* allocation than *DVB-T* using SFNs.

MOBILE TV

Mobile reception of digital stations using ATSC has (until now) been difficult to impossible, especially when moving at vehicular speeds. To overcome this, there are several proposed systems that report improved mobile reception: *Samsung/Rohde & Schwarz*'s *A-VSB*, *Harris/LG*'s *MPH*, and a recent proposal from *Thomson/Micronas*; all of these systems are expected to be submitted as candidates for a new ATSC standard, *ATSC-M/H*. This is in addition to other proprietary standards like *MediaFLO*, and worldwide open standards such as *DVB-H* and *T-DMB*. Like DVB-H and ISDB *1seg*, the proposed ATSC mobile standards are *backward-compatible* with existing tuners, despite being added to the standard well after the original standard was in wide use.

Mobile reception of some stations will still be more difficult, because 18 UHF channels in the U.S. have been removed from TV service, forcing some broadcasters to stay on VHF. This band requires larger antennas for reception, and is more prone to *electromagnetic interference* from *engines* and rapidly-changing *multipath* conditions (citations needed).

COUNTRIES AND TERRITORIES USING ATSC

Americas

- Argentina (experimental)
- Bahamas
- Bermuda
- Canada (To be completely transformed by 31 August 2011)
- Chile (experimental)
- Guatemala (experimental)
- Honduras
- Mexico
- Peru (experimental only in Lima)
- United States (To to be completely transformed by 17 February 2009)
    - Puerto Rico
    - U.S. Virgin Islands

Asia/Pacific

- American Samoa
- Guam
- Northern Mariana Islands
- South Korea

3

Cinematography, Film Editing and Filmmaking: Concepts, Tools and Techniques

CINEMATOGRAPHY

Cinematography [from Greek: *kinesis* κινησις (movement) and *grapho* γραφω (to record)], is the discipline of making lighting and camera choices when recording photographic images for the cinema. It is closely related to the art of still photography, though many additional issues arise when both the camera and elements of the scene may be in motion.

History

The first attempt at cinematography can be traced back to the world's first motion picture film, *Roundhay Garden Scene*. It was a sequence directed by Louis Le Prince, French inventor and showman, on October 14, 1888 in the garden at *Oakwood Grange* in Roundhay, Leeds, West Yorkshire, England. This groundbreaking event happened seven years before the Lumière Brothers' *Sortie de l'usine Lumière à Lyon* made the first paid exhibition on December 28, 1895 at Le Grand Café, in Paris, France. This date is known as the birth of cinema since it was the first time the cycle of production-distribution-exhibition happened. The European city soon became the motion picture capital of the world.

Cinematography is an art form unique to motion pictures. Although the exposing of images on light-sensitive elements dates back to the late 1600s, motion pictures demanded a new form of photography and new aesthetic techniques.

In the infancy of motion pictures, the cinematographer was usually also the director and the person physically handling the camera. As the art form and technology evolved, a separation between director and camera operator emerged. With the advent of artificial lighting and faster (more light sensitive) film stocks, in addition to technological advancements in optics and various techniques such as colour film and widescreen, the technical aspects of cinematography necessitated a specialist in that area.

Cinematography was key during the silent movie era—no sound apart from background music, no dialogue—the films depended on lighting, acting and set.

In 1919, in Hollywood, the new motion picture capital of the world, one of the first (and still existing) trade societies was formed: the American Society of Cinematographers (ASC), which stood to recognize the cinematographer's contribution to the art and science of motion picture making. Similar trade associations have been established in other countries, too.

The ASC defines cinematography as a creative and interpretive process that culminates in the authorship of an original work of art rather than the simple recording of a physical event. Cinematography is not a subcategory of photography. Rather, photography is but one craft that the cinematographer uses in addition to other physical, organizational, managerial, interpretive and image-manipulating techniques to effect one coherent process.

Aspects of Cinematography

Numerous aspects contribute to the art of cinematography.

Film Stock

Cinematography can begin with rolls of film or a digital imaging sensor. Advancements in film emulsion and grain structure have led to a wide range of film stocks available to cinematographers. The selection of a film stock is one of the first decisions they must make during any film production.

Aside from the film gauge seslection—8 mm (amateur), 16 mm (semi-professional), 35 mm (professional) and 65 mm (epic photography, rarely used except in special event venues)—the cinematographer has a selection of stocks in reversal (which, when developed, create a positive image) and negative formats along with a wide range of film speeds (varying sensitivity to light) from ISO 50 (slow, least sensitive to light) to 800 (very fast, extremely sensitive to light) and differing response to colour (low saturation, high saturation) and contrast [varying levels between pure black (no exposure) and pure white (complete overexposure)].

Advancements and adjustments to nearly all gauges of film created the "super" variety wherein the area of the film used to capture a single frame of an image is expanded, although the physical gauge of the film remains the same. Super 8 mm, Super 16 mm and Super 35 mm are all formats that utilize more of the overall film area for the image than their "regular" non-super counterparts. The larger the film gauge, the higher the overall image resolution clarity and technical quality. In the realm of digital imaging, various film stocks are no longer applicable, but the cameras themselves feature image adjustment capabilities that go far beyond the abilities of one particular film stock. The cameras can be adjusted to varying degrees of colour sensitivity, image contrast, light sensitivity and so on. One camera can achieve all the various looks of different emulsions, although it is heavily argued as to which method of capturing an image is the "best" method. It should be mentioned that the digital method of image adjustments (ISO, contrast etc.) are executed by estimating the same adjustments that would take place if actual film were in use and are thus vulnerable to the cameras sensor designers perceptions of various film stocks and image adjustment parameters. Sensors generally have an optimal ISO rating past which faster speeds will result in noticeable increases in image noise, thus compromising the quality.

The Lab

Laboratory work can also offer a considerable variance in the image produced. By controlling the temperature and varying the duration in which the film is soaked in the development chemicals and by skipping certain chemical processes (or partially skipping them), cinematographers can achieve very different looks from a single film stock in the laboratory.

Filters

Filters, such as diffusion filters or colour-effect filters, are also widely used to enhance mood or dramatic effects. Most photographic filters are made up of two pieces of optical glass glued together with some form of image or light manipulation material between the glass. In the case of colour filters, there is often a translucent colour medium pressed between two planes of optical glass. Colour filters work by blocking out certain colour wavelengths of light from reaching the film. With colour film, this works very intuitively wherein a blue filter will cut down on the passage of red, orange and yellow light and create a blue tint on the film. In black and white photography, colour filters are used somewhat counter intuitively; for instance a yellow filter, which cuts down on blue wavelengths of light, can be used to darken a daylight sky (by eliminating blue light from hitting the film, thus greatly underexposing the mostly blue sky), while not biasing most human flesh tone. Certain cinematographers, such as Christopher Doyle, are well known for their innovative use of filters. Filters can be used in front of the lens or, in some cases, behind the lens for different effects.

Lens

Focal Length

The camera does what a human eye does. That is, it creates perspective and spatial relations with the rest of the world. However, unlike one's eye, a cinematographer can select different lenses for different purposes. Variation in focal length is one of the chief benefits of such an advantage. The focal length of the lens in particular, determines the angle of view and, therefore, the field of view. Cinematographers can choose between a range of wide angle lenses, "normal" lenses and telephoto lenses, as well as macro lenses and other special effect lens systems such as borescope lenses. Wide-angle lenses have short focal lengths and make spatial distances more obvious. A person in the distance is shown as much smaller while someone in the front will loom large. On the other hand, telephoto lenses reduce such exaggerations, depicting far-off objects as seemingly close together and flattening perspective. The differences between the perspective rendering is actually not due to the focal length by itself, but by the distance between the subjects and the camera. Therefore, the use of different focal lengths in combination with different camera to subject distances creates these different rendering. Changing the focal length only while keeping the same camera position doesn't affect perspective but the angle of view only. A zoom lens allows a camera operator to change their focal length within a shot or quickly between setups for shots. As prime lenses offer greater optical quality and are "faster" (larger aperture openings, usable in less light) than zoom lenses, they are often employed in professional cinematography over zoom lenses. Certain scenes or even types of filmmaking, however, may require the use of zooms for speed or ease of use, as well as shots involving a zoom move.

Diaphragm Aperture

Like in photography, the control of the exposed image is done in the lens with the control of the diaphragm aperture. As to properly expose, the cinematographer needs that all lenses be engraved with T-Stop, not f-stop, so that the eventual light loss due to the glass doesn't affect the exposure control when setting it using the usual meters. The choice of the aperture also affects image quality (aberrations) and depth of field.

Depth of Field and Focus

Focal length and diaphragm aperture affect the depth of field of a scene—that is, how much the background, mid-ground and foreground will be rendered in "acceptable focus" (only one exact plane of the image is in precise focus) on the film or video target. Depth of field (not to be confused with depth of focus) is determined by the aperture size and the focal distance. A large or deep depth of field is generated with a very small iris aperture and focusing on a point in the distance, whereas a shallow depth of field will be achieved with a large (open) iris aperture and focusing closer to the lens. Depth of field is also governed by the format size. 70 mm film has much more depth of field for the same focal length lens than does 35 mm. 16 mm has even less and most digital video cameras have less depth of field than 16 mm. But if one considers the field of view and angle of view, the smaller the image is, the shorter the focal length should be, as to keep the same field of view. Then, the smaller the image is, the more depth of field is obtained, for the same field of view. Therefore, 70 mm as less depth of field than 35 mm for a given field of view, 16 mm more than 35 mm, and video cameras even more depth of field than 16 mm. As videographers try to emulate the look of 35 mm film with digital cameras, this is one issue of frustration—excessive depth of field with digital cameras and using additional optical devices to reduce that depth of field.

In *Citizen Kane,* cinematographer Gregg Toland used tighter apertures to create very large depth of field in the scenes, often rendering every detail of the foreground and background of the sets in sharp focus. This practice is known as deep focus. Deep focus became a popular cinematographic device from the 1940s onwards in Hollywood. Today, the trend is for more shallow focus.

To change the plane of focus from one object or character to another within a shot is commonly known as a *rack focus.*

Aspect Ratio and Framing

Aspect Ratio

The aspect ratio of an image is the ratio of its width to its height. Beginning in the 1910s, motion pictures settled on a ratio of four to three (four units wide to three units high). Often written as 4:3, this ratio may be reduced to 1.33:1 and this aspect ratio is commonly known as 1.33. The introduction of sound-on-film narrowed the aspect ratio briefly, before the Academy ratio of 1.37 was introduced in 1932 by means of thickening the frame line. For years, cinematographers were limited to this shape of image, but in the 1950s, thanks to the unanticipated popularity of Cinerama, widescreen ratios were introduced in an effort to pull audiences back into the theater and away from their home television sets. These new widescreen aspect ratios granted cinematographers a wider frame within which to compose their images. Many different proprietary photographic systems were invented and utilized in the 1950s to create widescreen movies, but one dominates today: the anamorphic process, which optically squeezes the image to photograph twice the horizontal area to the same size vertical as standard "spherical" lenses. The first commonly used anamorphic widescreen format was CinemaScope, which used a 2.35:1 aspect ratio, although it was originally 2.55:1. CinemaScope was used from 1953 to 1967, but due to technical flaws in the design and its ownership by Fox, several third-party companies, led by Panavision's technical improvements in the 1950s, now dominate the anamorphic cine lens market. Changes to SMPTE projection standards altered the projected ratio from 2.35:1 to 2.39:1 in 1970, although this did not change anything regarding the photographic anamorphic standards; all changes in respect to the aspect ratio of anamorphic 35 mm photography are specifically correlative to camera or projector gate sizes, not the optical system.

After the "widescreen wars" of the 1950s, the motion-picture industry settled into 1.85:1 (which is a cropped version of 1.37:1) as a standard for theatrical projection in the United States and the United Kingdom. Europe and Asia opted for 1.66:1 at first, although 1.85:1 has largely permeated these markets in recent decades. Certain "epic" or adventure movies utilized the anamorphic 2.39:1.

In the 1990s, with the advent of high-definition video, television engineers created the 1.78:1 (16:9) ratio as a mathematical compromise between the theatrical standard of 1.85:1 and television's 1.33:1, as it was not physically possible to safely create a television tube with a width of 1.85:1. Until that point, nothing had ever been originated in 1.78:1. Today, this is a standard for high-definition video and for widescreen television.

Lighting

Most likely the single most important aspect of cinematography is lighting. Light is necessary to create an image exposure on a frame of film or on a digital target (CCD, etc). The art of lighting for cinematography goes far beyond basic exposure, however, into the essence of visual storytelling. Lighting contributes considerably to the emotional response an audience has watching a motion picture. The control of light quality, colour, direction and intensity is a major factor in the art and science of cinematography.

Camera Movement

One aspect of cinematography that strongly separates it from still photography (aside from having a moving subject) is the ability to move the camera, which represents the audience's viewpoint or perspective, during the course of filming. This movement plays a considerable role in the emotional language of film images and the audience's emotional reaction to the action on the screen. From the most basic movements of panning (horizontal shift in viewpoint from a fixed position; like turning your head side-to-side) and tilting (vertical shift in viewpoint from a fixed position; like tipping your head back to look at the sky or tilting your head down to look at the ground) to dollying (placing the camera on a moving platform to move it closer or farther from the subject), trucking (placing the camera on a moving platform to move it to the left or right), craning (moving the camera in a vertical position; being able to lift it off the ground as well as swing it side-to-side from a fixed base position), and a combination of all of the above.

Cameras have been mounted to nearly every imaginable form of transportation. Most cameras can also be handheld, that is the camera operator literally holds the camera in their hands and moves from one position to another while filming the action. Personal stabilizing platforms came into being in the late 1970s through the invention of Garrett Brown, which became known as the Steadicam. The Steadicam is a body harness and stabilization arm that connects to the camera that allows the operator to move naturally while completely isolating the movements of their body from the movements of the camera. After the Steadicam patent expired in the early 1990s, many other companies began manufacturing their concept of the personal camera stabilizer.

Special Effects

The first special effects in the cinema were created while the film was being shot. These came to be known as "in-camera" effects. Later, optical and digital effects were developed so that editors and visual effects artists could more tightly control the process by manipulating the film in post-production.

Frame Rate Selection

Motion picture images are presented to an audience at a constant speed. In the theater, it is 24 frames per second, in NTSC (US) Television, it is 30 frames per second (29.97 to be exact), in PAL (Europe) television it is 25 frames per second. This speed of presentation does not vary.

However, by varying the speed at which the image is captured, various effects can be created knowing that the faster or slower recorded image will be played at a constant speed.

For instance, time-lapse photography is created by exposing an image at an extremely slow rate. If a cinematographer sets a camera to expose one frame every minute for four hours, and then that footage is projected at 24 frames per second, the event that took four hours to record will now take 10 seconds to present (1 frame per minute for 4 hours equals 240 frames, projected at 24 frames per second equals 10 seconds). This compresses the event that took place in four hours into just 10 seconds. At this speed, one can present the events of a whole day (24 hours) in just one minute. The inverse of this, if an image is captured at speeds above that at which they will be presented, the effect is to greatly slow down (slow motion) the image. If a cinematographer shoots a person diving into a pool at 96 frames per second, and that image is presented back at 24 frames per second, it will take 4 times as long to watch the dive as it did for it to actually happen.

In motion pictures the manipulation of time and space is a considerable contributing factor to the narrative storytelling tools. Film editing plays a much stronger role in this manipulation, but frame rate selection in the photography of the original action is also a contributing factor to altering time.

"Ramping" is a process whereby the capture frame rate of the camera changes over time. For example, if in the course of 10 seconds of capture, the capture frame rate is adjusted from 60 frames per second to 24 frames per second, when played back at the standard film rate of 24 frames per second, a unique time-manipulation effect is achieved. For example, someone pushing a door open and walking out into the street would appear to start off in slow-motion, but in a few seconds later within the same shot the person would appear to walk in "realtime" (normal speed). The opposite speed-ramping is done in *The Matrix* when Neo re-enters the Matrix for the first time to see the Oracle. As he comes out of the warehouse "load-point", the camera zooms into Neo at normal speed but as it gets closer to Neo's face time seems to slow down, perhaps visually accentuating Neo pausing and reflecting a moment, and perhaps alluding to future manipulation of time itself within the Matrix later on in the movie.

Role of the Cinematographer

In the film industry, the cinematographer is responsible for the technical aspects of the images (lighting, lens choices, composition, exposure, filtration, film selection), but works closely with the director to ensure that the artistic aesthetics are supporting the director's vision of the story being told. The cinematographers are the heads of the camera, grip and lighting crew on a set, and for this reason they are often called *directors of photography* or *DPs*.

Directors of photography make many creative and interpretive decisions during the course of their work, from pre-production to post-production, all of which affect the overall feel and look of the motion picture. Many of these decisions are similar to what a photographer needs to note when taking a picture: the cinematographer controls the film choice itself (from a range of available stocks with varying sensitivities to light and colour), the selection of lens focal lengths, aperture exposure and focus. Cinematography, however, has a temporal aspect, unlike still photography, which is purely a single still image. It is also bulkier and more strenuous to deal with movie cameras, and it involves a more complex array of choices. As such a cinematographer often needs to work co-operatively with more people than does a photographer, who could frequently function as a single person. As a result, the cinematographer's job also includes personnel management and logistical organization.

Evolution of Technology: New Definitions

Traditionally the term "cinematography" referred to working with motion-picture film emulsion, but it is now largely synonymous with videography and digital video due to the popularity of digital cinematography. Modern digital image processing has also made it possible to radically modify pictures from how they were originally captured. This has allowed new disciplines to encroach on some of the choices that were once the cinematographer's exclusive domain.

FILM

Film is a term that encompasses individual motion pictures, the field of film as an art form, and the motion picture industry. Films are produced by recording images from the world with cameras, or by creating images using animation techniques or special effects.

Films are cultural artifacts created by specific cultures, which reflect those cultures, and, in turn, affect them. Film is considered to be an important art form, a source of popular entertainment, and a powerful method for educating—or indoctrinating—citizens. The visual elements of cinema give motion pictures a universal power of communication; some movies have become popular worldwide attractions, by using dubbing or subtitles that translate the dialogue.

Traditional films are made up of a series of individual images called frames. When these images are shown rapidly in succession, a viewer has the illusion that motion is occurring. The viewer cannot see the flickering between frames due to an effect known as persistence of vision—whereby the eye retains a visual image for a fraction of a second after the source has been removed. Viewers perceive motion due to a psychological effect called beta movement.

The origin of the name "film" comes from the fact that photographic film (also called film stock) has historically been the primary medium for recording and displaying motion pictures. Many other terms exist for an individual motion picture, including *picture, picture show, photo-play, flick,* and most commonly, *movie.* Additional terms for the field in general include *the big screen, the silver screen, the cinema,* and *the movies.*

History

Mechanisms for producing artificially created, two-dimensional images in motion were demonstrated as early as the 1860s, with devices such as the zoetrope and the praxinoscope. These machines were outgrowths of simple optical devices (such as magic lanterns) and would display sequences of still pictures at sufficient speed for the images on the pictures to appear to be moving, a phenomenon called persistence of vision. Naturally, the images needed to be carefully designed to achieve the desired effect—and the underlying principle became the basis for the development of film animation.

With the development of celluloid film for still photography, it became possible to directly capture objects in motion in real time. Early versions of the technology sometimes required a person to look into a viewing machine to see the pictures which were separate paper prints attached to a drum turned by a handcrank. The pictures were shown at a variable speed of about 5 to 10 pictures per second depending on how rapidly the crank was turned. Some of these machines were coin operated. By the 1880s, the development of the motion picture camera allowed the individual component images to be captured and stored on a single reel, and led quickly to the development of a motion picture projector to shine light through the processed and printed film and magnify these "moving picture shows" onto a screen for an entire audience. These reels, so exhibited, came to be known as "motion pictures." Early motion pictures were static shots that showed an event or action with no editing or other cinematic techniques.

Ignoring Dickson's early sound experiments (1894), commercial motion pictures were purely visual art through the late 19th century, but these innovative silent films had gained a hold on the public imagination. Around the turn of the twentieth century, films began developing a narrative structure by stringing scenes together to tell narratives. The scenes were later broken up into multiple shots of varying sizes and angles. Other techniques such as camera movement were realized as effective ways to portray a story on film. Rather than leave the audience in silence, theater owners would hire a pianist or organist or a full orchestra to play music fitting the mood of the film at any given moment. By the early 1920s, most films came with a prepared list of sheet music for this purpose, with complete film scores being composed for major productions.

The rise of European cinema was interrupted by the breakout of World War I while the film industry in United States flourished with the rise of Hollywood. However in the 1920s, European filmmakers such as Sergei Eisenstein, F. W. Murnau, and Fritz Lang, along with American innovator D. W. Griffith and the contributions of Charles Chaplin, Buster Keaton and others, continued to advance the medium. In the 1920s, new technology allowed filmmakers to attach to each film a soundtrack of speech, music and sound effects synchronized with the action on the screen. These sound films were initially distinguished by calling them "talking pictures", or talkies.

The next major step in the development of cinema was the introduction of so-called "natural" colour. While the addition of sound quickly eclipsed silent film and theater musicians, colour was adopted more gradually as methods evolved making it more practical and cost effective to produce "natural colour" films. The public was relatively indifferent to colour photography as opposed to black-and-white, but as colour processes improved and became as affordable as black-and-white film, more and more movies were filmed in colour after the end of World War II, as the industry in America came to view colour as essential to attracting audiences in its competition with television, which remained a black-and-white medium until the mid-1960s. By the end of the 1960s, colour had become the norm for filmmakers.

Since the decline of the studio system in the 1960s, the succeeding decades saw changes in the production and style of film. New Hollywood, French New Wave and the rise of film school educated independent filmmakers were all part of the changes the medium experienced in the latter half of the 20th century. Digital technology has been the driving force in change throughout the 1990s and into the 21st century.

Theory

Film theory seeks to develop concise, systematic concepts that apply to the study of film as art. It was started by Ricciotto Canudo's *The Birth of the Sixth Art*. Formalist film theory, led by Rudolf Arnheim, Béla Balázs, and Siegfried Kracauer, emphasized how film differed from reality, and thus could be considered a valid fine art. André Bazin reacted against this theory by arguing that film's artistic essence lay in its ability to mechanically reproduce reality not in its differences from reality, and this gave rise to realist theory. More recent analysis spurred by Lacan's psychoanalysis and Ferdinand de Saussure's semiotics among other things has given rise to psychoanalytical film theory, structuralist film theory, feminist film theory and others.

Criticism

Film criticism is the analysis and evaluation of films. In general, these works can be divided into two categories: academic criticism by film scholars and journalistic film criticism that appears regularly in newspapers and other media.

Film critics working for newspapers, magazines, and mainly review new releases. Normally they only see any given film once and have only a day or two to formulate opinions. Despite this, critics have an important impact on films, especially those of certain genres. Mass marketed action, horror, and comedy films tend not to be greatly affected by a critic's overall judgement of a film. The plot summary and description of a film that makes up the majority of any film review can still have an important impact on whether people decide to see a film. For prestige films such as most dramas, the influence of reviews is extremely important. Poor reviews will often doom a film to obscurity and financial loss.

The impact of a reviewer on a given film's box office performance is a matter of debate. Some claim that movie marketing is now so intense and well financed that reviewers cannot make an impact against it. However, the cataclysmic failure of some heavily-promoted movies which were harshly reviewed, as well as the unexpected success of critically praised independent movies indicates that extreme critical reactions can have considerable influence. Others note that positive film reviews have been shown to spark interest in little-known films. Conversely, there have been several films in which film companies have so little confidence that they refuse to give reviewers an advanced viewing to avoid widespread panning of the film. However, this usually backfires as reviewers are wise to the tactic and warn the public that the film may not be worth seeing and the films often do poorly as a result.

It is argued that journalist film critics should only be known as film reviewers, and true film critics are those who take a more academic approach to films. This line of work is more often known as film theory or film studies. These film critics attempt to come to understand how film and filming techniques work, and what effect they have on people. Rather than having their works published in newspapers or appear on television, their articles are published in scholarly journals, or sometimes in up-market magazines. They also tend to be affiliated with colleges or universities.

Industry

The making and showing of motion pictures became a source of profit almost as soon as the process was invented. Upon seeing how successful their new invention, and its product, was in their native France, the Lumières quickly set about touring the Continent to exhibit the first films privately to royalty and publicly to the masses. In each country, they would normally add new, local scenes to their catalogue and, quickly enough, found local entrepreneurs in the various countries of Europe to buy their equipment and photograph, export, import and screen additional product commercially. The Oberammergau Passion Play of 1898 was the first commercial motion picture ever produced. Other pictures soon followed, and motion pictures became a separate industry that overshadowed the vaudeville world. Dedicated theaters and companies formed specifically to produce and distribute films, while motion picture actors became major celebrities and commanded huge fees for their performances. Already by 1917, Charlie Chaplin had a contract that called for an annual salary of one million dollars.

In the United States today, much of the film industry is centered around Hollywood. Other regional centers exist in many parts of the world, such as Mumbai-centered Bollywood, the Indian film industry's Hindi cinema which produces the largest number of films in the world. Whether the ten thousand-plus feature length films a year produced by the Valley pornographic film industry should qualify for this title is the source of some debate. Though the expense involved in making movies has led cinema production to concentrate under the auspices of movie studios, recent advances in affordable film making equipment have allowed independent film productions to flourish.

Profit is a key force in the industry, due to the costly and risky nature of filmmaking; many films have large cost overruns, a notorious example being Kevin Costner's Waterworld. Yet many filmmakers strive to create works of lasting social significance. The Academy Awards (also known as "the Oscars") are the most prominent film awards in the United States, providing recognition each year to films, ostensibly based on their artistic merits.

There is also a large industry for educational and instructional films made in lieu of or in addition to lectures and texts.

Production

The nature of the film determines the size and type of crew required during filmmaking. Many Hollywood adventure films need computer generated imagery (CGI), created by dozens of 3D modellers, animators, rotoscopers and compositors. However, a low-budget, independent film may be made with a skeleton crew, often paid very little. Also, an open source film may be produced through open, collaborative processes. Filmmaking takes place all over the world using different technologies, styles of acting and genre, and is produced in a variety of economic contexts that range from state-sponsored documentary in China to profit-oriented movie making within the American studio system.

A typical Hollywood-style filmmaking Production cycle is comprised of five main stages:

1. Development,
2. Pre-production,
3. Production,
4. Post-production, and
5. Distribution.

This production cycle typically takes three years. The first year is taken up with *development*. The second year comprises *pre-production* and *production*. The third year, *post-production* and *distribution*.

Crew

A film crew is a group of people hired by a film company, employed during the "production" or "photography" phase, for the purpose of producing a film or motion picture. *Crew* are distinguished from *cast*, the actors who appear in front of the camera or provide voices for characters in the film. The *crew* interacts with but is also distinct from the *production staff*, consisting of producers, managers, company representatives, their assistants, and those whose primary responsibility falls in pre-production or post-production phases, such as writers and editors. Communication between *production* and *crew* generally passes through the director and his/her staff of assistants. Medium-to-large crews are generally divided into departments with well defined hierarchies and standards for interaction and cooperation between the departments. Other than acting, the crew handles everything in the photography phase: props and costumes, shooting, sound, electrics (i.e., lights), sets, and production special effects. Caterers (known in the film industry as "craft services") are usually not considered part of the crew.

Independent

Independent filmmaking often takes place outside of Hollywood, or other major studio systems. An independent film (or indie film) is a film initially produced without financing or distribution from a major movie studio. Creative, business, and technological reasons have all contributed to the growth of the indie film scene in the late 20th and early 21st century.

On the business side, the costs of big-budget studio films also leads to conservative choices in cast and crew. There is a trend in Hollywood towards co-financing (over two-thirds of the films put out by Warner Bros. in 2000 were joint ventures, up from 10 per cent in 1987). A hopeful director is almost never given the opportunity to get a job on a big-budget studio film unless he or she has significant industry experience in film or television. Also, the studios rarely produce films with unknown actors, particularly in lead roles.

Before the advent of digital alternatives, the cost of professional film equipment and stock was also a hurdle to being able to produce, direct, or star in a traditional studio film. The cost of 35 mm film is outpacing inflation: in 2002 alone, film negative costs were up 23 per cent, according to *variety*.

But the advent of consumer camcorders in 1985, and more importantly, the arrival of high-resolution digital video in the early 1990s, have lowered the technology barrier to movie production significantly. Both production and post-production costs have been significantly lowered; today, the hardware and software for post-production can be installed in a commodity-based personal computer. Technologies such as DVDs, FireWire connections and non-linear editing system pro-level software like Adobe Premiere Pro, Sony Vegas and Apple's Final Cut Pro, and consumer level software such as Apple's Final Cut Express and iMovie make movie-making relatively inexpensive.

Since the introduction of DV technology, the means of production have become more democratized. Filmmakers can conceivably shoot and edit a movie, create and edit the sound and music, and mix the final cut on a home computer. However, while the means of production may be democratized, financing, distribution, and marketing remain difficult to accomplish outside the traditional system. Most independent filmmakers rely on film festivals to get their films noticed and sold for distribution. The arrival of internet-based video outlets such as YouTube and Veoh has further changed the filmmaking landscape in ways that are still to be determined.

Open Content Film

An open content film is much like an independent film, but it is produced through open collaborations; its source material is available under a license which is permissive enough to allow other parties to create fan fiction or derivative works, than a traditional copyright. Like independent filmmaking, open source filmmaking takes place outside of Hollywood, or other major studio systems.

Fan Film

A fan film is a film or video inspired by a film, television programme, comic book or a similar source, created by fans rather than by the source's copyright holders or creators. Fan filmmakers have traditionally been amateurs, but some of the more notable films have actually been produced by professional filmmakers as film school class projects or as demonstration reels. Fan films vary tremendously in length, from short faux-teaser trailers for non-existent motion pictures to rarer full-length motion pictures.

Animation

Animation is the technique in which each frame of a film is produced individually, whether generated as a computer graphic, or by photographing a drawn image, or by repeatedly making small changes to a model unit, and then photographing the result with a special animation camera. When the frames are strung together and the resulting film is viewed at a speed of 16 or more frames per second, there is an illusion of continuous movement (due to the persistence of vision). Generating such a film is very labour intensive and tedious, though the development of computer animation has greatly speed up the process.

File formats like GIF, QuickTime, Shockwave and Flash allow animation to be viewed on a computer or over the Internet.

Because animation is very time-consuming and often very expensive to produce, the majority of animation for TV and movies comes from professional animation studios. However, the field of independent animation has existed at least since the 1950s, with animation being produced by independent studios (and sometimes by a single person). Several independent animation producers have gone on to enter the professional animation industry.

Limited animation is a way of increasing production and decreasing costs of animation by using "short cuts" in the animation process. This method was pioneered by UPA and popularized by Hanna-Barbera, and adapted by other studios as cartoons moved from movie theaters to television.

Although most animation studios are now using digital technologies in their productions, there is a specific style of animation that depends on film. Cameraless animation, made famous by moviemakers like Norman McLaren, Len Lye and Stan Brakhage, is painted and drawn directly onto pieces of film, and then run through a projector.

Venues

When it is initially produced, a feature film is often shown to audiences in a movie theater or cinema. The first theater designed exclusively for cinema opened in Pittsburgh, Pennsylvania in 1905. Thousands of such theaters were built or converted from existing facilities within a few years. In the United States, these theaters came to be known as nickelodeons, because admission typically cost a nickel (five cents).

Typically, one film is the featured presentation (or feature film). Before the 1970s, there were "double features"; typically, a high quality "A picture" rented by an independent theater for a lump sum, and a "B picture" of lower quality rented for a percentage of the gross receipts. Today, the bulk of the material shown before the feature film consists of previews for upcoming movies and paid advertisements (also known as trailers or "The Twenty").

Historically, all mass marketed feature films were made to be shown in movie theaters. The development of television has allowed films to be broadcast to larger audiences, usually after the film is no longer being shown in theaters. Recording technology has also enabled consumers to rent or buy copies of films on VHS or DVD (and the older formats of laserdisc, VCD and SelectaVision), and Internet downloads may be available and have started to become revenue sources for the film companies. Some films are now made specifically for these other venues, being released as made-for-TV movies or direct-to-video movies. The production values on these films are often considered to be of inferior quality compared to theatrical releases in similar genres, and indeed, some films that are rejected by their own studios upon completion are distributed through these markets.

The movie theater pays an average of about 50-55 per cent of its ticket sales to the movie studio, as film rental fees. The actual percentage starts with a number higher than that, and decreases as the duration of a film's showing continues, as an incentive to theaters to keep movies in the theater longer. However, today's barrage of highly marketed movies ensures that most movies are shown in first-run theaters for less than 8 weeks. There are a few movies every year that defy this rule, often limited-release movies that start in only a few theaters and actually grow their theater count through good word-of-mouth and reviews. According to a 2000 study by ABN AMRO, about 26 per cent of Hollywood movie studios' worldwide income came from box office ticket sales; 46 per cent came from VHS and DVD sales to consumers; and 28 per cent came from television (broadcast, cable, and pay-per-view).

Technology

Film stock consists of transparent celluloid, acetate, or polyester base coated with an emulsion containing light-sensitive chemicals. Cellulose nitrate was the first type of film base used to record motion pictures, but due to its flammability was eventually replaced by safer materials. Stock widths and the film format for images on the reel have had a rich history, though most large commercial films are still shot on (and distributed to theaters) as 35 mm prints.

Originally moving picture film was shot and projected at various speeds using hand-cranked cameras and projectors; though 1000 frames per minute ($16\frac{2}{3}$ per second) is generally cited as a standard silent speed, research indicates most films were shot between 16 and 23 fps and projected from 18 fps on up (often reels included instructions on how fast each scene should be shown). When sound film was introduced in the late 1920s, a constant speed was required for the sound head. 24 frames per second was chosen because it was the slowest (and thus cheapest) speed which allowed for sufficient sound quality. Improvements since the late 19th century include the mechanization of cameras—allowing them to record at a consistent speed, quiet camera design—allowing sound recorded on-set to be usable without requiring large "blimps" to encase the camera, the invention of more sophisticated filmstocks and lenses, allowing directors to film in increasingly dim conditions, and the development of synchronized sound, allowing sound to be recorded at exactly the same speed as its corresponding action. The soundtrack can be recorded separately from shooting the film, but for live-action pictures many parts of the soundtrack are usually recorded simultaneously.

As a medium, film is not limited to motion pictures, since the technology developed as the basis for photography. It can be used to present a progressive sequence of still images in the form of a slideshow. Film has also been incorporated into multimedia presentations, and often has importance as primary historical documentation. However, historic films have problems in terms of preservation and storage, and the motion picture industry is exploring many alternatives. Most movies on cellulose nitrate base have been copied onto modern safety films. Some studios save colour films through the use of separation masters—three B&W negatives each exposed through red, green, or blue filters (essentially a reverse of the Technicolour process). Digital methods have also been used to restore films, although their continued obsolescence cycle makes them (as of 2006) a poor choice for long-term preservation. Film preservation of decaying film stock is a matter of concern to both film historians and archivists, and to companies interested in preserving their existing products in order to make them available to future generations (and thereby increase revenue). Preservation is generally a higher-concern for nitrate and single-strip colour films, due to their high decay rates; black and white films on safety bases and colour films preserved on Technicolour imbibition prints tend to keep up much better, assuming proper handling and storage.

Some films in recent decades have been recorded using analog video technology similar to that used in television production. Modern digital video cameras and digital projectors are gaining ground as well. These approaches are extremely beneficial to moviemakers, especially because footage can be evaluated and edited without waiting for the film stock to be processed. Yet the migration is gradual, and as of 2005 most major motion pictures are still recorded on film.

Future State

While motion picture films have been around for more than a century, film is still a relative newcomer in the pantheon of fine arts. In the 1950s, when television became widely available, industry analysts predicted the demise of local movie theaters. Despite competition from television's increasing technological sophistication over the 1960s and 1970s, such as the development of colour television and large screens, motion picture cinemas continued. In the 1980s, when the widespread availability of inexpensive videocassette recorders enabled people to select films for home viewing, industry analysts again wrongly predicted the death of the local cinemas.

In the 1990s and 2000s, the development of digital DVD players, home theater amplification systems with surround sound and subwoofers, and large LCD or plasma screens enabled people to select and view films at home with greatly improved audio and visual reproduction. These new technologies provided audio and visual that in the past, only local cinemas had been able to provide: a large, clear widescreen presentation of a film with a full-range, high-quality multi-speaker sound system. Once again, industry analysts predicted the demise of the local cinema. Local cinemas will be changing in the 2000s and moving towards digital screens, a new approach which will allow for easier. quicker distribution of films (via satellite or hard disks), a development which may give local theaters a reprieve from their predicted demise.

FILMMAKING

Filmmaking is the process of making a film, from an initial story idea or commission through scriptwriting, shooting, editing and finally distribution to an audience. Typically it involves a large finally distribution to an audience. Typically it involves a large number of people and can take anywhere between a few months and several years to complete. Filmmaking takes place all over the world in a huge range of economic, social and political contexts, using a variety of technologies and techniques.

Stages of Filmmaking

Filmmaking consists of five main stages:

1. *Development*. The script is written and drafted into a workable blueprint for a film.
2. *Pre-production*. Preparations are made for the shoot, in which cast and crew are hired, locations are selected, and sets are built.
3. *Production*. The raw elements for the finished film are recorded.
4. *Post-production*. The film is edited, sound effects, music and any computer effects are added, and the film is completed.
5. *Sales and distribution*. The film is picked up by a distributor and reaches its audience.

1. Development

This is the stage where an idea is fleshed out into a viable script. The producer of the movie will find a story, which may come from books, plays, other films, true stories, original ideas, etc. Once the theme, or underlying message, has been identified, a synopsis will be prepared. This is followed by a step outline, which breaks the story down into one-paragraph scenes, concentrating on the dramatic structure. Next, a treatment is prepared. This is a 25 to 30 page description of the story, its mood and characters, with little dialogue and stage direction, often containing drawings to help visualize the key points.

The screenplay is then written over a period of several months, and may be rewritten several times to improve the dramatization, clarity, structure, characters, dialogue, and overall style. However, producers often skip the previous steps and develop submitted screenplays which are assessed through a process called script coverage. A film distributor should be contacted at an early stage to assess the likely market and potential financial success of the film. Hollywood distributors will adopt a hard-headed business approach and consider factors such as the film genre, the target audience, the historical success of similar films, the actors who might appear in the film and the potential directors of the film. All these factors imply a certain appeal of the film to a possible audience and hence the number of "bums on seats" during the theatrical release. Not all films make a profit from the theatrical release alone, therefore DVD sales and worldwide distribution rights need to be taken into account.

The movie pitch is then prepared and presented to potential financiers. If the pitch is successful and the movie is given the "green light", then financial backing is offered, typically from a major film studio, film council or independent investors. A deal is negotiated and contracts are signed.

2. *Pre-Production*

In pre-production, the movie is designed and planned. The production company is created and a production office established. The production is storyboarded and visualized with the help of illustrators and concept artists. A production budget will also be drawn up to cost the film.

The producer will hire a crew. The nature of the film, and the budget, determine the size and type of crew used during filmmaking. Many Hollywood blockbusters employ a cast and crew of thousands while a low-budget, independent film may be made by a skeleton crew of eight or nine. Typical crew positions include:

1. The director is primarily responsible for the acting in the movie and managing the creative elements.
2. The assistant director (AD) manages the shooting schedule and logistics of the production, among other tasks.
3. The casting director finds actors for the parts in the script. This normally requires an audition by the actor. Lead actors are carefully chosen and are often based on the actor's reputation or "star power."
4. The location manager finds and manages the film locations. Most pictures are shot in the predictable environment of a studio sound stage but occasionally outdoor sequences will call for filming on location.

5. The production manager manages the production budget and production schedule. He or she also reports on behalf of the production office to the studio executives or financiers of the film.
6. The director of photography (DP or DOP) or cinematographer creates the photography of the film. He or she cooperates with the director, director of audiography (DOA) and AD.
7. The art director manages the art department, which makes production sets, costumes and provides makeup and hair styling services.
8. The production designer creates the look and feel of the production sets and props, working with the art director to create these elements.
9. The storyboard artist creates visual images to help the director and production designer communicate their ideas to the production team.
10. The production sound mixer manages the audio experience during the production stage of a film. He or she cooperates with the director, DOP, and AD.
11. The sound designer creates new sounds and enhances the aural feel of the film with the help of foley artists.
12. The composer creates new music for the film.
13. The choreographer creates and coordinates the movement and dance—typically for musicals. Some films also credit a fight choreographer.

3. *Production*

In production the movie is created and shot. More crew will be recruited at this stage, such as the property master, script supervisor, assistant directors, stills photographer, picture editor, and sound editors. These are just the most common roles in filmmaking; the production office will be free to create any unique blend of roles to suit a particular film. A typical day's shooting begins with an assistant director following the shooting schedule for the day. The film set is constructed and the props made ready. The lighting is rigged and the camera and sound recording equipment are set up. At the same time, the actors are wardrobed in their costumes and attend the hair and make-up departments.

The actors rehearse their scripts and blocking with the director. The picture and sound crews then rehearse with the actors. Finally, the action is shot in as many takes as the director wishes. Each take of a shot follows a slating procedure and is marked on a clapperboard, which helps the editor keep track of the takes in post-production. The clapperboard records the scene, take, director, director of photography, date, and name of the film written on the front, and is displayed for the camera. The clapperboard also serves the necessary function of providing a marker to sync up the film and the sound take. Sound is recorded on a separate apparatus from the film and they must be synched up in post-production. The director will then decide if the take was acceptable or not. The script supervisor and the sound and camera teams log the take on their respective report sheets. Every report sheet records important technical notes on each take.

When shooting is finished for the scene, the director declares a "wrap." The crew will "strike," or dismantle, the set for that scene. The director approves the next day's shooting schedule and a daily progress report is sent to the production office. This includes the report sheets from continuity, sound, and camera teams. Call sheets are distributed to the cast and crew to tell them when and where to turn up the next shooting day. For productions using traditional photographic film, the unprocessed negative of the day's takes are sent to the film laboratory for processing overnight. Once processed, they return from the laboratory as *dailies* or *rushes* (film positives) and are viewed in the evening by the director, above the line crew, and, sometimes, the cast. For productions using digital technologies, shots are downloaded and organized on a computer for display as dailies. When the entire film is *in the can,* or in the completion of the production phase, the production office normally arranges a wrap party to thank all the cast and crew for their efforts.

4. Post-Production

Here the film is assembled by the film editor. The modern use of video in the filmmaking process has resulted in two workflow variants: one using entirely film, and the other using a mixture of film and video. In the film workflow, the original camera film (negative) is developed and copied to a one-light workprint (positive) for editing with a mechanical editing machine. An edge code is recorded onto film to locate the position of picture frames.

Since the development of non-linear editing systems such as Avid, Quantel or Final Cut Pro, the film workflow is used by very few productions. In the video workflow, the original camera negative is developed and telecined to video for editing with computer editing software. A time code is recorded onto video tape to locate the position of picture frames. Production sound is also synced up to the video picture frames during this process. The first job of the film editor is to build a rough cut taken from sequences (or scenes) based on individual "takes" (shots). The purpose of the rough cut is to select and order the best shots. The next step is to create a fine cut by getting all the shots to flow smoothly in a seamless story. Trimming, the process of shortening scenes by a few minutes, seconds, or even frames, is done during this phase. After the fine cut has been screened and approved by the director and producer, the picture is "locked," meaning no further changes are made. Next, the editor creates a negative cut list (using edge code) or an edit decision list (using time code) either manually or automatically. These edit lists identify the source and the picture frame of each shot in the fine cut.

Once the picture is locked, the film passes out of the hands of the editor to the sound department to build up the sound track. The voice recordings are synchronized and the final sound mix is created. The sound mix combines sound effects, background sounds, ADR, dialogue, walla, and music. The sound track and picture are combined together, resulting in a low quality answer print of the movie. There are now two possible workflows to create the high quality release print depending on the recording medium:

1. In the film workflow, the cut list that describes the film-based answer print is used to cut the original colour negative (OCN) and create a colour timed copy called the colour master positive or interpositive print. For all subsequent steps this effectively becomes the master copy. The next step is to create a one-light copy called the colour duplicate negative or internegative. It is from this that many copies of the final theatrical release print are made. Copying from the internegative is much simpler than copying from the interpositive directly because it is a one-light process; it also reduces wear-and-tear on the interpositive print.

2. In the video workflow, the edit decision list that describes the video-based answer print is used to edit the original colour tape (OCT) and create a high quality colour master tape. For all subsequent steps this effectively becomes the master copy. The next step uses a film recorder to read the colour master tape and copy each video frame directly to film to create the final theatrical release print.

Finally the film is previewed, normally by the target audience, and any feedback may result in further shooting or edits to the film.

5. Distribution

This is the final stage, where the movie is released to cinemas or, occasionally, to DVD, VCD or VHS (though VHS tapes are less common now that more people own DVD players). The movie is duplicated as required for theatrical distribution. Press kits, posters, and other advertising materials are published and the movie is advertised. The movie will usually be launched with a launch party, press releases, interviews with the press, showings of the film at a press preview, and/or at film festivals. It is also common to create a website to accompany the movie. The movie will play at selected cinemas and the DVD is typically released a few months later. The distribution rights for the film and DVD are also usually sold for worldwide distribution. Any profits are divided between the distributor and the production company.

Independent Filmmaking

Filmmaking also takes place outside of the studio system and is commonly called independent filmmaking. Since the introduction of DV technology, the means of production have become more democratized. Filmmakers can conceivably shoot and edit a movie, create and edit the sound and music, and mix the final cut on a home computer. However, while the means of production may be democratized, financing, distribution, and marketing remain difficult to accomplish outside the traditional system. Most independent filmmakers rely on film festivals to get their films noticed and sold for distribution. However, the Internet has allowed for relatively inexpensive distribution of independent films; many filmmakers post their films online for critique and recognition. Although there is little profitability in this, a filmmaker can still gain exposure via the web.

February 29, 2008—The first student to complete the basic filmmaking course (pre-production) is Mohamed Alsayed of Cairo, Egypt. The final assignment of the course is to create an animatic (which is a movie of the storyboards produced with the free version of FrameForge 3D Studio).

You can see Mohamed's animatic movie (with instructor's corrections) at Mohamed's Animatic. (This file requires the ability to play OGG movies on your computer. Updated March 8: 1.7 MB, 1 minute 13 seconds, stereo, 320×240 letterboxed with subtitles).

Courses in Filmmaking?

Course #1: Basic filmmaking (pre-production)
Course #2: Film editing introduction
Course #3: Film scoring for dramatic scenes
Exercise: Script writing for high school dramas
Project: The storyboard artwork project
Future: Poser / DAZ Studio animation.

Anyone can Learn to be a Filmmaker

Filmmaking is easy

Filmmaking is not rocket science. Everything about filmmaking is extremely easy to learn. Anyone can do it if they wish.

The challenge of learning filmmaking

The challenge is filmmaking requires learning a huge number of skills. If you want to be an independent filmmaker, you must learn the equivalent of 20 different careers.

Telling a story

In a dramatic motion picture, the story is told by many people. The cinematographer tells the story with the camera. The lighting person tells the story with lighting. The film composer tells the story with music. The actors tell the story with action and dialogue. The editor tells the story with editing. The sound effects person tells the story with sound.

You have to learn all of this

And as an independent filmmaker, you have to learn to all of these skills. If you fail to learn even one of these skills, people will notice and be turned off by your movie. You must learn everything!!!!

Film School Preparatory

Wikiversity Film School is a preparatory school for budding filmmakers who plan to go to film school or take classes in motion picture production. Each year, USC Film School receives 800 applicants to fill just 50 undergraduate positions. We teach you the things that film schools expect you to know before you get to film school.

Learning Filmmaking Software

Intel processor: First, you need to do is learn about the computer software for filmmaking.

Designed for the Macintosh: The film scoring course is designed for Apple's GarageBand with Jam Pack: Symphony Orchestra. The Film Editing course is designed for Apple's Final Cut Pro or Adobe Premiere.

Linux: Where possible, free Linux software is listed. However, there is still no standard movie file format for Linux and nothing which matches the quality and usefulness of Apple's GarageBand for film scoring. Therefore, Linux is currently not a good choice for filmmakers.

Where to start?

Filmmaking, editing, and scoring: Budding filmmakers should start with the basic filmmaking course. For the first lesson, you will format a very short motion picture script. After that, take the pop quiz where you tell me how you would begin to film this scene. If you want to be a film composer (but you are not a musician), screen writer, or a film editor, you can go directly to the courses in film editing or film scoring or the script writing exercise.

Cost

Lessons

These filmmaking courses are free. The only requirement is you submit your homework assignments so others can benefit.

The Disks

If you do not wish to purchase the required disks from the Star Movie Shop, you can borrow the disks from the instructor. You will have one month before you must return each disk.

Software

I always try to select programmes which are free.

Sharing Your Work

Your Homework Assignments

Your completed assignments must be submitted under the Free Documentation License or as Public Domain. This allows what you have learned to be shared by others.

There is some of free software used at Wikiversity Film School. Sometimes, this software is demo versions or simplified versions of software but this is good enough to complete these lessons. Using free software, you can learn a tremendous amount about filmmaking.

FrameForge 3D Studio Free Demo Version

Basic filmmaking (pre-production)

The heart of the Wikiversity Film School's basic filmmaking course (pre-production) is FrameForge 3D Studio 2 Demo Version. This is the most educational programme used at Wikiversity Film School. And the demo version is free for both the Macintosh and Windows operating system.

This programme simulates the motion picture camera, the movie set, and the actors. The programme is useful for experimenting with the different lenses on your motion picture camera. And the final output of FrameForge 3D Studio 2 Demo Version is completely frame accurate (including depth of field effects) ready to give your cinematographer for creating all the shots of your movie.

The free demo version is limited to 20 uses. Other limitations apply. However, this is more than enough to complete your assignments at Wikiversity Film School. Download this free programme today and begin learning how to use it.

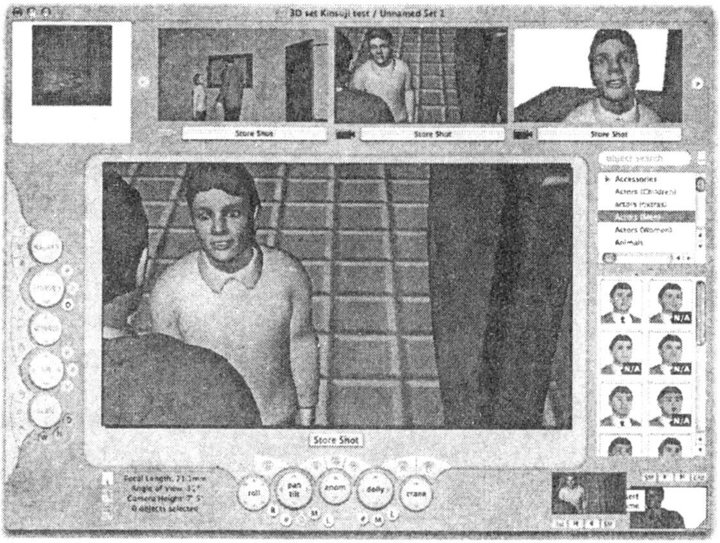

Apple's GarageBand

Film Scoring

All film scoring lessons at Wikiversity Film School is done using Apple's GarageBand which is free with each new Macintosh PC. Starting in 2008, if you are going to buy a PC, you might as well purchase a Macintosh PC. You will also need the musical instruments of the symphony orchestra. Some sources of musical software instruments of the symphony orchestra are free (such as the packages from Boldt) and some are not. I recommend Apple's Jam Pack: Symphony Orchestra. I have not tried Apple's new Jam Pack for voices which might also be useful.

- Filmmakers should not use Apple's Logic 7 which is poorly designed and exceedingly awkward.

Film Dailies

Film Editing

The filmmaking, film editing and film scoring courses use disks from the Star Movie Shop. The Star Movie Shop is not open to the public. It is only open to serious film students.

The disks contain unedited scenes from television dramas for editing and scoring on the Macintosh computer. This is the real thing. Most film dailies require QuickTime. Files can be converted to other formats for Windows using additional software (not provided.) Except for the actual film dailies, all the contents of these disks is distrubuted under the NGU Open Source Document License.

Animation

Starting in 2009, Wikiversity Film School will have a simple course in 3D animation. This will use the free programmes of DAZ Studio and Bryce 5.5. If you have Poser and Vue, you can use those programmes but they are not free.

DAZ Studio and Bryce take time to learn so if you are interested in working with 3D, you should download these free programmes and begin to learn them.

Other useful Programmes

- ArtRage2 Free is used for matte painting and creating the movie poster. This is a simple and fun artistic painting programme. Feels very natural. Extremely useful. If you need any kind of digital painting with traditional artist materials, this is your first choice. This is the free version which is fully working but more limited than the full version which is also remarkably inexpensive.
- GIMP is a free paint programme comparable to Adobe Photoshop. Surprisingly mature programme but definitely not to the level of Photoshop. Requires X-11. If you do not have Adobe Photoshop 4 or later, this programme is absolutely necessary for some of the classes at Wikiversity Film School.
- Audacity is a free useful utility for working with audio and converting audio to OGG files. It is a bit awkward but it is free.
- Tux Paint is a free fun paint programme for kids. It has the added advantage of using rubber stamps and creating matte paintings easily. Has the unique feature of doing rough storyboards with special storyboard artwork. Also useful for one of the lessons about learning matte painting at Wikiversity Film School for kids.

FILM PRODUCTION OVERVIEW

Who are these People?

First there is the movie's producer. The producer hires the line producer to be in charge of the crew but the producer is still going to be hanging around the movie set each day. The line producer must hire all the people on the crew. And the line producer must also worry about keeping the crew happy! The producer hired the movie's director. Over the years, the role of director has changed. And depending on how the deal was set up, the director can have other titles and duties as well. In the simplest case, the director simply controls the performance of the actors and focuses the actors. The director must be good at directing actors. The director will do the blocking for the scene. Each director has his own shooting style. The cinematographer is in charge of everything related to creating and capturing the image on film (or digital video, etc.). Therefore, the cinematographer must worry about lighting, the camera, the lenses, film stock, cameras and formats, power sources, the film, filteration etc. and everything which effects the look of the movie. The cinematographer is in charge of the camera crew and renting a camera, no matter if it is film, HD and DV. If your movie is low budget, guess who worries about Shooting on Film on a low budget? The cinematographer is responsible for monitoring and measuring exposure. The cinematographer must do all the in-camera special effects such as filming or faking rain or shooting underwater. For more information on learning to be a cinematographer, here is a list of books. Other things to consider are Movie Making Manual/ HDV I HDV *vs.* DVCproHD. To do the sound recording, the sound mixer records the dialogue while the boom operator holds the microphone over the actors but out of sight of the camera (hopefully). The slate person operates the clapper board and quietly through this entire process, a still photographer takes the stills.

The Daily Grind

Each day, according to the call sheet that was distributed the night before, the actors arrive very early in the morning for make-up and costumes. Last night, the actors have memorized their lines for today based on the scene list in the call sheet. In the meantime, the director, producer and studio executives are looking at the film dailies from yesterday to see what went right and what went wrong. At the same time, the light people are finishing the rough setup of the lighting. And the construction crew is finishing any last minute changes to the movie set. Finally, everyone gets together and begins blocking the scene and final rehearsals (if any.)

If lighting adjustments are needed based on the blocking, the actors go to their trailers while their stand-ins stay to help with the lighting. Finally the filming of the scene begins. Long before now, the director has broken down the scene into a series of shots. For each shot, the cinematographer positions the camera and the boom operator positions the microphone.

Filming Procedure

When everyone is ready, the Cinematographer tells, "Set" to mean that the everything on the set is ready. The tape recorder for the boom microphone is turned on when the director yells, "Roll Sound." When the audio tape recorder has reached the proper speed, the sound mixer yells, "Rolling." Then the director yells, "Roll Camera." The camera is started. The camera is turned on after the audio tape recorder because the film is more expensive than the audio tape. When the camera is rolling, the camera operator will yell, "Rolling." Then the director will yell, "Slate" and the slate operator will announce which scene this is (having first gotten that information from the script supervisor). This same information is written on the slate of the clapper board. The reason for announcing the scene number is for the lab technician who will listen to the audio tape to find the start of the correct scene when the lab operator syncs the audio to the picture that night.

Then the slate operator will close the clapper sticks with a loud clapping sound so that the camera sees the closing of the clapper sticks and the audio tape records the noise of the sticks hitting together. Then the director will inform the actors that they can begin the scene. When the director feels like it, the director will yell, "Cut." If the movie is being shot on 35 mm film which is very expensive, and the director likes the actor's performance and the cameras performance, the director will also yell, "Print" which means that this is a good take and everyone including the script supervisor, the sound person and the camera assistant will circle this take number on their logs or notes. If the director feels like it, he will ask everyone do to this again. If the director is satisfied, then director will yell, "Next" and everyone will set up for the next shot. If the same scene will be filmed from a different angle, the script supervisor will create a number Take Number usually by adding an alphabetic letter to the take number. Take 32A is will be roughly the same as Take 32 but from a different camera angle.

If there are multiple takes, if the slate is not at the beginning of the shot, it will be at the end of the shot but upside down. If the movie has a really low budget and the audio or the camera are not running accurately, there might be two slates, one at the beginning and one at the end so the audio can be stretched to fit the video. (This is very rare but realize it is possible.)

Visiting the Movie Set

The best way to see all of this is to visit the movie set. If you don't have the time to become a Production Assistant, take the tours of movie studios. Some tours can be very interesting.

Hollywood Studio Tours

While the Universal Studio Tour is more entertainment than actual examples of filming, you can pick up tickets to filming as you leave Universal Studio Tour area. Most are for Sitcoms which are filmed totally different from a motion picture. Yet they are very educational and entertaining to watch. At one time, the best tour in Hollywood (and the most expensive) was at Warner Bros. Their website does not work well but you can try it at Warner Bros. If you have been on this tour recently, please tell us. NBC Studio has a ticket office which gives out free ticket. However, these are mostly for sitcoms. If anyone has been to the filmings in LA, please give us a list of where you go to get tickets and what is available currently.

Japan

Don't overlook the studio tours in other lands. Eiga Mura, the Toei Studio Movie theme park in the northwest part of Kyoto is great fun. Years ago, you could actually see post production if you waited and watched very carefully in one of the distant buildings. If anyone has gone visited this movie village recently, please describe what you saw. Here is an article on this movie village in 2005. Many of the movie are filmed in plain sight of the crowds of tourists. Great fun!

India

Ramoji Film City in Hyderabad does have a tour facility. The main hub of Indian Cinema is Mumbai—A unguided tour of Film City, off the Western Express Highway in Goregaon (E), Mumbai is a good place to start off with. Spread over acres and acres of lush green forests on mountains there are sets of various film and TV productions at any point in time with shoots going on. One of India's largest film processing labs, Adlabs is located here along with sets of Balaji (India's tele soap factory) and many others. One can also move from here to Mehboob Studios, Bandra where there are often lavish sets of various film songs are set up. Then on it is a process of ask the locals and try your luck.

England

I believe that Pinewood Studios has a studio tour. Anyone been there? Please tell us more.

Visiting the Movie Set by Watching Film Dailies

You can also get an understanding of the way that movies are filmed if you watch film dailies. You see everything that the camera sees for all of the circle takes.

Watching the Movie Set—Film Dailies on eBay

Sometimes these tapes (given as souvineers to the cast and crew) become available on eBay. If you also plan to edit the scenes for practice, be sure to get only originals, not copies.

Watching the Movie Set—Digitized Film Dailies

If you have no other way to watch what happens on the movie set of television dramas, look at Disk #2 from the Star Movie Shop which shows how 24 different scenes were filmed from a variety of television dramas. It is amazing to watch how perfectly the actors repeat their lines. After only one night of memorization and one mornings rehearsal, they hit their mark perfectly.

Note: If you shoot your own movie, the dailies will never look as good as dailies from a television drama which is filmed fast and efficiently after years of practice for both the cast and crew. Your first day of filming on a low budget movie with a new crew and inexperience actors will look more like a disaster movie than a motion picture set.

Animated Motion Pictures

If you are making an animated movie, the production is done differentlly. Animation for an animated motion picture is done during production (not post-production) and it is very different from the animation which is done for visual effects in post-production.

FILM PRE-PRODUCTION

Pre-production is the process of preparing all the elements involved in a film, play, or other performance. In the film industry, pre-production usually only commences once a project has been developed and is greenlit. At this stage a project will generally be fully financed and have most of the key elements such as principal cast, director and cinematographer in place, as well as a screenplay which is satisfactory to all the financiers. During pre-production, the script is broken down into individual scenes and all the locations, props, cast members, costumes, special effects and visual effects are identified. An extremely detailed schedule is produced and arrangements are made for the necessary elements to be available to the filmmakers at the appropriate times. Sets are constructed, the crew are hired, financial arrangements are put in place and a start date for the beginning of principal photography is set. At some point in pre-production there will be a read-through of the script which is usually attended by all cast members with speaking parts, all heads of departments, financiers, producers, publicists, and of course the director.

Even though the writer may still be working on it, the screenplay is generally *page-locked* and *scene-numbered* at the beginning of pre-production to avoid confusion. This means that even though additions and deletions may still be made, any particular scene will always fall on the same page and have the same scene number.

UNTITLED FILM STUDIO IN PRE-PRODUCTION

For clarification, Currently Untitled Studio means just that, not that CUS is the name of the studio. The name will be changed as work progresses. In either case, this is a case study/log of events concerning production of a series of shorts undertaken by DorianGray (director) and a group of volunteers.

Note: The first few weeks of work are not dated, or have only been dated by the accuracy of memory. Specific items such as previous ideas, names, and storylines/scripts will not be mentioned or changed for privacy, liability and copyright reasons. These will possibly be changed as work progresses/finishes.

Development

(*a*) Finding a Story
(*b*) Begging for Backing
(*c*) Contracts

Pre-Production

(*a*) Storyboarding
(*b*) Casting
(*c*) Location Scouting
(*d*) Budgeting
(*e*) Schedule
(*f*) Paperwork

Production

(*a*) Cinematography etc.
(*b*) Sound Recording
(*c*) Tracking and Management

Post-Production

(*a*) Soundtrack
(*b*) Editing
(*c*) Formatting

Exhibition and Release

(*a*) Exhibition
(*b*) Distribution

FILM POST-PRODUCTION

Post-production occurs in the making of audio recordings, films/ movies, photography and digital art, videos and television programmes. It is the general term for all stages of production occurring after the actual recording and ending with the completed work.

Post-production is in fact many different processes grouped under one name. These typically include:

(*a*) Editing the picture/TV programme.
(*b*) Editing the soundtrack.
(*c*) Writing and recording the soundtrack music.
(*d*) Adding visual special effects—mainly computer generated imagery (CGI) and digital copy from which release prints will be made (although this may be made obsolete by digital cinema technologies).

Typically, the post-production phase of creating a film takes longer than the actual shooting of the film, and can take several months to complete.

Other film production stages include (very broadly)—writing the screenplay, script development (rewriting), financing, pre-production, the actual shooting and film distribution/marketing.

INTRODUCTION TO FILM SCORING

This course is for high school students and first year college students. This course is *Film scoring for musicians.*

Course Contents

1. Introduction to film scoring
2. Exercise: The sound of fear
3. Exercise: Other moods from a single note
4. Exercise: The sound of joy

5. Exercise: Other moods from delicate rhythm
   Fun pop quiz: Music which tells a story
6. Exercise: Creating a mood or story with a melody
   Creative pop quiz: The Spy Story - Who is who?
   FREE: Entrance Exam disk for film editing and scoring
7. Exercise: Creating a motive
8. Exercise: Creating continuity
9. Exercise: Foreground/Background music
   Watch a movie: George Lucas in Love
   Film scoring with actual scenes from television dramas
10. Exercise: What is a "Spotting Session"? - Only A Dream
11. Exercise: Write two musical cues for Home Wrecker
    More Musical Theory
    Exercise: Butchering Midi
12. Exercise: How would you score Green Tea Smoothie?
13. Exercise: Write a film score for Blindman's Bluff
    Exercise: Write a film score for Seduced by the Dark Side!

"What music does in film or commercials is supplant the emotion that is lost on camera. My job is to create the mood and direct your feelings. If it is working beautifully, you do not even realize it is there." - Brian Banks, *Fortune Magazine*, April 30, 2007.

The Ideal Student

This course is only for people who want to make musical sound effects.

The Wrong Student

If you enjoy writing songs, do not take this course.

If you ever attended a music school, do not take this course.

If you enjoy playing music, do not take this course.

Frequently Changing Moods

In a television drama with dialogue (with a conversation), there is an average of one edit every three seconds. The longest edit is six seconds. Movies for the younger generation have one edit every 1.5 seconds. That means the MOOD will change every three seconds to six seconds. And that means the mood of your music must change every three to six seconds. A song has only ONE (1) mood. Therefore, songs are useless for a scene with dialogue.

Are you able to change your mood every three to six seconds?

Use MIDI, not DAW

For this course, you need a MIDI setup which will sync to digital video (QuickTime or WAV) such as GarageBand. If you play lots of instruments, you can use a DAW such as GarageBand. But this is only for advanced users. Most people should use MIDI with software instruments. And you should have the sounds of a symphony orchestra (starting with a nice violin trill).

GarageBand

Your instructor recommends Apple's GarageBand with Jam Pack Symphony Orchestra for beginners. It is reasonably simple yet surprisingly powerful... once you find the hidden features.

No Linux

There is no programmes for Linux that will do film scoring with software instruments in sync with QuickTime, WAV, or OGG movies. With Ubuntu Linux, you can try Rosegarden to make the midi files. Then use TiMidity++ (a command line application) to change midis to oggs, and Audacity for some final effects (mostly amplifying and adjusting the envelope). Not easy!

It is not about you!

This course is not about you or your music. This is not a place to show how great you are. This course explains what the director/ producer of the motion picture needs. You learn to create the music that they want, not the music you want.

About this Course

Which kind of film scoring? This course teaches you how to score a conversation from a narrative motion picture or narrative television drama. This course teaches how to use musical sound effects to create moods for dramatic scenes where people are talking. That is all! Creating the mood for a conversation is the most challenging job of a film composer. Everything else is much easier. That is why the course focuses on just this one kind of film scoring—conversations.

Film scoring made easy

Film scoring is easy. Anyone can do it. You just need someone to tell you the theory and then show you how to apply it to real scenes from television dramas.

The Secret of Film Scoring

All you have to do is learn the secret of film scoring:

1. The only purpose of a film score is to create the moods for a scene.
2. Single notes are best. (Usually, a single note is all that will fit.)
3. Delicate rhythms also work well. (No drums or other percussion, including piano)
4. Melodies can do lots of special things.

Preparing the Viewer Emotionally

Explaining the Story with Music

This course deals with dramatic TV shows (cop, lawyer, medical shows). This is a medium where sounds are used to cue the viewer emotionally. That is your job! The best way to do this is to keep your music short and simple. That is why this course is emphasizes the basics. You simply add moods to a scene. I cannot stress this enough. This course is not about making music. Instead, this course is about creating moods. In this course, you create most of your film score by creating musical sound effects, not music. That is all that is needed. Do not get carried away with your own brilliance. Please keep it simple!

The Disks are on Loan

The disks for this course come from the Star Movie Shop. I can loan them to you if you promise to return each disk in one month. (All of the disks are not copy protected.) Otherwise, you must purchase the disks from them.

You Begin at the Beginning

Start with the Basics

I can teach you film scoring. But you must start with the basics. For the moment, forget about John Williams and Danny Elfman.

Instead, think Schroeder (of the "Peanuts" cartoons). Just a 5-year-old kid pounding on a toy piano to create musical sound effects. These musical sound effects create moods. That is your goal. To create moods for your audience.

Requirement for this course

To take this course, you must become a 5-year-old kid who likes to create wonderful moods just by pounding on your Midi keyboard.

The Theory of Film Scoring

Mood, Mood, Mood

The only purpose of music in a motion picture is to explain the moods of the scene. The composer tells the audience what they should be feeling when they watch the movie. That's it! Therefore, you have to learn to create moods with your music.

Most Important

It is not the music which is important but only the mood which it creates. Most of the time, your music must be kept short and simple. Musicians have very little time and space in a motion picture. Most musicians/composers find this very frustrating. Get over it.

It is not about You

Film scoring is not about your music. Film scoring is only about creating the moods that the director needs in his movie. If you can accept this, you can be a great film composer.

So keep it simple. Just create moods.

Required Software

Symphony Orchestra

For this course, you should be able to create realistic sound of a symphony orchestra on your computer. Lots of programmes do this. Even GarageBand with Jam Pack: Symphony Orchestra or the free Boldt packages can do this very well.

LEARNING THE BASICS OF FILMMAKING

March 27, 2008—This course requires the installation of the FREE demo version of FrameForge 3D Studio. Many people have problems with this so download this free programme as soon as possible to see if it will work on your computer.

Course in Basic Filmmaking (Pre-production)
Lesson: Formatting the Script.
Pop Quiz: Pop Quiz—What is the first shot?
Lesson: Creating the thumbnail storyboards
Lesson: Creating the 3D storyboards
Free: Entrance Exam disk
Lesson: Learning about camera lenses
Lesson: Record the dialogue for the animatic
Lesson: Intro to narrative filmmaking
Lesson: Draw the movie poster for "Star Wars"
Lesson: Understanding dailies
Lesson: Create a matte painting
Lesson: Understanding editing
Pop Quiz: Pop Quiz—Creating the moods (film scoring)
Lesson: Understanding "L-Cuts"
Lesson: Create the animatic

Lessons in Basic Filmmaking

Course #1 "Basic Filmmaking" starts by showing you all the *pre-production steps* for making a short motion picture.

- Begin learning filmmaking by formatting the script using the free demo version of Final Draft (or CeltX for people who have Linux.)
  First lesson: Formatting the movie script.

Your Instructor Says

- Please use the free demo version of Final Draft rather than CeltX.
  1. The free Final Draft demo has fewer bugs than the beta version of CeltX.
  2. You will learn much more from Final Draft because it has many more features than CeltX.
  3. It takes longer to learn to use Final Draft than CeltX but Final Draft has better.

The Story of "Seduced by the Dark Side!"

An old (yet wise) person and a young (but curious) person are outside a movie theater where they have just seen the movie "Star Wars." Now they stand looking at the movie poster on the wall outside the theater.

The younger person says, "That was a great movie... but I don't understand one thing." The older person says, "Hum, what's that?" The young person says, "I don't understand how anyone can be 'seduced by the dark side'".

The older person thinks for a while and then answers, "What computer do you use at home?"

The young person immediately responds eagerly, "A Macintosh."

Then the older person slowly says, "But what computer does your father use at work?"

The young person thinks for a while and then smiles in amazement, exclaiming loudly, "Seduced by the Dark Side!"

The older person smiles knowingly at the young person. The young person is very happy knowing he has just learned a very important lesson. Now the two have formed a bond that will last a lifetime.

They begin walking slowly home together.

Purpose and Goal of this Filmmaking Course

The Purpose (pre-production)

The purpose of this course is to learn the steps needed to prepare to make a motion picture. This is called "Pre-Production".

The final product of this course is a movie of the storyboards which is called an "Animatic."

The heart of this course is the free demo version of FrameForge 3D Studio. You must use this programme to create the high-quality storyboards needed for the animatic.

Download the free demo version of FrameForge 3D Studio today and take a look.

Note: As we walk through all the steps of making this movie, you will prepare yourself for entering film school.

The Story

The story of our motion picture: The story is simple. A young person and an old person talk about the meaning of the motion picture "Star Wars." That is how the story gets the name "Seduced by the Dark Side!."

Time to Completion

Work at your own pace: There are many steps to make a movie. Go at your own pace. Eventually, you will need to complete all the courses at the Wikiversity Film School to complete this movie.

The Software

The software is free. Most of the software for this course is free. We use trial version and free versions when we can.

BLOCKING

Blocking is the act of walking the actors through the scene before it is shot in order to make sure the lighting is sufficient and the camera is able to get the desired focus required. That's close: Blocking is for all departments to be sure that they are prepared for the scene to be shot. Taking the extra 3-5 minutes to block a scene can save you time, money and patience later. It is not uncommon for blocking to last days for a big scene, such as the scene in Jarhead where the soldiers all met in a tent "in country." Sam Mendes blocked that scene for 4 days before they shot it. Still closer: Blocking a scene for film also must afford the camera the most aesthetically interesting compositions that flow before the lens. It is not only the movement of actors and props to achieve optimum efficiency on the set.

FILM EDITING

Film editing is the connecting of one or more shots to form a sequence, and the subsequent connecting of sequences to form an entire movie. Film editing, by definition, is the only art that is unique to cinema and which defines and separates filmmaking from almost all other art forms (such as: photography, theater, dance, writing, and directing). The job of an editor is not merely to mechanically put pieces of a film together, nor to just cut off the film slates, nor merely to edit dialogue scenes. Film editing is an art form which can either make or break a film. A film editor works with the layers of images, the story, the music, the rhythm, the pace, shapes the actors' performances, "re-directing" and often re-writing the film during the editing process, honing the infinite possibilities of the juxtaposition of small snippets of film into a creative, coherent, cohesive whole.

Film Editor

A film editor is a person who practices film editing by assembling footage into a coherent film. Film editors often are responsible for pulling together all of the elements of story, dialogue, music, sound effects, visual effects, rhythm and pace of a film. In the making of a film, the editors usually play a dynamic and creative role.

History of Film Editing Technology

Film editing evolved from the process of a film editor physically cutting and taping together pieces of film, using a splicer and threading the film on a machine with a viewer such as a Moviola, or "flatbed" machine such as a Kem or Steenbeck.

Before the widespread use of non-linear editing systems, the initial editing of all films was done with a positive copy of the film negative called a film workprint (cutting copy in UK). Today, most films are edited digitally (on systems such as Avid or Final Cut Pro) and bypass the film positive workprint altogether. In the past, the use of a film positive (not the original negative) allowed the editor to do as much experimenting as he or she wished, without the risk of damaging the original.

When the film workprint had been cut to a satisfactory state, it was then used to make an Edit Decision List (EDL). The negative cutter referred to this list while processing the negative, splitting the shots into rolls, which were then contact printed to produce the final film print or answer print. Today, production companies have the option of to bypass negative cutting altogether. With the advent of digital intermediate or "DI," the physical negative does not necessarily need to be physically cut and hot spliced together; rather the negative is optically scanned into computer(s) and a cut list is conformed by a DI editor.

Edwin S. Porter

Edwin S. Porter is generally thought to be the American filmmaker who first put film editing to use. Porter migrated to the United

States as a young sailor and worked as a mechanic before joining the film laboratory of Thomas Alva Edison in the late 1890s.

Early Edison films were short films that were typically shot in one long static locked down shot. When Edison's motion picture studio wanted to increase the length of the short films he came to Porter. Porter made the breakthrough film *Life of an American Fireman* in 1902. The film was among the first that had a plot, action, and even a closeup of a hand pulling a fire alarm.

Other films were to follow. Porter's ground-breaking film, *The Great Train Robbery* is still shown in film schools today as an example of early editing form. It was produced in 1903 and was one of the first examples of dynamic, action editing (the piecing together scenes shot at different times and places and for emotional impact unavailable in a static long shot). Being one of the first film hyphenates (film director, editor and engineer) Porter also invented and utilized some of the very first (albeit primitive) special effects such as double exposures, miniatures and split-screens.

Post-Production

The Editor's Cut

There are several editing stages and the editor's cut is the first. An editor's cut (sometimes referred to as the "assembly edit" or "rough cut") is normally the first pass of what the final film will be when it reaches picture lock. The film editor usually starts working while principal photography (shooting) starts. In the first stage of editing the film editor will usually work alone (save for his or her own team of assistant editors, associate or co-editors and/or visual effects and music editors). Likely, prior to cutting, the editor and director will have seen and/or discussed "dailies" (raw footage shot each day) as shooting progresses. Screening dailies gives the editor a ballpark idea of the director's intentions.

Because it is the first pass, the editor's cut might be somewhat longer than the final film. The editor continues to refine the cut while shooting continues, and often the entire editing process goes on for many months and sometimes more than a year, depending on the film.

The Director's Cut

When shooting is finished, the director can then turn his or her full attention to collaborating with the editor and further refining the cut of the film. This is the time that is set aside where the film editor's first cut is molded to fit the director's vision, and before the studio and/or producers are generally allowed to have input. In the United States, under DGA rules, directors receive a minimum of ten weeks after completion of principal photography to prepare their first cut.

While collaborating on what is referred to as the "director's cut," the director and the editor go over the entire movie with a fine tooth comb; scenes and shots are re-ordered, removed, shortened and otherwise tweaked. Often it is discovered that there are plot holes, missing shots or even missing segments which might require that new scenes be filmed. Because of this time working closely and collaborating—a period that is normally far longer, and far more intimately involved, than the entire production and filming—most directors and editors form a unique artistic bond.

The Producers vs. The Director

Often after the director has had his or her chance to oversee a cut, the subsequent cuts are supervised by one or more producers, who represent the production company and/or movie studio. At times, the final cut of films produced by the major studios is the one that most closely represents what the studio wants from the film and not necessarily what the director wants. Because of this, there have been several conflicts in the past between the director and the studio, sometimes leading to the use of the "Alan Smithee" credit signifying when a director no longer wants to be associated with the final release.

Continuity

Often a film editor is blamed for improper continuity. For example, cutting from a shot where the beer glass is empty to one where it is full. Continuity is, in fact, very nearly last on a film editor's list of important things to maintain. Continuity is typically the business of the script supervisor and film director, who are together responsible for preserving continuity and preventing errors from take to take and shot to shot. Generally speaking, the editor utilizes the script supervisor's notes during post-production to log and keep track of the vast amounts of footage and takes that a director might shoot. However, to most editors what is more important than continuity is the editing of emotional and storytelling aspects of any given film—something that is much more abstract and harder to judge—which is why films often take much longer to edit than to shoot. Often a film editor will used this to focus on the theme of the film.

Methods of Montage

In motion picture terminology, a montage (from the French for "putting together" or "assembly") is a film editing technique.

There are at least three senses of the term:

1. In French film practice, "montage" has its literal French meaning and simply identifies a movie's editor.
2. In Soviet filmmaking of the 1920s, "montage" was a method of juxtaposing shots to derive new meaning that did not exist in either shot alone.
3. In classical Hollywood cinema, a "montage sequence" is a short segment in a film in which narrative information is presented in a condensed fashion. This is the most common meaning among laymen.

Soviet Montage

Lev Kuleshov was among the very first to theorize about the relatively young medium of the cinema in the 1920s. For him, the unique essence of the cinema—that which could be duplicated in no other medium—is editing. He argues that editing a film is like constructing a building. Brick-by-brick (shot-by-shot) the building (film) is erected. His often-cited established that montage can lead the viewer to reach certain conclusions about the action in a film. Montage works because viewers infer meaning based on context.

Although, strictly speaking, U.S. film director D.W. Griffith was not part of the montage school, he was one of the early proponents of the power of editing—mastering cross-cutting to show parallel action in different locations, and codifying film grammar in other ways as well. Griffith's work in the teens was highly regarded by Kuleshov and other Soviet filmmakers and greatly influenced their understanding of editing. Sergei Eisenstein was briefly a student of Kuleshov's, but the two parted ways because they had different ideas of montage. Eisenstein regarded montage as a dialectical means of creating meaning. By contrasting unrelated shots he tried to provoke associations in the viewer, which were induced by shocks.

Montage Sequence

A montage sequence consists of a series of short shots that are edited into a sequence to condense narrative. It is usually used to advance the story as a whole (often to suggest the passage of time), rather than to create symbolic meaning. In many cases, a song plays in the background to enhance the mood or reinforce the message being conveyed. Classic examples are the training montages in Sylvester Stallone's *Rocky* series of movies.

Continuity Editing

What became known as the popular 'classical Hollywood' style of editing was developed by early European and American directors, in particular D.W. Griffith in his films such as *The Birth of a Nation* and *Intolerance*. The classical style ensures temporal and spatial continuity as a way of advancing narrative, using such techniques as the 180 degree rule, Establishing shot, and Shot reverse shot.

Alternatives to Continuity Editing (Non-traditional or Experimental)

Early Russian filmmakers such as Lev Kuleshov further explored and theorized about editing and its ideological nature. Sergei Eisenstein developed a system of editing that was unconcerned with the rules of the continuity system of classical Hollywood that he called Intellectual montage. Alternatives to traditional editing were also the folly of early surrealist and dada filmmakers such as Luis Buñuel (director of the 1929 *Un chien andalou*) and René Clair (director of 1924's *Entr'acte* which starred famous dada artists Marcel Duchamp and Man Ray). Both filmmakers, Clair and Buñuel, experimented with editing techniques long before what is referred to as "MTV style" editing.

The French New Wave filmmakers such as Jean Luc Godard and François Truffaut and their American counterparts such as Andy Warhol and John Cassavetes also pushed the limits of editing technique during the late 1950s and throughout the 1970s. French New Wave films and the non-narrative films of the 1960s used a carefree editing style and did not conform to the traditional editing etiquette of Hollywood films. Like its dada and surrealist predecessors, French New Wave editing often drew attention to itself by its lack of continuity, its demystifying self-reflexive nature (reminding the audience that they were watching a film), and by the overt use of jump cuts or the insertion of material not often related to any narrative.

Editing Techniques

Stanley Kubrick noted that the editing process is the one phase of production that is truly unique to motion pictures. Every other aspect of filmmaking originated in a different medium than film (photography, art direction, writing, sound recording), but editing is the one process that is unique to film. In Alexender Walker's *Stanley Kubrick Directs,* Kubrick was quoted as saying, "I love editing. I think I like it more than any other phase of filmmaking. If I wanted to be frivolous, I might say that everything that precedes editing is merely a way of producing film to edit."

In his book, *On Film Editing,* stipulates seven "rules of cutting" that a good editor should follow:

(*a*) "Rule 1: *Never* make a cut without a positive reason."
(*b*) "Rule 2: When undecided about the exact frame to cut on, cut *long* rather than short" (Dmytryk, 23).
(*c*) "Rule 3: Whenever possible cut 'in movement'" (Dmytryk, 27).
(*d*) "Rule 4: The 'fresh' is preferable to the 'stale'" (Dmytryk, 37).
(*e*) "Rule 5: All scenes should begin and end with continuing action" (Dmytryk, 38).
(*f*) "Rule 6: Cut for proper values rather than proper 'matches'" (Dmytryk, 44).
(*g*) "Rule 7: Substance first—then form" (Dmytryk, 145).

According to Walter Murch, when it comes to film editing, there are six main criteria for evaluating a cut or deciding where to cut. They are (in order of importance, most important first):

(*a*) *Emotion*—Does the cut reflect what the editor believes the audience should be feeling at that moment?

(*b*) *Story*—Does the cut advance the story?
(*c*) *Rhythm*—Does the cut occur "at a moment that is rhythmically interesting and 'right'" (Murch, 18)?
(*d*) *Eye-trace*—Does the cut pay respect to "the location and movement of the audience's focus of interest within the frame" (Murch, 18)?
(*e*) *Two-dimensional place of the screen*—Does the cut respect the 180 degree rule?
(*f*) *Three-dimensional space of action*—Is the cut true to the physical/spatial relationships within the diegesis?

Murch assigned notional percentage values to each of the criteria. Emotion, with 51 per cent, outweighed the combined value of all the other criteria.

EDITING AND PROGRAMME CONTINUITY

Editing a television programme is much more than just putting shots together on a single piece of tape so they can be viewed as a whole. It is in the editing phase that a production is finally made to conform to the producer's vision of it. Editing is both the last and one of the most powerful opportunities the producer has to influence whether a programme will communicate the information it was meant to convey successfully, and whether it will affect the emotions and moods of the audience as the producer wished. The editing process is also a difficult and demanding craft, and presents many opportunities for the unprepared to go astray. Indeed, the failure to communicate effectively in many beginners' television programmes is much more often a failure of the editor to develop a coherent conception of the flow of the programme than of any problem with other technical aspects of the art of television, such as camera work or sound recording.

Conversely, it is possible for a skilled editor to take even seriously flawed original footage and produce a programme which still manages to say what the writer and director had in mind—but we certainly hope you will never be forced to work that way.

In commercial television and film production, the "shooting ratio," or amount of film or tape shot divided by the length of the finished programme, averages about 10:1. In other words, for every minute of edited programme you see, ten minutes or more of tape was recorded by the camera crew. In some specialized and difficult programmes the ratio routinely climbs above 100:1. On the other hand, in live television production in the relatively comfortable atmosphere of a studio, it is often possible to use every second of the original recording with a shooting ratio of 1:1.

Actually both of these represent extremes which you will not ordinarily encounter. Ways to reduce editing time include keeping the overall shooting ratio as low as practical, grouping scenes shot in the same place or time together on the original tape, and, when possible, "slating" shots by holding up a card in front of the camera showing the place, time, date, and crew members present and any other information you think may be helpful in identifying material later.

You may have inferred from the above that the process of editing in a sense begins long before any tape is recorded. In those productions which are scripted in detail before shooting, the script may in fact dictate almost exactly how the finished programme will be edited. So a knowledge of some of the rules of visual and aural continuity is as essential for the script writer, director, and camera operator as for the editor. Again, the more planning and preparation before entering the editing room, the less time and money spent there. Even if your programme does not lend itself well to detailed scripting in advance, it is usually possible to write up an outline, or perhaps even an exact "editing script," based on several viewings of the original footage, which can guide the editor in putting things together properly in the minimum amount of time. This is not to imply that many decisions won't have to be made during the process of editing—especially the specifics of exactly on which frame to make cuts—but good planning can make the actual work with the editing machines much quicker and more pleasant.

There are basically three purposes in editing a programme. The are:

1. To eliminate material which is unusable because it is technically flawed;
2. To remove footage which is irrelevant to the information to be presented in the programme;
3. To assemble what is left in a way which communicates the important information in the programme and, at worst,

the editing is not distracting to viewers and, at best, the programme is both interesting and entertaining.

There is almost never a justifiable reason for making a programme longer than the absolute minimum necessary to cover the topic adequately. If in doubt about the relevance of a particular shot or sequence, it is almost always better to leave it out. Keep cutting away at what you have available (while watching the shooting ratio soar) until every frame of the remaining tape has something valuable to say. Your audience will be grateful for it, and may reward you by staying awake through the whole programme.

What follows is a selection of various rules and concepts of editing which have been developed through experience over the last century of editing motion pictures and, more recently, television programmes. The rules are, to some degree, flexible, but they should be violated blatantly only with great trepidation and after carefully considering all of the alternate ways of editing the sequence. However, if you have something important to say, and only unconventional editing will communicate it effectively, then the content should take precedence over any editing rules. Remember, your final consideration is your audience and their reactions.

1. WS-MS-CU Sequences; Using Close-Ups

Beginning television news camera people are always taught to take three shots of each subject, using different distances, angles, or lens settings to yield a long shot, medium shot, and close-up of the subject. Then these three pieces of tape are edited together in that order to give the viewer an impression of moving in on the action from the outside, finally becoming involved (through the close-ups) in the action itself. Watch television news coverage of a fire or similar event the next time you can. Typically, you will see something like:

LONG SHOT, the burning building;

MEDIUM SHOT, firefighters pulling hoses off the truck and carrying them toward the fire;

CLOSE-UP, firefighter's face or hands as he wrestles with the hose.

Additional shots would tend to be more close-ups: equipment on the truck, hands holding the hose, the faces of spectators, etc. At some time, determined by the pacing of the editing and, in this case, the severity of the fire, there might be a return to the long shot to reestablish the overall layout of the scene in the viewer's mind. Notice the emphasis on close-ups. Television is a relatively low-definition medium, and subjects seen in medium shots or wider just do not come across powerfully on a television screen. It is details, sometimes shot at very close distances, which are most effective in adding visual interest to a story. Use close shots—details of objects, a person's surroundings, or especially of the human face—whenever it is possible and meaningful to do so. They do more than anything else to add excitement and interest to your programme. As the amount of information on the screen , decreases, so does the viewer's ability to watch it for a long time. This implies that close-ups, which contain relatively little visual information but spread it over the entire area of the screen, should not be held on the screen for a very long time. When presented with a single detail of something, an audience can look at it for no more than three or four seconds before it becomes bored and turns away. Exceptions to this rule occur when there is something going on to maintain interest. For example, moving objects can be held longer than totally inanimate ones. A narrator heard in a voice over may point out interesting details in what is shown so that the audience is continually discovering new aspects of the picture. In these cases, even extreme close-ups can remain on the screen for a relatively long time.

Close-ups of faces, on the other hand, can be held for along time, as we seem to find endless fascination in that particular subject. Close-ups are very powerful and revealing for interviews and tend to give at least the illusion of great insight into the speaker. By contrast, long and medium shots are used less in television, although they certainly have a very important place in most programmes. The audience can become disoriented if they are not occasionally reminded of where they are, the overall arrangement of objects and people in the location and the relationships between them. This is the purpose of the long shot. Medium shots reveal more about a single subject, without the emotional commitment of a close-up and they are also most often used for showing the progress of action, as in our fire example above. Of course, there are an infinite number of possible variations. It is the subject matter and overall mood and structure of your programme which determine in the end how sequences of different angles views will fit together.

2. Jump Cuts and the Thirty-Degree Rule

One of the most distracting mistakes it is possible to make in editing is called a "jump cut." If you have watched commercial television all you life, you may in fact never have seen a jump cut. They are so visually distracting, and such pains are taken to avoid them, that this particular error almost never makes it to your home screen.

A jump cut happens when you attempt to edit together two shots which are too similar in visual content. The most obvious example might occur if you remove a single sentence from an interview shot while the camera (which recorded the interview originally as a single shot) remained static. What would happen is that the background would remain still, while the subject's head might "jump" a bit to one side, or lips which were closed might appear instantly to open.

The result is a very jarring interruption in the otherwise smooth flow of action. There are several solutions to this problem. In the case of the interview, an appropriate response would be a cutaway shot—about which more will be said later. In other situations application of the "rule of thirty degrees" can help.

The Thirty-Degree Rule

The thirty-degree rule states that if you make sure that the angle of view of the camera to the subject changes by thirty degrees or more between two shots cut together, the background will move enough that the shots will cut together well without any apparent visual discontinuity. Failure to move the camera at least thirty degrees between shots almost invariable leads to a jump cut. There are exceptions, of course. Cutting from a medium shot to a close-up, for example, can be done even if the camera is not moved an inch. The point is to make each shot as visually different from the one preceding it as possible, so that the viewer's point of view of the scene appears to change in a natural manner. Notice that if you invariably follow the long shot—medium shot—close-up sequence suggested earlier, the problem of jump cuts caused by violations of the thirty degree rule never develops. And cutting from one subject to an entirely different one, or from one location to another, rarely presents any problems.

There are other types of visual discontinuities you must guard against. Most of these are essentially the responsibility of the camera crew at the time of shooting, and the editor's only involvement is to try to cover them up when they occur.

Errors of this sort usually creep in when shooting is spread out over several hours, days, or months. A typical problem might be shooting part of an interview one day, then coming back a few days later to get additional material and finding the subject dressed in different clothing. (Invariably the clothes the subject wore the first time will be in the laundry and totally unavailable.) You cannot cut together parts of the two interviews without making it look as though the subject instantly changed clothes. Errors like these can only be avoided if you are aware of them and plan around their occurrence. It is also among the editor's responsibilities to point out continuity problems when they occur, so that a way can be found to avoid them or minimize their effects. (For example, in this case, it might be possible to group the footage in such a way that the clothing appears to change during a long interlude while other subjects are being shown. When the action returns to the interview the change won't be obvious.)

3. Direction of Motion and The 180 Degree Rule

By this time you may think that editors and directors have to be experts in geometry. Not so! There is really only one other "angle rule," which is designed to keep people facing and moving in the same direction on the screen. One of the more distressing visual discontinuities is reversal in direction of motion, or in screen position of people.

Someone walks out of one room and into another. In the first shot, you set up the camera in the middle of the first room and the subject walks from the left side of the screen and exits through a door on the right. Now on entering the second room, into which the subject is to walk, you find a large expanse of windows on one wall, with the door on the left as you face them. You don't want to shoot into those bright windows, as the camera will give you a poor picture, so you set up the camera on the window side of the room looking toward the middle. Now the subject walks in, but this time WILL BE ENTERING FROM THE RIGHT SIDE OF THE SCREEN. When this is edited together with the previous shot, it will look like the subject changed direction in mid-stride.

The solution is to keep the camera always on the same side of the moving subject. If something is travelling from left to right, it should continue to go in the same direction in every shot you think might be edited into the same sequence. Sometimes, as in our window example, this takes considerable pre-planning and can be something of a headache if there are many locations involved. But it is necessary if the audience is to be able to follow the action without confusion. Again, if you just cannot think of any other way, a cutaway may be used between two shots where the action reverses direction. But this technique is all too obvious to the viewer much of the time.

A somewhat related situation arises when you are dealing with multiple subjects, perhaps in a discussion situation. It is necessary to arrange your shots, and their editing, so that subjects do not appear to be moving from one side of the screen to the other, or looking in different directions at different times.

Study the diagram below, which represents a simple situation with two people seated at a table. If the camera always stays in the area indicated by the number "1" no matter what two shots you cut together, subject "A" will be looking toward the right side of the screen at subject "B," who faces left. This will result in proper visual continuity.

If, however, the camera crosses over to the other side of the table, the apparent positions of the two subjects will be reversed. If you cut two shots of "B" together in succession, "B" will suddenly appear to be looking at himself, but from opposite directions.

This is called the 180 degree rule. When dealing with two or more subjects, visualize a straight line drawn through both of them. As long as the camera always stays on one side or the other of this line, apparent visual continuity can be maintained. The name derives from the fact that the camera can move through an arc of 180 degrees relative to the center point between the subjects.

Now remember the thirty degree rule. We have set up a situation in which, in order to maintain effective visual continuity, the camera has to move at least thirty degrees between shots but has an overall field of only 180 degrees to work in. It can be frustrating, to say the least, to the editor who has to work with material shot without regard for these two rules. Yet the editor, too, has the responsibility of putting shots together in such a sequence that these rules are observed, while still trying to make sense out of the overall meaning of the programme. Good luck!

4. Cutaways and Inserts

Often the availability of proper cutaway or insert shots is the only thing which saves the editor from, at best, profound frustration, or possible even insanity.

You see cutaways frequently in television news interviews. These are the shots of the interviewer looking at his notes, or nodding at what the subject is saying. Usually the cutaway shot has been used to cover up an edit in a continuous shot of the interview subject when removing a few words or sentences would otherwise have produced an unacceptable jump cut. As such, the cutaway is a valuable device, but it should be used with great discretion, as it looks rather contrived. (Often these shots are done after the interview is completed, and the interviewer isn't really reacting to anything—which often shows.) Over-the-shoulder shots are common too—and also often don't work because the sound is noticeably out of sync with the subject's body or facial movements.

It is also possible to cut away to other subjects, like the crowd reacting to a speaker's words, or a close-up of the subject's hands. These sometimes work well and can cover many otherwise embarrassing gaps in visual continuity.

Insert shots have another function in that they actually contribute to the meaning of the programme. Inserts are shots, or sequences, which usually show something that a speaker is talking about. While an interview subject describes a process, an insert sequence can be designed to show that process actually taking place. While these segments can be used to cover continuity difficulties they also tend to make a programme more interesting and meaningful.

Achieving the proper balance between "people" footage (interviews and speakers) and "process" material is difficult, and of course depends on the nature of the specific programme you are making. In general, though, it is better to show something than to talk about it; television is a visual medium and only by making use of its ability to show things as they actually happen can it truly be distinguished from radio or audio tape. Of course, there are programmes where the emphasis is on the people involved as much as the things they are doing, and in these cases there is nothing more beautiful or interesting than the human face. So keep your purpose in mind when deciding on an overall plan for the editing of your programmes.

Insert and cutaway footage is so important in editing that it is essential to be aware of the need to produce this type of material at the time of shooting. Many discontinuities are not the result of ignorance of the rules on the part of the editor, but happen simply because the required quantity or quality of insert material was never shot. Much of a good camera person's time is spent looking for and recording reaction shots and various close-ups and cutaways which can be used by the editor to cover any difficulties later. It is definitely something to keep in mind when you start to shoot tape.

5. Shot Timing and Pacing

The need to keep certain shots fairly short was discussed earlier. In general, close-ups do not hold interest as long as medium shots and it is uncommon to see any shot that lasts longer than about ten seconds, but certain types of action can be held longer if it seems appropriate. It is a good idea to vary the length of shots, particularly if many of your shots are fairly short, unless the building of a definite and predictable rhythm is what you have in mind. One final note. Changes in shots that are too frequent and done for no apparent reason can be worse than long static shots. Editing should never be allowed to interfere with or distract from programme content.

6. Cutting Sound

In professional film editing, it is not considered much of a problem at all to restructure sentences or even words by precise editing to change the meaning of what someone says. Digital audio files and the audio portion of digital video files can be processed using computers to change not only the sequence of sounds, but volume, pitch, and other characteristics. Even so, most audio editing for video is restricted to making cuts between phrases or sentences, trying to fit together the sometimes random-sounding ramblings of your subjects into a smooth whole.

It is beyond the scope of this chapter to try to dictate how your subjects' thoughts should be fitted together, so we will concentrate on a few rules and suggestions as to how the continuity of sound fits into the overall production of a programme.

Most programmes of the informational or educational genre have their continuity dictated almost entirely by the content of the sound track. In fact, the spoken word probably conveys most of the actual information in most of the television programmes you have seen.

This is a difficult problem, because errors in visual continuity (which is what most of this chapter has been about) are usually much more obvious and distracting to the viewer than a more abstract lack of logic or coherence in what the interview subjects or narrator say. So in many cases the content will have to be adapted to the needs of maintaining a smooth VISUAL flow. Cutting within interview footage, which is often necessary from a content perspective, almost always generates a visually offensive jump cut which requires a cutaway or something similar to reduce the distraction.

The use of sound other than voices should be considered. The natural sounds of many settings—chirping crickets or the cacophony of a factory—can be used to make some kinds of points more effectively than any narration. The use of music in setting moods is fairly obvious; indeed it is possible, and often very powerful, to edit the visual portion of a programme to fit, in both rhythm and content, a prerecorded piece of music.

One technical detail about editing sound which seems relevant here involves the timing of different spoken segments to be edited together. In average conversation, most people pause about half a second between sentences. If you are trying to edit dialogue together so that it still sounds natural and flowing, you should try to maintain the time between utterances at about this figure. Most people do not pause noticeably between individual words, although a gap of a tenth of a second or so will go unnoticed if it does not occur too often. Naturally, these times have to be adjusted somewhat to fit the specific speech patterns of the individuals involved, so they are only a guide.

A second consideration in sound editing might be thought of as an audio jump cut. Every recording location has a characteristic sound, or presence which may even change slightly during different times of the day. People, too, vary the quality of their voices according to many conditions from stuffy noses to fatigue or emotion. Very few narrators can duplicate the sound of their own voices from one day to the next. Even though two sequences might be recorded using the same equipment in the same location, the quality of the audio may well be so different that a noticeable and objectionable change in sound occurs at an edit point. In editing narrative sequences, the speaking pace must also be fairly constant if the edit is to be "believable."

This barely begins to scratch the surface of the field of editing, yet the rules and ideas presented here are basic ones you will have to keep in mind while shooting and editing videotape. Watching television critically, with an eye toward the contribution of the editor to the finished programme, then editing your own work, will teach you more about the craft than any stack of books could. Do not be afraid of all those buttons!

Editing

Video editing is the selective copying of material from one videotape (or computer file) to another. The process is entirely electronic. Nothing is cut, glued, or pasted. The original is not altered in any way by the editing process. Successful and efficient editing requires some specialized equipment, some knowledge of how the equipment works, and a great deal of planning and preparation both in shooting original footage and in editing itself.

Tape-to-Tape Editing

The necessary editing equipment includes two videotape recorders, two television monitors, and an edit controller. The original tape is played back on the source recorder, which is sometimes called the master recorder. This recorder must be designed to be run by remote control. The audio and video outputs of the source recorder are connected to the inputs on the editing recorder, sometimes called the slave recorder. The editing recorder, in addition to being operated by remote control, also needs some features not found on most videotape recorders. First, it must operate in sync with the playback recorder. That is, its internal timing circuits have to lock to the sync portion of the incoming composite video signal. Second, to make clean edits between old and new video, it must be able to go from the playback mode to the record mode and back only in the vertical interval, or the brief time between pictures. Finally, to accomplish this, it must have special erase heads, called "flying" erase heads, actually mounted on the video head assembly. Most videotape recorders have erase heads that are fixed and erase the entire width of the tape. Because the video signal is laid down on tape in long diagonal passes across the tape, the conventional erase head would erase portions of many frames of video. The erase heads mounted on the video drum can erase video one field at a time, allowing very clean transitions between old and new video.

The audio and video signals from each recorder are also connected to television monitors. This allows the operator to see and hear what is on either tape at any time. Finally, both recorders are connected to a compatible edit controller. The controller includes the basic transport controls for both recorders, such as fast forward, rewind, play, pause, and stop, plus special editing functions.

Editing Modes

In the ASSEMBLE mode it is assumed that there is nothing recorded on the edited videotape after the selected edit point. Each new sequence is edited onto the end of the previous sequence until the tape is completed. No picture of sound which might already have been on the tape is used.

In the INSERT mode, it is assumed that material already on the tape is to be retained. New material is inserted into old. Not all of the signals during the edit need to be replaced. The operator sets the editing machine to change the picture or either of the sound channels or any combination of the three. At the end of the edit, the recorder will return from the record mode to the playback mode.

The Control Track

Almost all videotape recorders record and play back a special sixty hertz pulse called the control track. This track is used in playback to make sure the video heads are positioned correctly to read video information recorded on the tape. Any break in the control track, or sudden shift in phase, or loss of signal level will cause a videotape recorder to vary its speed until it returns to lock. This in turn usually causes the picture to break up or disappear entirely. The essential difference between the assemble and insert edit modes is that in the assemble mode new control track is recorded from the edit point on, while in the insert mode prerecorded control track is used and no new control track is generated. Therefore, the picture will always break up at the end of an assemble edit and, conversely, there must always be good continuous control track already on the tape throughout an insert edit or the picture will break up on later playback wherever the control track was flawed, even though no trouble was observed during the actual insert edit.

Many editors commonly in use are called control track editors because they use the control track as a reference for all of the editing functions. It is critical to know and understand this. Without a good and continuous control track from at least six seconds prior to an edit point to at least two or three seconds after an edit point it may be impossible to make an edit at all. Actual requirements vary from machine to machine, so it is advisable to make sure there is always at least ten seconds of control track in front of and behind every shot recorded.

SMPTE Editing

The Society of Motion Picture and Television Engineers devised a special audio signal that can be recorded on tape and used to identify the location of each frame of video precisely. This SMPTE code is used in many edit suites for three reasons. First, edits using SMPTE code are frame-accurate and repeatable. Second, the code can be used to trigger events in other equipment, such as special effects generators, computers, and audio recorders. Third, preview copies of raw tapes can be made with the frame numbers showing on the screen, so you can make editing decisions "off-line."

Most SMPTE code is recorded on a linear audio channel. That means you have to have two audio channels to use it. Three are better. Most one inch and many 3/4 inch VTR's have three audio channels, leaving two for programme content.

SMPTE is not the only time code in use today. A number of companies have their own proprietary codes. They all serve the same purpose—allowing precise control over editing equipment.

Computer Editing

The rules for editing are the same for film, videotape, and computer editing. The medium changes, not the message. In addition to playback and record VCR's, video monitors and audio gear, computer editing requires a computer that is fast enough and has enough memory to process video, a device to capture video and audio and turn them into computer files, and hard drives that are big enough and fast enough to handle all of the video and audio you will need to store. On Windows computers you want to make sure your capture drive uses the NTFS file format. Editing video on a computer offers several advantages over using videotape. The first is the ability to change the content or length of any part of a programme without having to re-edit everything from that point to the end. In computer editing you are constructing a list of instructions, describing how the programme is to be assembled by the computer. Because you can work on any part of the programme without adversely affecting subsequent parts, computer editing is commonly referred to as "non-linear editing."

A second advantage of computer-based editing is the ability to use more audio and video tracks. Tape-to-tape editing allows for only one or two video tracks and (for most systems) two monaural audio tracks. In theory, computer-based editors could have virtually unlimited audio and video tracks available. In practice, four or five video tracks and the same number stereo audio tracks are usually sufficient. On the video side, this allows the usual "A" and "B" video rolls, the transitions between the A and B rolls, a track for titles and other luminance or chroma keys, and even enough tracks to do a "quad split." Audio would generally consist of the location sound (two tracks to cross fade with the video transitions), the narration, and two music tracks (to cross fade between cuts).

A third advantage of computer editing lies in the ability to duplicate files without loss. As you move files from memory to a hard drive or to tape backup or to a CD or DVD-ROM and back again, there is no loss of quality.

On the "down" side, video has to be "captured," or transferred from tape into the computer. Capturing is in itself an editing process. Clips have to be identified and transferred in real time. You might expect capturing to take up to twice as long as the total length of the video you are transferring even if the process is automated.

The way video is captured and stored in one editing system may not be compatible with another. In other words, while you can be sure that an NTSC VHS videocassette can be played back on any NTSC VHS machine, a video computer file may not be readable by any software other than the software used to create it.

Almost all video on computers is "compressed." Uncompressed video is equivalent, more or less, to a 20 Megabytes per second data stream. The fastest "safe" video data rate for most hard drives is half of the tested sustained speed, or between two and eight Megabytes per second. Compression schemes that reduce the effective data rate to three to six Megabytes per second produce excellent video and manageable file sizes. For example, one hour of video at four Megabytes per second would fit on a fifteen gigabyte hard drive.

Depending on the sophistication of your editing hardware, some, most, or all, of the transitions, keys, and other effects you apply to clips in your editing programme have to be created and saved on disk by the programme before they can be viewed or played back. This process is called "rendering." It can be quite time-consuming, especially in low-end editing systems.

As far as creating a "first draft" is concerned, non-linear, or computer editing is not really any faster than tape-to-tape editing, especially when the time required to digitize clips is considered. It is much more powerful and more flexible.

The first step in nonlinear editing is capturing the source video and audio. There are, broadly speaking, two types of video; analogue and digital.

Analogue Video Capture

To capture analogue video you will need a video capture card that can convert composite video or S-video to digital video. High-end cards may also be able to convert component video to digital. Some capture cards convert both audio and video and some rely on your sound card to handle the audio. The conversion process may be carried out entirely by the hardware on the card, or by software running on your computer, or by some combination of both. In general, hardware conversion is more reliable than software conversion. On windows computers the digital conversion product is generally an AVI file. An AVI (Audio Video Interleaved) file is a sound and motion picture file that conforms to the Microsoft Windows Resource Interchange File Format (RIFF) specification. MacIntosh files conform to their Quicktime format.

In either case, the converted file is almost always compressed. That is, much of the picture information is truncated or discarded according to a compression scheme called a codec. If the file format is dependant on hardware on the capture card or deviates from one of the generally accepted codecs your ability to play back files will be limited. Do not assume that all AVI files are alike in the way that all VHS tapes are alike. They are not.

Most capture cards do not compress audio. In fact, rather than using the 44100 Hz sample rate found on commercial CD audio disks, audio for video is sampled at 48000 Hz. That equates to 1.536 Mbps. You probably will not be able to monitor audio or video levels on the computer as your video is captured. If possible, you should use a time base corrector and waveform monitor to make sure the signal going to the computer meets broadcast standards. Although some capture cards have time base correctors built in, most do not. It is not sufficient to monitor the audio input, since the computer has software audio level and balance controls.

Audio Recording Control

In general, the audio signal can be recorded only if "line in" is selected in the audio recording window. This is true whether or not playback of "line in" is muted. Use an audio recording programme to verify the presence of the signal and to check the loudest part of your programme.

Windows Sound Recorder

These programmes will show you a graphic representation of audio amplitude in real time. Set the incoming audio at zero VU if you can, then adjust the line in record level to make sure the loudest audio on your tape is not "clipped." The dynamic range from noise to clipping is so great in digital audio that there is no excuse for clipping a digital audio signal. Only when you are satisfied that the record audio level is correct should you begin the capture process.

Among the options you can select in most capture programmes is the division of the source video into discrete clips. When capturing composite or S-Video, the capture programme attempts to detect scene changes by measuring the difference between frames. You may also be able to set an arbitrary interval and create a new clip, for example, every ten or twenty seconds. There are two types of clips. In some programmes each clip is a separate file. In others the captured video is a single file with software-defined clips. You should consider your application before using video clip detection. If, for example, you are going to be making minor changes to an event video you would not want to have to re-assemble the event from a large number of discreet clips. On the other hand, if you are looking for short segments from your tape to be used in another programme or you need to alter the sequence of events, clip detection can be very helpful.

Your digital recording will never be better than the tape you digitize. Because of the rapid degradation of the quality of the tape signal from one generation to the next you should make every reasonable effort to digitize the original raw video and audio.

Except in rare cases you will not have computer control over your video playback machine. You will have to start the tape machine and the digitizing process separately. Some capture programmes will detect absence of video. Some will wait to begin digitizing until the video signal amplitude is greater than colour black. Your goal should be to start digitizing before any useful video or audio begins and, obviously, to stop within five or ten seconds of the end of your material. You are going to be consuming enormous chunks of hard drive. You do not want to waste it with colour black or snow.

You can estimate the amount of disk space you will need. At 4.5 MBps for audio and video you will use 270 MB per minute and 16 GB per hour of recording. Your digital file may hang around on your hard drive for weeks or months.

Digital Capture

Digital capture is a much simpler process than analogue capture. The most common digital recording format is "DV." This format is already digital and already compressed to about 4 MB/sec and already compatible with the Microsoft AVI format. To move it to your computer you need to connect your camcorder or DV recorder to your computer using the IEEE-1394. Interface, also called "FireWire." There is no loss of audio or video quality in the transfer. That is the good news. The bad news is that there is no way to adjust the video (level, setup, chroma, hue) or audio (level, balance, equalization).

Capture software for digital transfer generally offers the additional advantage of "machine control." The playback device can be controlled by the computer. DV tapes can have two different times embedded in the video signal. One is zeroed at the beginning of the recording and shows the time on tape. It can be displayed on the camcorder monitor in the upper right hand corner. Your capture software depends on the tape time recorded on your DV tape. If that signal is not continuous it will zero itself and start over. This is confusing for people. It is fatal for some digital capture software, since tape times are not unique and the software uses the machine control interface to search the tape for specific time points on the tape.

DV tapes can also have a digital time stamp that records the actual date and time each frame is recorded. Clip detection can be based on the digital time stamp on the tape. A discontinuity in the time stamp indicates the tape was stopped and restarted, ending one clip and beginning a new one. It may also be possible to detect clips by looking for sudden changes in video content. Whether you want to detect clips depends on how your software treats clips and the nature of your project.

CONTINUITY CONSIDERATIONS

A good videographer and editor will look for movements within a sequence that tie the shots together.

- When changing to a different shot within a sequence, you should plan to have things in the same position. For example, when switching from a medium shot to a close-up of someone writing, their hand should be in the same place when the edit is made.
- Make sure movement in the frame goes in the same direction. For example, have your talent walk out of the frame to the left and into the next shot from the right.
  - *Establishing Shot:* Your audience is limited to what you show them so it is important to let them know where you are. Usually a long shot.
  - *Continuity Considerations*: Plan how you enter and exit the frame so the edited sequence looks like one continuous action.

- *Long Shot*: A long shot allows your audience to see everything. It shows the big picture.
- *Continuity Considerations*: This shot allows the editor to match the action in the previous shot. The edit should take place when the man is in approximately the same location in each shot.
- *Medium Shot*: This shot gets rid of any distractions in the picture and starts the process of zeroing in on the action.
- *Continuity Considerations*: The editor should allow the man to walk out of the previous shot then walk into this shot. This helps the audience get a sense of the size of the room.
- *Extreme Close-up*: Use this shot to focus attention on what is important. It enlarges small objects to show details.
- *Continuity Considerations*: The editor should match the hand location in the previous shot.
- *Close-up*: This shot cuts out extraneous visual material. Faces should fill up the screen. Who wants to see a person's feet when they are saying something we need to hear?
- *Continuity Considerations*: This close-up is used as a cutaway. A cutaway is any shot that covers an edit. It is most commonly used to shorten interviews.
- *Reestablishing Shot*: This shot reminds people where you are.
- *Continuity Considerations*: It is good to end with a shot that reminds people where you are. Exiting the frame is also a good closer.

SHOOTING VIDEO FOR EDITING

Now that computer based editing is affordable, you do not have to shot video in sequence. It is much simpler to shot a series of scenes and then edit them together later. However, to do this you must preplan your shots. Think in terms of the type of shots you will need to tell the story and what happens in the frame to show continuity. In other words, to shoot for editing you need to be aware of how the finished sequence will look before you take the camera out of the box.

- Each time you start and stop the videotape, you have created a shot, you edit shots together into sequences that tell a story.
- To produce really good edited video you need to start with a storyboard. Storyboards are a tool to help you think visually. Draw pictures of what you are going to see. Next to your pictures write down what you want the shot to look like and what audio will be heard. Here is a sample storyboard.
- Your shots need to link together to make your audience believe it is one continuous scene. People, hands, etc. should remain in the relative same place within a series of shots in order to have continuity in the sequence.
- A cutaway is a shot that allows you to cover up an edit. They are very useful when editing interviews. Always be thinking of cutaways you can get when on location.

FUNDAMENTALS OF NARRATIVE FILM EDITING

Editing Dramatic Scenes Only

Which Type of Editing?

This course covers only one (1) type of film editing: editing scripted dialogue (drama).

For people who want to make narrative motion pictures, editing a dramatic conversation is the most important and the most challenging form of film editing.

Not for Documentaries Nor Multi-Media

This course is only for editing of a dramatic conversation. If you are interested in other documentaries nor multi-media, do not take this course. Editing a conversations is completely backwards to editing everything else.

Real Hands-on Editing

This course quickly goes through all the basics of editing a dramatic scene from TV dramas.

These lessons gives you hands-on experience editing actual motion pictures and television dramas. It is the real thing!

Required Disks

Each lesson requires a disk. After the first disk, I will loan you the disks but you must return them. To get the first one, see the qualification to the left.

What are Practice Scenes?

Practice scenes are the film dailies from actual motion pictures or television dramas. These are unedited scenes which have been digitized, ready for editing on your computer.

Drama, not Documentaries

These scenes are not from documentaries. Instead, they contain scripted dialcgue from narrative productions. That means a dramatic conversation. Editing a dramatic scene is totally different from editing a documentary which is a completely different technology using completely different methods. If you want to learn to edit documentaries, corporate video, event video or multimedia, these lessons will only confuse you.

Editing for Motion Pictures

Narrative film editing gives you an understanding of the basic concepts of telling a dramatic story. Once you have learned to edit a conversation, you are ready for more advanced editing of motion pictures (action scenes which are not covered here).

Disks Requires

Not available to the public. This course uses the disks from the Star Movie Shop. As far as I know, this is the only company in the world which offers unedited scenes for film students to practice dialogue editing from dramatic scenes.

The Star Movie Shop is not open to the general public. They only sell through selected film schools or to qualified film students. You can qualify by purchasing the Entrance Exam Disk and editing the short scene on the disk.

I will loan you the Disks

So for this course, I will loan you the disks. When you are finished with a lesson, you return the disk to receive the next lesson.

Quick Time Pro Required

Most of the film dailies require QuickTime to play. Fortunately, QuickTime film clips can be converted to other formats by using Movie Player with QuickTime Pro or other utilities programmes.

SCREENPLAY

A screenplay or script is a written plan, authored by a screenwriter, for a film or television programme. Screenplays can be original works or adaptations from existing works such as novels. A screenplay differs from a script in that it is more specifically targeted at the visual, narrative arts, such as film and television, whereas a script can involve a blueprint of "what happens" in a comic, an advertisement, a theatrical play and other "blueprinted" creations.

The major components of a screenplay are action and dialogue, with the "action" being "what we see happening" and "dialogue" being "what the characters say." The characters, when first introduced in the screenplay, may also be described visually. Screenplays differ from traditional literature conventions in ways described below; however, screenplays may not involve emotion-related descriptions and other aspects of the story that are, in fact, visual within the end-product.

In the United States, the Writers Guild of America (WGA) has final control on whom may be awarded screenwriting credit for a screenplay in a union production. The WGA is one of several organizations in the U.S. and worldwide which recognize screenplays with awards.

A script for television is sometimes called a teleplay.

Writing on Spec or Assignment

Screenplays can be written either on "spec" (speculative) or as assignment ("Commissioned"). The Variety language dictionary defines "spec script" as "a script shopped or sold on the open market, as opposed to one commissioned by a studio or production company."

Writing on Assignment

Assignments are commissioned by production companies or studios on the basis of pitches from producers or writers, or literary properties they already own. Most established writers do most of their work on assignment and will only "spec" scripts which they think no-one will pay them to write, or if they cannot find assignment work. There are exceptions: some very famous writers only write on spec because they know that they can get a better price for their work this way. Other writers spec scripts that they care deeply about so that they do not have to bend to the whims of executives and producers.

An assignment may be for an original screenplay, or for an adapted screenplay based on another work such as a novel, film, short story, comic book, magazine article or, increasingly, video game. It may also, however, be for a rewrite of an existing script, and in fact this is how a large proportion of writers in the modern studio system make their living. Rewriting scripts is an art in itself and an extremely lucrative one at that: it is not unknown for trusted writers in the higher echelons of the industry to receive $200,000 a week (2004 numbers) for their efforts. $50,000 per week is not uncommon.

Rewriting is difficult because executives often have very clear ideas about what is wrong with a script, however, they are usually unable to provide detailed prescriptions for ways it can be fixed. This is not surprising, because screenwriting is not the expertize of the executive, but of the screenwriter. The writer is therefore usually expected to come up with a detailed prescription for how the script can be improved, and then execute this in a timely fashion. During the process of choosing a writer to rewrite a script the executives may ask several writers for their 'take' and choose the one who appears to have the greatest likelihood of moving the script forward to the point where it may be greenlit for production.

Before 'going to script' a writer may be asked to write a treatment, an outline, or a step outline describing the script in various granularities of detail. Some writers resist this process and will do anything to avoid it and get down the writing the script itself; others embrace the process and even deliver fairly elaborate treatments, the so-called scriptments. It is fair to say that producers tend to be wary of the former and pleasantly surprised by the latter.

Spec Scripts

Many Spec scripts (short for speculative) are written independently by screenwriters in hopes of optioning and eventually outright selling them to producers or studios. Other spec scripts are written by writer-directors who plan to direct the film themselves. Many so-called "art films", films fall into this latter category, whereas the former category tends to be filled with "high concept" scripts—mostly action or comedy, to which a star or A-list director can be attached. However, most of the hundreds of thousands of spec scripts penned each year are written by unknowns who are trying to attract attention and find it difficult to generate the kind of "buzz" that more established scribes count on to sell their scripts.

The Development Process

Once a studio has purchased or commissioned a script, it goes through the process of revisions and rewriting until all stakeholders are satisfied and ready to proceed. It is not uncommon for a script to go through many, many drafts on its journey to production. Very few scripts improve steadily with each draft, and when a certain avenue has been exhausted the writer will often be replaced and another brought in to do a rewrite.

Occasionally it becomes impossible to satisfy all such parties, and the project enters development hell.

If a studio decides it does not wish to proceed to production with the script, the project enters 'turnaround'. Another studio may purchase the script from its original owner, but the script is encumbered with the development costs the studio has already incurred. At a certain point, it may simply be uneconomic for anyone to purchase the script, even if it is a very good one. This goes part of the way to explaining why some of the best scripts in Hollywood remain unproduced.

The Shooting Script

Once a script has been approved for production, camera directions and notes may be inserted by the Director, and each scene is assigned a number to provide a convenient way for the various production departments to reference individual scenes. When a scene is omitted, its number is retained labeled with "OMITTED", so that it would not be assigned to any newly added scenes.

When the shooting script is distributed, its pages are locked, meaning that any subsequent revisions will apply to the first set of revision pages. When revisions are distributed, the pages are swapped into the outstanding drafts, and the script is once again locked. The process is repeated for each new round of revisions.

Each round of revisions is distributed on different coloured paper. The progression of colours varies from one production to the next. Since rewrites often continue throughout principal photography, most shooting scripts evolve into a rainbow of gold, pink, blue, green and cherry pages.

Transcripts

A screenplay is different from a *transcript*. A transcript is simply a copy of what dialogue finally appeared onscreen, without regard to the original script, the stage directions or action. A full *post-production transcript* may also include descriptions of the action onscreen, but since it is generally not written by a professional writer but either a production assistant or a fan, it may not be particularly entertaining to read. Many published screenplays available at booksellers or downloaded from the internet are in fact glorified post-production transcripts rather than shooting scripts. Transcripts and screenplays often differ radically because scenes are frequently re-ordered or dropped entirely during the editing process. Moreover, actors may change lines or simply improvise dialogue, and many directors will make their own changes to the script on the fly during rehearsal or shooting. It can be extremely revealing to compare a shooting script with the film as finally distributed.

Screenwriting Software

Detailed computer programmes are designed specifically for screenplays, and many have templates for teleplays and stageplays. These programmes have been designed to create industry standard screenplays and are used by professional screenwriters. What should be remembered is that all such software is an aid in the *formatting* of a screenplay and not the actual *creation* of it. A number of these programmes offer access to online screenwriter communities where feedback from fellow screenwriters is availabe. Some examples of screenwriting software are: Celtx, DramaScript, Final Draft and Montage. Furthermore, screenwriting software is available for handheld devices (Palm OS, and Windows Mobile/Pocket PC).

BASIC FILMMAKING FOR HIGH SCHOOL DRAMA DEPARTMENTS

Welcome to the "Filmmaking for High School Drama Departments"

A Film and a Play

Wikiversity Film School is developing a new way for drama departments to create short motion pictures at the same time they produce a school play. The idea is to create a 5-minute motion picture using the same set, lights, costumes and props as the current school play. After the school play begins its run, rehearsals on a short movie can begin with new actors. Once the play is over, the shooting of the movie can begin. Since the set and the lights and the costumes are all ready, filming can be done very quickly during the weeks that follows the closing of the play.

Once the short movie is filmed, the raw footage can be put on DVD-Video disks for people around the world to edit. To do this, schools need 5-minute motion picture scripts which can be filmed on stage for the most popular school plays.

Script Writing

We need you to write a script which a high school drama department will turn into a 5-minute motion picture. But not just any script. Your script must use the same movie set, lights, costumes, and props for popular schools plays such as:

1. Grease
2. Peter Pan
3. The Sound of Music
4. Little Red Ridinghood
5. Rumplestiltsikn
6. Cinderella

7. Christmas Carol
8. Fiddler on the Roof
9. Romeo and Juliet
10. Annie
11. Music Man
12. Death of a Salesman
13. Our Town
14. Godspell
15. You're a Good Man, Charlie Brown

The Situation

It has been 15 years since digital video came to personal computers. Yet today, few high school drama departments create their own motion pictures. (I have only heard of one in Lawrence, Tennessee). There must be an easier way for drama departments to begin making movies. Each year, high school drama departments put on outstanding plays by extremely talented students. These plays have beautiful and expensive stage sets, very extensive lighting, and wonderful costumes. So why not use all of this to make a very short motion picture once the play is finished?

Right now, the missing ingredient is a movie script for each of the popular school plays. Once we have scripts, we can begin to create the storyboards and all the rest of the pre-production elements for the movie.

Getting Started: The Story

The first step is to think of a story for one of the popular school plays. This can be similar to the play or completely different. The only requirement is the movie must be able to be filmed on the same stage, with the same lights and costumes as the play.

Format the Script

Then type the story as a movie script. When formatted, it should be one to five pages long. Two or three pages is best.

CHARACTER ANIMATION

There are two kinds of animation used in the making of a motion picture. Animated movies have a special produced and the animation is done in Production. This section covers the procedure for creating an animated movie. Animation is also done in Post-Production as part of visual effects. For visual effects, go to Animation for Visual Effects.

Overall Procedure of an Animated Motion Picture

An animated motion picture starts out like any other motion picture. Pre-production is the same... and that includes storyboarding. The only difference is storyboarding for an animated motion picture is much more intense. In live action filming, the storyboards are only an approximation. In an animated motion picture, the storyboards eventually become the keyframes of the animation.

Dialogue Recording

All textbooks on making an animated motion picture explain that before the animation can begin, the dialogue of the script must be recorded by the actors. The textbooks say that only after the actor's dialogue has been recorded does work begin on the animation.

The problem in this method does not work. Actors have too much trouble visualizing who they are and their surroundings in an animated movie. Their performance is terrific when they can see the animation but not good when they cannot see anything.

Therefore, in almost all cases, the dialogue must be recorded a second time after the animation is finished. To see that this is true, go through the "making of the movie" articles for all the successful animated movies and you will learn that they recorded the dialogue a second time while the actors watch the animation.

Dialogue Recording vs. ADR Session

To keep the two recording sessions separate, I will call the first recording of the dialogue, the "Dialogue Recording". And the second recording of the dialogue after the movie is almost finished, the "ADR Session" since the second recording of the dialogue is very much like a normal ADR session with a few exceptions.

Dialogue Recording Procedure

There are two different ways to record the initial dialogue for an animated motion picture.

One Actor at a Time

The first way is the easy way. This is to bring in each actor, one at a time, and record that persons dialogue. This recording session is with the director who will coach the actor by either reading the other character's dialogue or will explain each scene to the actor.

Multiple Actors

This is much more difficult. Two or more actors are brought into the recording studio and if possible, put into separate (isolated) recording booths connected to the same recording console. The actors can hear each other as they record their dialogue together. This way, the two actors interact with each other but their voices are recorded on separate tracks. If the two actors are in the same recording booth, and if the actors happen to be speaking at the same time (as people often do in a heated conversation), this become locked into the dialogue recording. There can be no adjustment during the editing of the movie. Therefore, recording each actor on a separate track is preferable.

The other Steps of Making the Animated Movie

Here are the steps for creating the animated movie once the dialogue has been recorded.

Animatic Creation Procedure

Using the still images from the storyboard, an animatic is created using the recorded dialogue. Another way to explain this is the movie is made using just still pictures along with the dialogue as well as with a temp film score and rough sound effects.

Timing Procedure

Once the dialogue is recorded and the animatic completed, the dialogue must be timed. For each scene, each syllable of the dialogue must be timed from the beginning of the scene. This is needed for the animators to create the animation and rough lip sync.

Animation Procedure

Once the timing of each scene is complete the animation is started. For 3D animation, each shot is rendered just like a motion picture shot on film with live actors. Then these shots are edited together.

This is very different from 2D animation where each frame is carefully planned out and no extra frames are created. In 3D animation, about 10 per cent of the rendered frames are removed (trimmed off the two ends of the shot) during editing. If ADR will be used, the actual lip sync can still be very rough or not at all.

Editing Procedure

For 3D animation, a regular digital video editing programme (such as Final Cut Pro) is used to edit the movie. The sound effects and the musical score are added now. The musical score might even have been created before the editing so that the movie will be edited to match the film score.

Dialogue Recording Procedure

Once the animation is done and the movie has been edited, all the actors return, one at a time, to an ADR session where the actors see everything that is happening on the screen and they react to it.

Lip Sync Timing Procedure

Now the final timing of the lip sync is calculated. Then the animation for the mouth movements is done to match the timing. Some animation software have faster ways to do this. This is the last step in the animation process by Mein Hart Joseph I. Santos—Philippines sa AMA marami pang secret na ibubunyag sa pag gawa na animation.

Types of Animation

There are two kinds of 3D character animation.

1. *General Purpose 3D Animation Programmes*: This is done with programmes such as Maya, LightWave, and 3D Studio Max. In this case, all characters in the movie are custom made. All the movie sets and the scenery are created from scratch.

2. *Special Purpose 3D Animation Programmes*: This is done with specialized programmes such as Poser and DAZ Studio. In this case, most all the characters are purchased off the shelf from companies such as RuntimeDNA. Frequently, specialized programmes are also used to create the movie set. These programmes are Vue and Bryce. For low budget animation, the movie sets will be rendered as multi-layered still images which are composited with the character animation and (at the same time) animated with Adobe After Effects.

    - Examples of animation motion pictures created with general purpose 3D animation programme are Polar Express and Aero-Troopers. Polar Express uses realistic human figures while Aero-Troopers uses cartoon-like characters which are easier to animate.
    - Examples of animation motion pictures created with special purpose 3D animation programme can be seen overseas in television dramas.

DIGITAL PUPPET ANIMATION

Mostly Free Software

In this course, we will create a movie using Digital Puppets and a scenery generator. For this course, we will recommend software which is free or very low cost. If you want to do more, contact us before you buy anything.

Basic Requirements

- DAZ Studio for character animation
- Bryce 5.5 for scenery generation
- AfterEffects (not free) for compositing

Digital Puppet Animation

- *History*: Digital Puppets (also know as Poser figures) is a unique form of 3D animation. We will use digital puppets to create a motion pictures based on everything you have learned so far.

- *Prerequisites*: To begin this class, you must have completed all the other courses. This is because you will need the animatic which you created in the course on Basic Filmmaking which relies on the editing course and the film scoring course.
- *Animation vs. Live Action*: When you attend film school, you will learn all about live action filming. You will learn to work in a team and become a team player.
  Therefore, for this course, you will work alone to create the entire motion picture by using digital actors on your personal computer.

Casting

The first step will be to find the digital actors you want for your motion picture. This requires the same care as casting live action actors. You need to find the characters which help tell the story you want to tell. When you select the characters, these characters will greatly shape the meaning of the motion picture.

Also the selection of the characters for your motion picture will decide what kind of voices you need for the characters. As an example, look at the list of possible characters for this movie. See how each of the options gives a completely new feeling to the motion picture.

DIRECTING ACTORS

If you have done the casting correctly and your actor has the ability—let them express it. An actor will respond far better if they are given a degree of freedom to bring their creativity to the process. A good director will encourage this without, however, letting it go too far. The challenge here is to find the balance between allowing the actor to express themselves and serving the scene. The scene is part of a greater whole and their performance should be in balance with the other elements of the film.

Casting Actors

Next to having a great screenplay and a clear vision, casting great actors is the best thing you can do to improve the odds of your film succeeding. Casting good actors is 80 per cent of the directing process because once you have cast actors who understand what they are doing, the director's job is almost done. External reference on Auditioning and Casting actors.

Inexperienced Actors

Inexperienced actors nearly always err on the side of overacting, putting too much into the role. Your task is often to convince them to be more naturalistic. Be clear and do not baffle them with technical terms. Explain how tight the shot is and their range of movement within the frame and they should be able to gauge how to behave. One very effective way to get truthful acting from inexperienced actors is to let them improvise their own lines around a specifically designed situation. It works! Guaranteed.

Another rule of thumb is to compliment generally, but criticize specifically. For example, telling an actress that you liked how she flipped her hair will cause her to do it again and again in subsequent takes, and it would not look as natural as it did the first time. Just tell her how great she did and hopefully she will unconciously continue what she was doing. However, you will want to be precise (but gentle) when pointing out the things you are certain you do not want.

If you have not done it already, making a backstory for the characters is always useful.

Troubleshooting

These tricks should be a last resort; the best way to work is through honest and open communication. Being sneaky can sometimes lose you the trust of your cast.

There is a great story about an actor who was so nervous he was having trouble remembering his lines and was getting flustered. The director gave him a coin to flip and asked him to keep flipping it throughout the scene. This sucessfully made the actor less self conscious and the scene flowed after that.

If an actor continually overdoes it, quietly start the camera, keep it rolling and do a "walkthrough" of the scene. Some of the footage might be quite usable.

SLATE

The clapper board (AKA Clap slate) is a well-recognized icon of filming, but serves many purposes beyond its appearance. A clapper board is made up of two parts: The slate and the clapper.

The slate's most obvious purpose is the documentation it provides on what scene is being filmed, when it was filmed, what take it was, which film reel it was, etc. The "clapper" provides an easily identified audio marker, which is useful when filming with multiple cameras and you must synchronize them during post-production, and is more commonly used to synchronize the sound and picture since they are usually recorded on separate devices. The black-and-white stripes on the clapper provide a reference for setting the white balance on the camera.

Increasingly in the modern digital age, the clapper becomes less useful as footage can be digitally marked by the camera and audio synchronization is no longer a problem due to the digital nature of the footage. However, for the sake of your editor, you may wish to continue using a clapper to make any possible problem easier to fix.

How to Use a Clapper Board?

While a clapper board seems simple, its use is more complex than it looks. When motion picture film is developed, the lab technician who is developing the film, printing the film, and syncing the audio to the film, must have all the necessary information to sync the audio to the picture. If you want to see your dailies the first thing in the morning and you want everything to work properly, you must never confuse the lab technician.

Verbal Slate

While the clapper board provides information for the picture, there must also be a verbal slate for the audio. This verbal slate must provide the scene and take number for the lab technician. The verbal slate must also make it clear if multiple cameras are used. The verbal slate must also make it clear if multiple tracks of audio are used. "Stereo Split" means one track of a stereo track has the audio from one microphone and the other track has audio from the other microphone.

A and B Cameras

If there are two or more cameras, sometimes a common slate is used. Both the slate and the verbal slate must make this clear.

Using a common slate is not good because it can be confusing. With a common slate, there is no camera number ("Camera A" *vs.* "Camera B') and no film reel number. Therefore, each camera should have its own slate. The slate information for one camera must never be seen by the other camera. The same rule applies for showing the clapper closing. Therefore, when one camera is slated, someone puts their hand over the lens of the other camera to block the view of the other camera's slate.

Tail Slates

Sometimes, when it is impossible to use a clapper board at the beginning of a shot, someone will yell "Tail Slate" at the beginning of the shot and at the end of the shot, the slate will be clapped upside down so that the film laboratory will know that this is the slate at the end of a shot rather than the slate for the beginning of the next shot. The verbal slate is always done at the same time as the clapper board.

Any Pulse will Do

On shots where a clapper board is not practical, the actors will use their arms as a huge clapper. The film lab can easily see when the actor's hands come together. This noise is loud enough and concentrated enough to be accurate for syncing the audio to the picture.

Wildtrack

If there is no clapper for a shot, then the sound is wild. The lab technician might try to do a rough sync. Or the technician will create a separate section of the dailies for the audio from wildtracks. When you hear a wild track on the dailies, you see only a card saying Wildtrack as you hear the audio.

Re-Syncing Sound

For motion picture film, the closing of the clapper (as seen on the film) must be aligned with the audio pulse (which shows up on the audio tape as a blip). Since audio travels at about 40 feet per frame of motion picture film (1/24th of a second), the audio pulse should be less than one frame after the closing of the slate unless the microphone is far from the camera (and the audience.) Yet, when you watch dailies made using digital slates in Hollywood, you will find that most film labs sync the audio so it is late by one or two frames because the electronics in the slate are slow. Therefore, before you begin editing your movie, you must resync each take based on the actual clapper closing and the pulse on the audio track.

DV Camcorders

DV Camcorders often are supplemented with a separate audio recording device in order to record better sound quality. In this case it is nessasary to use a clapper in the beginning (or at the end if you are tailslating) in order to sync the sound up with the video.

Watch Dailies

If you want to see how the clapper board is used, simply look at film dailies from motion pictures and television dramas. You can buy motion picture and television drama dailies on tape at almost any second-hand video store in Hollywood.

KEEPING THE CREW HAPPY

Food

Never underestimate the importance of good food. If your crew is working for free then you must feed them well and at well defined times. If you are going to overrun then stop and ask your crew if they mind working for another hour before lunch. Always try to provide hot food. Sandwiches are your last resort. Good food need not cost a lot. See if you can get your Mum involved or your best friend's mate who is an out-of-work chef. Remember also that some of your cast and crew (especially the clapper-loader) may have to work though their food breaks and so will need easy-to-eat food. Oh, and is do not forget to check on allergies. Check here for advice on good food which is affordable and works on set—Ultra Low Budget Production Recipies. Also remember to have a snack table (called craft services table in the USA). This may seem insignificant, however, film sets bring together very different personalities and egos, both technical and artistic, in very intense situations over a short period of time. Tempers will flare. They always do. Humans when upset or dealing with any extreme emotion in all cultures like to do one thing: put something in their mouth. A drink, a smoke, a chocolate, a thumb... whatever. The craft services table provides this option. Coffee, tea, water, donuts, pastries, water, chocolates, sweets, juice, fruit and water. Do not underestimate it. Try to put the emphasis on healthy food like fruit rather than chocolates and crisps—junk food may give a quick 'high' but would not sustain that high so your crew will become irritable as the day progresses.

Another option (if you are lucky) is to get a deal with a local restaurant or pizza place, perhaps exchanging discounts on food for product placement in your film or advertising in the credits, brochures or your film's website. Local pizza places are a good first stop. This can get costly if done too often. Some consider this option selling out, which is fair, however, it is not a bad way to get some grub for the crew. No matter what your position on set try to offer others a tea or coffee whenever you can. As a runner you will quickly gain the enthusiasm of others by offering tea and coffee. As a more senior crew member you will show that you are not a snobby nosed, status-obsessed fool in it only for the power, but a good natured human who likes to get along with people and do the best job possible.

But be warned—never eat in front of a hungry camera crew. Why? The camera crew do not have the option of quickly picking up a sandwich because their hands must be kept very clean whilst on set and handling camera kit. Once, on my first ADing job, I was casually nibbling on a sandwich when the DoP gave me a loud and public telling off. You have been warned!

Hours

Do not overwork your crew. Your job as a filmmaker is to get the very best out of your cast and crew—as a producer or director you actually do *very little* hands-on filmmaking. So the best thing you can do is create a productive, exciting and comfortable environment for your cast and crew. The one thing that will destroy the mood on set (and destroy your film) is exhaustion. If your schedule demands 20 hour days then cut the script or increase the number of shooting days.

It is important to remember that the hours worked also include the 'wrapping out' time: not all crew just walk away when 'wrap' is called, spark (electricians), camera crew, grips, makeup, wardrobe and others still have a lot of work to pack up from the day and clean and prepare for the next day. So an estimated wrap time of say, 22.00 hours really means an end of shooting at 21.00 to allow for the wrapping-out. Expecting a 12 hour on-camera day to then be followed by an hour's worth of putting away the gear is a surefire way to spark a mutiny!

Communication

Give the cast and crew as much information as possible, especially when things are going wrong. If you can then print and distribute the schedule to every crew member at the start of each day, if not far earlier. If you are going run over schedule then first explain the situation to your crew, then ask very nicely if they mind working longer and then tell your crew the new estimate wrap time.

Drugs

You cannot stop everyone from taking loads of drugs but do your best to dissuade your cast and crew. Drugs and alcohol on set will void most insurance policies. You must get your crew to never ever take any kind of extreme mind altering substances while anywhere near set. I would advise firing anyone that does not heed this warning. This has nothing to do with moral or social issues it has to do with running a business. Until the insurance contracts change no drugs or alcohol on set.

Drinking

This is a dodgy one. Going out for drinks every night of the shoot is a good way to get to know everyone. But do not over do it. What you do as a director or producer is up to you. You will certainly increase your chances of getting on well with your cast and crew if you go out drinking with them. But, then again, you have probably got to spend every evening preparing the next day's shot list.

DIGITAL CINEMA

Digital cinema refers to the use of digital technology to distribute and project motion pictures. The final movie can be distributed via hard drives, DVDs or satellite and projected using a digital projector instead of a conventional film projector. Digital cinema is distinct from high-definition television and in particular, is not dependent on using television or HDTV standards, aspect ratios, or frame rates. Digital projectors capable of 2K resolution began deploying in 2005, and since 2006, the pace has accelerated. HDTV and pre-recorded HD disks could put pressure on movie theaters to offer something to compete with the home HD experience.

In this article, 2K and 4K refer to images with 2048 and 4096 horizontal pixel resolution, respectively.

Technology

To match or improve the theater experience of movie audiences, a digital cinema system must provide high quality image, sound, subtitles, and captions. Theater managers require server controls for managing and displaying content in multiple theaters, and studios want their content encrypted with secure delivery, playback, and reporting of play times to the distribution company.

Digital Cinema Initiatives (DCI), a joint venture of the six major studios, published a system specification for digital cinema. Briefly, the specification calls for picture encoding using the ISO/IEC 15444-1 "JPEG2000" (.jp2) standard and use of the CIE XYZ colour space at 12 bits per component encoded with a 2.6 gamma applied at projection, and audio using the "Broadcast Wave" (.wav) format at 24 bits and 48 kHz or 96 kHz sampling, controlled by an XML-format Composition Playlist, into an MXF-compliant file at a maximum data rate of 250 Mbit/s. Details about encryption, key management, and logging are all discussed in the specification as are the minimum specifications for the projectors employed including the colour gamut, the contrast ratio and the brightness of the image. While much of the specification codifies work that had already been ongoing in the Society of Motion Picture and Television Engineers (SMPTE), the specification is important in establishing a content owner framework for the distribution and security of first-release motion picture content.

Digital cinema conforming to the DCI Standard is referred to within the film industry as D-Cinema while all other forms of digital cinema are referred to as E-Cinema. Thus, while D-Cinema is a defined standard, though one that is still partly being framed by SMPTE as of 2007, E-Cinema may be anything, ranging from a

DVD player connected to a consumer projector to something that approaches the quality of D-Cinema without conforming to some of the standards. Even D-Cinema itself has evolved over time before the DCI standards were framed. However, the current DCI standards were made with the intention of standing the test of time, much like 35 mm film which has evolved but still retained compatibility over a substantial part of a century.

In addition to DCI's work, the National Association of Theatre Owners (NATO) released its Digital Cinema System Requirements. The document addresses the requirements of digital cinema systems from the operational needs of the exhibitor, focusing on areas not addressed by DCI, including access for the visually impaired and hearing impaired, workflow inside the cinema, and equipment interoperability. In particular, NATO's document details requirements for the Theatre Management System (TMS), the governing software for digital cinema systems within a theatre complex, and provides direction for the development of security key management systems. As with DCI's document, NATO's document is also important to the SMPTE standards effort.

Digital Capture

As of 2007 the most common acquisition medium for digitally projected features is 35 mm film scanned and processed at 2K or 4K via digital intermediate. Most digital features to date have been shot at 1920x1080 HD resolution using cameras such as the Sony CineAlta, Panavision Genesis or Thomson Viper. New cameras such as the Arriflex D-20 and Silicon Imaging's SI-2K can capture 2K resolution images, and the Red Digital Cinema Camera Company's Red One can record 4k RAW. Thus the future of digital cinema can be expected to have as a standard 4K capture and 4K projection. Currently in development are other cameras capable of recording 4K RAW, such as Dalsa Corporation's *Origin,* and cameras capable of recording 5k RAW, such as the RED EPIC , and cameras capable of recording 3k RAW (for budget filmmakers) such as the RED SCARLET.

Digital Post-Production

Film is scanned from camera-original film negatives into a digital format on a scanner or high-resolution telecine. Data from digital motion picture cameras may be converted to a convenient image file format for work in a facility. All of the files are 'conformed' to match an edit list created by the film editor, and are then colour corrected under the direction of the film's staff. The end result of post-production is a digital intermediate used to record the motion picture to film and/or for the digital cinema release.

Digital Mastering

When all of the sound, picture, and data elements of a production have been completed, they may be assembled into a *Digital Cinema Distribution Master* (DCDM) which contains all of the digital material needed for a show. The images and sound are then compressed, encrypted, and packaged to form the *Digital Cinema Package* (DCP).

Digital Cinema Distributors

Technicolour, Deluxe Entertainment Services Group Inc., XDC and Access Integrated Technologies are the leading companies in digital distribution. Other companies currently distributing digital cinema include Kodak, DTS, Ascent Media, Dolby, Arts Alliance Media and Motion Picture Solutions.

Digital Projection

There are currently two types of projectors for digital cinema. Early DLP projectors, which were deployed primarily in the U.S., used limited 1280×1024 resolution which are still widely used for pre-show advertising but not usually for feature presentations. The DCI specification for digital projectors calls for three levels of playback to be supported: 2K (2048×1080) at 24 frames per second, 4K (4096×2160) at 24 frames per second, and 2K at 48 frames per second.

Three manufacturers have licensed the TI-developed DLP Cinema technology. Christie Digital Systems, Barco and NEC. Christie is the maker of the CP2000 line of 2K DCI-compliant Digital Cinema Projectors, and long established in traditional film projector technology throughout the U.S. and is the market leader in terms of units sold and deployed internationally. NEC manufactures the Starus NC2500S, NC1500C and NC800C 2K projectors for large, medium and small screen respectively and the Starus Digital Cinema Server system, as well as other equipment to connect PCs, analogue/digital tape decks and satellite receivers, DVD, and off-air broadcast, etc. for pre-show and special presentations. While NEC is a relative newcomer to Digital Cinema, Christie is the main player in the U.S. and Barco takes the lead in Europe and Asia. In addition Digital Projection Incorporated (DPI) designed and sold a few DLP Cinema units when TI's 2K technology first debuted but then abandoned the D-Cinema market while continuing to offer DLP-based projectors for non-cinema purposes. Although based on the same 2K TI "light engine" as those of the major players they are so rare as to be virtually unknown in the industry.

The other technology is from Sony and is labeled "SXRD" technology. Their projector provides 4096 × 2160 4K resolution and is priced very competitively with the lower resolution 2K 2048 × 1080 DLP projectors.

Other manufacturers have been developing digital projector technology, but these have not yet been deployed into motion picture theaters and are not commercially available in versions that conform to the DCI specification.

As of July 2007, there are some cinemas in Singapore showing digital 4K films to public using Sony's CineAlta 4K digital projector. They are located at Golden Village Cinema in Vivocity (Hall 11), Eng Wah Cinema in Suntec (Hall 3), Shaw Cinema in Bugis (Hall 1 & 3) and at Cathay Cineplex (Hall 7).

In September 2007, Muvico Theaters Rosemont 18 in Rosemont, Illinois became the first theater in North America to have Sony's CineAlta 4K digital projectors for all 18 screens. Muvico Theaters intends on opening more theaters in the last quarter of 2008 and well into 2009 all utilizing Sony's CineAlta 4K digital projector.

Live Broadcasting to Movie Theaters

Digital cinemas can deliver live broadcasts from performances or events. For example, there are regular live broadcasts to movie theaters of Metropolitan Opera performances.

Current Developments

By October 2007, DG2L Technologies was reported to have supplied 1500 Digital Cinema Systems to UFO Moviez Ltd. in India and Europe. As of July, 2007, 1400 screens in the U.S. have been equipped with digital cinema projectors including a dozen theaters where the Sony 4K projector has been installed. In continental Europe, XDC is servicing over 300 screens in 10 countries, where Germany has the leading territory with over 100 installations. The UK is home to Europe's first DCI compliant fully digital multiplex cinemas, Odeon Hatfield and Odeon Surrey Quays (London) have a total of 18 digital screens and were both launched on Friday 9 February 2007.

In June 2007, Arts Alliance Media announced the first European commercial digital cinema VPF agreements (with Twentieth Century Fox and Universal Pictures). As of March 2007, with the release of Disney's *Meet the Robinsons*, about 600 screens have been equipped with 2K digital projectors that are equipped with Real D Cinema's stereoscopic 3D technology, marketed under the Disney Digital 3-D brand. In mid 2006, about 400 theaters have been equipped with 2K digital projectors with the number increasing every month. In February 2005, Arts Alliance Media was selected to roll out the UK Film Council's Digital Screen Network (DSN), a $20M contract to install and operate Europe's largest 2K digital cinema network. By March 2007, 230 of the 241 screens had been installed on schedule, with the remaining 11 to be installed later in 2007 when cinemas have completed building works or construction.

Chicken Little from Disney, with its experimental release of the film in digital 3D, increased the number of projectors using the 2K format. Several digital 3D films will surface in 2006 and several prominent filmmakers have committed to making their next productions in stereo 3D. By early 2006, Access Integrated Technologies (AccessIT) had announced agreements with nearly all of the major film studios and several exhibitors that enable the company to roll-out its end-to-end digital cinema systems. In August 2006, the Malayalam digital movie *Moonnamathoral* was distributed via satellite to cinemas; thus becoming the first Malayalam digital film to be so distributed. This was done using the end-to-end digital cinema system developed by Singapore based DG2L Technologies.

On May 1, 2008, Public Radio International (PRI) spearheaded the first-ever digital cinema event in public media by working with Ira Glass and Chicago Public Radio on This American Life Live!

The event was presented exclusively in select theatres by National CineMedia's (NCM) Fathom, in partnership with BY Experience and Chicago Public Radio, and in association with Public Radio International.

Economics

Savings in Distribution

Digital distribution of movies has the potential to save money for film distributors. A single film print can cost around US$1200 or $30,000 for a 1-time print of an 80-minute feature, so making 4000 prints for a wide-release movie might cost $5 million. In contrast, at the maximum 250 megabit-per-second maximum data rate defined by DCI for digital cinema, a typical feature-length movie could fit comfortably on an off the shelf 300 GB hard drive—which cost as low as $70—which could even be returned to the distributor for reuse after a movie's run. With several hundred movies distributed every year, industry savings could potentially reach $1 billion or more.

Alternative Content

An added incentive for exhibitors is the ability to show alternative content such as live special events, sports, pre-show advertising and other digital or video content. Some low-budget films that would normally not have a theatrical release because of distribution costs might be shown in smaller engagements than the typical large release studio pictures. The cost of duplicating a digital "print" is very low, so adding more theaters to a release has a small additional cost to the distributor. Movies that start with a small release could scale to a much larger release quickly if they were sufficiently successful, opening up the possibility that smaller movies could achieve box office success previously out of their reach.

Greater Protection for Content

A last incentive for digital distribution is the possibility of greater protection against piracy. With traditional film prints, distributors typically stagger the film's release in various markets, shipping the film prints around the globe. In the subsequent markets, pirated copies of a film (i.e. a cam) may be available before the movie is released in that market. A simultaneous worldwide release would mitigate this problem to some degree. Simultaneous worldwide releases on film have been used on *The Da Vinci Code, Lord of the Rings: Return of the King, Star Wars: Revenge of the Sith, Charlie's Angels: Full Throttle* and *Mission: Impossible III* amongst others. With digital distribution, a simultaneous worldwide release would not cost significantly more than a staggered release.

Costs

On the downside, the initial costs for converting theaters to digital are high: up to $150,000 per screen or more. Theaters have been reluctant to switch without a cost-sharing arrangement with film distributors. Recent negotiations have involved the development of a *Virtual Print License* fee which the studios will pay for their products which allows financiers and system developers to pay for deployment of digital systems to the theaters, thus providing investors a certain payback.

While a theater can purchase a film projector for US$50,000 and expect an average life of 30-40 years, a digital cinema playback system including server/media block/and projector can cost 3-4 times as much, and is at higher risk for component failures and technological obsolescence. Experience with computer-based media systems show that average economic lifetimes are only on the order of 5 years with some units lasting until about 10 years before they are replaced.

Archiving digital material is also turning out to be both tricky and costly. In a 2007 study, the Academy of Motion Picture Arts and Sciences found the cost of storing 4K digital masters to be "enormously higher—1100 per cent higher—than the cost of storing film masters." Furthermore, digital archiving faces challenges due to the insufficient temporal qualities of today's digital storage: no current media, be it optical discs, magnetic hard drives or digital tape, can reliably store a film for a hundred years, something that properly stored and handled film can do.

History

Digital media playback of hi-resolution 2K files has at least a twenty year history with early RAIDs feeding custom frame buffer systems with large memories. Content was usually restricted to several minutes of material. Transfer of content between remote locations was slow and had limited capacity. It was not until the late 1990s that feature length projects could be sent over the 'wire' (Internet or dedicated fiber links).

There were many prototype systems developed that claim a *first* in some form of digital presentation. However, few of these had a significant impact on the advance of the industry. Key highlights in the development of digital cinema would likely include: demonstrations by TI of their DMD technology, real-time playback of compressed hi-resolution files by various vendors, and early HD presentations from D5 tape to digital projectors.

Standards Development

The Society of Motion Picture and Television Engineers began work on standards for digital cinema in 2001. It was clear by that point in time that HDTV did not provide a sufficient technological basis for the foundation of digital cinema playback. (In Europe and Japan however, there is still a significant presence of HDTV for theatrical presentations. Agreements within the ISO standards body have led to these systems being referred to as Electronic Cinema Systems (E-Cinema).)

Digital Cinema Initiatives (DCI) was formed in March 2002 as a joint project of the motion picture studios (Disney, Fox, MGM, Paramount, Sony Pictures Entertainment, Universal and Warner Bros. Studios) to develop a system specification for digital cinema. In cooperation with the American Society of Cinematographers, DCI created standard evaluation material (the ASC/DCI StEM material) and developed tests of 2K and 4K playback and compression technologies. DCI published their specification in 2005.

Claims to Significant Events

One claim for the first digital cinema demonstration comes from JVC. On March 19, 1998, they collaborated on a digital presentation at a cinema in London. Several clips from popular films were encoded onto a remote server, and sent via fibre optic for display to a collection of interested Industry parties.

The Last Broadcast made cinematic history on October 23, 1998, when it became the first feature to be theatrically released digitally, via satellite download to theaters across the United States. An effort headed by Wavelength Releasing, Texas Instruments, Digital

Projection Inc. and Loral Space, it successfully demonstrated what would become a template for future releases. In 1999, it was repeated utilizing QuVIS technology across Europe, including the Cannes Film Festival, making *The Last Broadcast* the first feature to be screened digitally at the Cannes Film Festival.

Several feature films were shown in 1999 using DLP prototype projectors and early wavelet based servers. For example, Walt Disney Pictures *Bicentennial Man* was presented using a Qubit server manufactured by QuVIS of Topeka, Kansas. DVD ROM was used to store the compressed data file. The DVD ROMs were loaded into the QuBit server hard drives for playout. The file size for *Bicentennial Man* was 42 GB with an average data rate of 43 Mbit/s. In 2000, Walt Disney, Texas Instruments and Technicolour with the cooperation of several U.S. and international exhibitors, began to deploy prototype Digital Cinema systems in commercial theatres. The systems were assembled and installed by Technicolour using the TI mark V prototype projector, a special Christie lamphouse, and the QuBit server with custom designed automation interfaces.

Technicolour manufactured the DVDs for uploading on these test systems and was responsible for sending technicians out to the locations for every new feature film that was played. The technicians would typically spend ten or so hours to load the files from the DVD to the QuBit, set up the server to play the files, and then set up the projector. A full rehearsal screening of the feature was mandatory as was the requirement to have back up DVDs and backup QuBits available should something fail.

The systems were eventually replaced or upgraded after TI made improvements to the projectors and Technicolour developed a purpose-built digital cinema server in a venture with Qualcomm, the engineering giant from San Diego best known for advanced mobile phone technology. The new systems were called *AMS* for *Auditorium Management Systems* and were the first digital cinema servers designed to be user friendly and operate reliably in a computer-hostile environment such as a projection booth. Most importantly, they provided a complete solution for content security. The AMS used removable hard disk drives as the transport mechanism for the files. This eliminated the time required to upload the DVD ROMs to the local hard drives and provided the ability to switch programmes quickly. For security, the AMS used a media block type system that placed a sealed electronics package within the projector housing. The server output only 3DES encrypted data and the media block did the decryption at the point just before playout.

The first secure encrypted digital cinema feature was *Star Wars Episode II: Attack of the Clones*. The system functioned well but was eventually replaced because of the need to create a standard data package for D-cinema distribution.

Universal Pictures used their film *Serenity* as the first DCI-compliant DCP to be delivered shown to an audience at a remote theater, although it was not distributed this way to the public. *Inside Man* was their first DCP cinema release, and was transmitted to 20 theatres in the United States along with two trailers.

In April 2005, DG2L Technologies announced that it had been awarded the multi-million dollar contract for the world's largest satellite based MPEG4 digital cinema deployment to be done in India, which encompassed 2000 theaters for UFO (United Film Organizers), a subsidiary of the Valuable Media Group. In March 2006, United Film Organizers Moviez (UFO Moviez), had reached a significant milestone—surpassing 30,000 shows using the DG2L Cinema System platform. This figure increased to 100,000 shows in August 2006. In September 2006, UFO Moviez acquired 51 per cent stake in DG2L Technologies in a deal estimated at around $50 million.

Stereo 3-D Images

In late 2005, interest in digital 3-D stereoscopic projection has led to a new willingness on the part of theaters to co-operate in installing a limited number of 2K stereo installations to show Disney's *Chicken Little* in 3-D film. Six more digital 3-D movies are slated for 2006 or 2007 release (including Beowulf, *Monster House* and *Meet the Robinsons*). The technology combines two digital projectors fitted with polarizing filters with the use of polarized glasses and silver screens. A single projector can also be used in conjunction with a simple adapter in the front (a single-cell LCD screen that acts as a quarter-wave retarder, also known as a Z screen) that rotates the polarity of projector's light output several times per second to alternate quickly the left-and-right-eye views. Another system used by DOLBY makes use of a special colour filter and glasses and has the advantage that does not require a silver screen. Also, some theaters use a system that requires no modification on the screen or the projector but uses active liquid crystal shutter glasses that quickly block the views of each eye alternatively.

List of Digital Cinema Companies

- Access Integrated Technologies, Inc. (AccessIT)—theater system integrator
- Arts Alliance Media (Arts Alliance Digital Cinema)—theater system integrator
- Barco—digital projector manufacturer
- Christie—digital projector manufacturer
- d2—digital cinema integrator
- Deluxe Digital Studios—distributor and theater system integrator
- Digital Genius—digital cinema integrator
- Doremi Cinema—manufacturer of digital cinema servers and mastering systems
- Dolby Laboratories—theater system integrator
- GDC Technology (gdc-tech.com)—manufacturer of digital cinema servers and mastering systems
- intoPIX—JPEG 2000 compression for theater system
- Kodak—theater system integrator
- Motion Picture Solutions—Digital Cinema Mastering
- NEC—digital projector manufacturer
- RED Digital Cinema Camera Company—digital cinema camera manufacturer
- Sony—digital projector manufacturer
- Technicolour—distributor and theater system integrator
- Texas Instruments—developers of DLP projector technology
- Qube Cinema—manufacturer of digital cinema servers and mastering systems
- XDC—theater system integrator
- Ymagis—theater system integrator.

DIGITAL CINEMATOGRAPHY

Digital cinematography is the process of capturing motion pictures as digital images, rather than on film. Digital capture may occur on tape, hard disks, flash memory, or other media which can record digital data. As digital technology has improved, this practice has become increasingly common. Several mainstream Hollywood movies have now been shot digitally, and many vendors have brought products to market, including traditional film camera vendors like Arri and Panavision, new vendors like RED and Silicon Imaging, and companies which have traditionally focused on consumer and broadcast video equipment, like Sony and Panasonic. The benefits and drawbacks of digital vs. film acquisition are still hotly debated, but digital cinematography cameras sales have surpassed mechanical cameras in the classic 35 mm format.

History

Beginning in the late 1980s, Sony began marketing the concept of "electronic cinematography", utilizing its analogue HDTV cameras. The effort was met with very little success. In 1998, with the introduction of HDCAM recorders and 1920 × 1080 pixel digital video cameras based on CCD technology, the idea, now re-branded as "digital cinematography", finally began to gain traction in the market. In May 2002 *Star Wars Episode II: Attack of the Clones* became the first high-profile, high-budget movie released that was shot on 24 frame-per-second high-definition digital video, using a Sony HDW-F900 camera. The lesser-known 2001 movie Vidocq was shot with the same camera.

In parallel with these developments in the world of traditional high-budget cinematography, a digital cinema revolution was occurring from the bottom up, among low budget filmmakers outside of the Hollywood system. Beginning in the mid-1990s, with the introduction of Sony's DCR-VX1000, the digital MiniDV format began to emerge. MiniDV offered much greater quality than the analogue formats that preceded it, at the same price point. While its quality was not considered as good as film, these MiniDV camcorders, in conjunction with non-linear editing software that could run on personal computers, allowed a large number of people to begin making movies who were previously prevented from doing so by the high costs involved with shooting on film.

Today, cameras from companies like Sony, Panasonic, JVC and Canon offer the prosumer market a variety of choices for shooting high-definition video with less than $10,000 worth of camera equipment. At the high-end of the market, there has been an emergence of cameras aimed specifically at the digital cinema market. These cameras from Arri, Panavision, Grass Valley and RED offer resolution and dynamic range that exceeds that of traditional video cameras, which are designed for the limited resolution and dynamic range of broadcast television.

Technology

Digital cinematography captures motion pictures digitally, in a process analogous to digital photography. While there is no clear technical distinction that separates the images captured in digital cinematography from video, the term "digital cinematography" is usually applied only in cases where digital acquisition is substituted for film acquisition, such as when shooting a feature film. The term is not generally applied when digital acquisition is substituted for analogue video acquisition, as with live broadcast television programmes.

Sensors

Digital cinematography cameras capture images using CMOS or CCD sensors, usually in one of two arrangements. High-end cameras designed specifically for the digital cinematography market often use a single sensor (much like digital photo cameras), with dimensions similar in size to a 35 mm film frame or even (as with the Vision 65) a 65 mm film frame. An image can be projected onto a single large sensor exactly the same way it can be projected onto a film frame, so cameras with this design can be made with PL, PV and similar mounts, in order to use the wide range of existing high-end cinematography lenses available. Their large sensors also let these cameras achieve the same shallow depth of field as 35 or 65 mm motion picture film cameras, which is important because many cinematographers consider selective focus an essential visual tool.

Prosumer and broadcast television cameras typically use three 1/3" or 2/3" sensors in conjunction with a prism, with each sensor capturing a different colour. Camera vendors like Sony and Panasonic, which have their roots in the broadcast and consumer camera markets, have leveraged their experience with these designs into three-chip products targeted specifically at the digital cinematography market. The Thomson Viper also uses a three-chip design. These designs offer benefits in terms of colour reproduction, but are incompatible with traditional cinematography lenses (though new lines of high-end lenses have been developed with these cameras in mind), and incapable of achieving 35 mm depth of field unless used with depth-of-field adaptors, which can lower image sharpness and result in a loss of light.

Acquisition Formats

While many people make movies with MiniDV camcorders and other consumer and prosumer products that have lower resolutions or shoot interlaced video, cameras marketed as digital cinematography cameras typically shoot in progressive HDTV formats such as 720p and 1080p, or in higher-end formats created specifically for the digital cinematography market, such as 2K and 4K.

Data Storage

Tape vs. Data-Centric

Broadly, there are two paradigms used for data storage in the digital cinematography world. Many people, particularly those coming from a background in broadcast television, are most comfortable with video tape based workflows. Data is captured to video tape on set. This data is then ingested into a computer running non-linear editing software, using a deck. Once on the computer, the footage is edited, and then output in its final format, possibly to a film recorder for theatrical exhibition, or back to video tape for broadcast use. Original video tapes are kept as an archival medium. The files generated by the non-linear editing application contain the information necessary to retrieve footage from the proper tapes, should the footage stored on the computer's hard disk be lost.

Increasingly, however, digital cinematography is shifting toward "tapeless" workflow, where instead of thinking about digital images as something that exists on a physical medium like video tape, digital video is conceived of as data in files. In tapeless workflow, digital images are usually recorded directly to files on hard disk or flash memory based "digital magazines." At the end of a shooting day (or sometimes even during the day), the digital files contained on these digital magazines are downloaded, typically to a large RAID connected to an editing system. Once data is copied from the digital magazines, they are erased and returned to the set for more shooting. Archiving is accomplished by backing up the digital files from the RAID, using standard practices and equipment for data backup from the Information Technology industry, often to data tape.

Compression

Digital cinema cameras are capable of generating extremely large amounts of data; often hundreds of megabytes per second.To help manage this huge data flow, many cameras or recording devices designed to be used in conjunction with them offer compression. Prosumer cameras typically use high compression ratios in conjunction with chroma sub-sampling. While this allows footage to be comfortably handled even on fairly modest personal computers, the convenience comes at the expense of image quality.

High-end digital cinematography cameras or recording devices typically support recording at much lower compression ratios, or in uncompressed formats. Additionally, digital cinematography camera vendors are not constrained by the standards of the consumer or broadcast video industries, and often develop proprietary compression technologies that are optimized for use with their specific sensor designs or recording technologies.

Lossless vs. Lossy Compression

A lossless compression system is capable of reducing the size of digital data in a fully reversible way—that is, in a way that allows the original data to be completely restored, byte for byte. This is done by removing redundant information from a signal. Digital cinema cameras rarely use only lossless compression methods, because much higher compression ratios (lower data rates) can be achieved with lossy compression. With a lossy compression scheme, information is discarded to create a simpler signal. Due to limitations in human visual perception, it is possible to design algorithms which do this with little visual impact.

Chroma Subsampling

Some digital cinematography systems further reduce data rate by subsampling colour information. Because the human visual system is much more sensitive to luminance than to colour, lower resolution colour information can be overlaid with higher resolution luma (brightness) information, to create an image that looks very similar to one in which both colour and luma information are sampled at full resolution. This scheme may cause pixelation or colour bleeding under some circumstances, however, and the highest quality digital cinematography systems are capable of recording full resolution colour data (4:4:4) or raw sensor data.

Bitrate

Video and audio compression systems are often characterized by their bitrates. Bitrate describes how much data is required to represent one second of media. One cannot directly use bitrate as a measure of quality, because different compression algorithms perform differently. A more advanced compression algorithm at a lower bitrate may deliver the same quality as a less advanced algorithm at a higher bitrate.

Intra- vs. Inter-Frame Compression

Most compression systems used for acquisition in the digital cinematography world compress footage one frame at a time, as if a video stream is a series of still images. Inter-frame compression systems can further compress data by examining and eliminating redundancy between frames. This leads to higher compression ratios, but displaying a single frame will usually require the playback system to decompress a number of frames that precede it. In normal playback this is not a problem, as each successive frame is played in order, so the preceding frames have already been decompressed.

In editing, however, it is common to jump around to specific frames and to play footage backwards or at different speeds. Because of the need to decompress extra frames in these situations, inter-frame compression can cause performance problems for editing systems. Inter-frame compression is also disadvantageous because the loss of a single frame (say, due to a flaw writing data to a tape) will typically ruin all the frames until the next keyframe occurs. In the case of the HDV format, for instance, this may result in as many as 6 frames being lost with 720p recording, or 15 with 1080i recording.

Table 3.1 : Digital Acquisition Codecs Compared

Format	Bit depth	Resolution	Chroma sampling	Bitrate	Inter-frame?	Algorithm type
DV	8 bit	720×480 (NTSC)/720×576 (PAL)	4:1:1 or 4:2:0	3.75 Mbit/s	No	DCT (lossy)
DVCPRO50	8 bit	720×480 (NTSC)/720×576 (PAL)	4:2:2	50 Mbit/s	No	DCT (lossy)
DVCPRO HD	8 bit	960×720, 1280×1080 or 1440×1080	4:2:2	100 Mbit/s	No	DCT (lossy)
AVCHD	8 bit	1920x1080,1440x1080,1280x720	4:2:0	24 Mbit/s	Yes	DCT (lossy)
AVC Intra	10 bit	1920x1080,1440x1080,1280x720	4:2:2	50 or 100 Mbit/s	No	DCT (lossy)
HDV	8 bit	1280×720 or 1440×1080	4:2:0	19-25 Mbit/s	Yes	DCT (lossy)
XDCAM EX	8 bit	1280x720 or 1920×1080	4:2:0	25-35 Mbit/s	Yes	DCT (lossy)
HDCAM	8 bit	1440×1080	3:1:1	144 Mbit/s	No	DCT (lossy)
HDCAM SR	10 bit	1920×1080	4:2:2 or 4:4:4	440 or 880 Mbit/s	No	DCT (lossy)
CineForm RAW (SI-2K)	10 bit Log	2048×1152	Raw Bayer	100-140 Mbit/s	No	Wavelet (lossy)
REDCODE RAW	12 bit	4096×2304	Raw Bayer	220 Mbit/s	No	Wavelet (lossy)

Distribution Formats

Movies shot digitally may be released theatrically, on DVD VHS or in a High Definition format like Blu-Ray or HD-DVD.

Digital Theatrical Distribution

For the over 4000 theaters with digital projectors in the USA, digital films may be distributed digitally, either shipped to theaters on hard drives or sent via the Internet or satellite networks. Digital Cinema Initiatives, LLC, a joint venture of Disney, Fox, MGM, Paramount, Sony Pictures Entertainment, Universal and Warner Bros. Studios, has established standards for digital cinema projection. In July 2005, they released the first version of the Digital Cinema System Specification, which encompasses 2K and 4K theatrical projection. They also offer compliance testing for exhibitors and equipment suppliers.

Distributors naturally prefer digital distribution, because it saves them the expense of making film prints, which may cost as much as $2000 each. Digital projection also offers advantages over traditional film projection such as lack of jitter, flicker, dust, scratches, and grain. They are also far more flexible with regard to running trailers, pre-feature advertisements and the like.

However theater owners initially balked at the high cost and potential reliability problems of installing digital projection systems, since they normally do not contribute directly to print costs, simply splitting admission proceeds with the distributors in an agreed ratio. Nonetheless, the number of digitally equipped venues is now growing (as of September 2007), at a rate of around 400 screens a month in the United States. It is important to note that in the majority of cases, rather than being a complete conversion to digital projection, the more likely scenario is digital projectors sitting side-by-side with film projectors in the projection booths (often replacing the pre-feature slide projector), or only some units in a multiplex being Digital only. Currently, (2008) even new cinema installations typically use a mixture of film and digital projection.

Film-based Theatrical Distribution

Since not all theaters currently have digital projection systems, even if a movie is shot and post-produced digitally, it must be transferred to film if a large theatrical release is planned. Typically, a film recorder will be used to print digital image data to film, to create a 35 mm internegative. After that the duplication process is identical to that of a traditional negative from a film camera.

Digital Cinematography Cameras

Professional cameras include the Sony HDCAM Series, RED One, Panavisions Genesis, SI-2K, Thomson Viper, Vision Research Phantom, Weisscam, GS Vitec noX, and the Fusion Camera System. Independent filmmakers have also pressed low-cost consumer and prosumer cameras into service for digital filmmaking.

Digital vs. Film Cinematography

Technical Considerations: Predictability

When shooting on film, response to light is determined by what film stock is chosen. A cinematographer can choose a film stock he or she is familiar with, and expose film on set with a high degree of confidence about how it will turn out. Because the film stock is the main determining factor, results will be substantially similar regardless of what camera model is being used. However, the final result cannot be controlled when shooting with mechanical cameras until the film negative has been processed at a laboratory. Therefore, damage to the film negative, scratches which are generated by faulty camera mechanics etc. cannot be controlled.

In contrast, when shooting digitally, response to light is determined by the CMOS or CCD sensor(s) in the camera and recorded and "developed" directly. This means a cinematographer can measure and predict exactly how the final image will look by eye if familiar with the specific model of camera being used or able to read a vector/waveform.

On-set monitoring allows the cinematographer to see the actual images that are captured, immediately on the set, which is impossible with film. With a properly calibrated high-definition display, on-set monitoring, in conjunction with data displays such as histograms, waveforms, RGB parades, and various types of focus assist, can give the cinematographer a far more accurate picture of what is being captured than is possible with film. However, all of this equipment may impose costs in terms of time and money, and may not be possible to utilize in difficult shooting situations.

Film cameras do often have a video assist that captures video though the camera to allow for on-set playback, but its usefulness is largely restricted to judging action and framing. Because this video is not derived from the image that is actually captured to film, it is not very useful for judging lighting, and because it is typically only NTSC-resolution, it is often useless for judging focus.

Portability

Ultra-lightweight and extremely compact digital cinematography cameras, as the SI:2K mini, are much smaller and lighter than mechanical film cameras. Other High-end digital cinema cameras can be quite large, and some models require bulky external recording mechanisms (though in some cases only a small strand of optical fiber is necessary to connect the camera and the recording mechanism).

Compact 35 mm film cameras that produce the full 35 mm film resolution and accept standard 35 mm lenses cannot be sized down below a certain size and weight, as they require at least space for the film negative and basic mechanics.

Smaller form-factor digital cinema cameras such as the Red One and SI-2K have made digital more competitive in this respect. The SI-2K, in particular, with its detachable camera head, allows for high-quality images to be captured by a camera/lens package that is far smaller than is practically achievable with a 35 mm film camera and is used in many scenarios to replace film—especially for stereoscopic productions.

Dynamic Range

The sensors in most high-end digital video cameras have less exposure latitude (dynamic range) than modern motion picture film stocks. In particular, they tend to 'blow out' highlights, losing detail in very bright parts of the image. If highlight detail is lost, it is impossible to recapture in post-production. Cinematographers can learn how to adjust for this type of response using techniques similar to those used when shooting on reversal film, which has a similar lack of latitude in the highlights. They can also use on-set monitoring and image analysis to ensure proper exposure. In some cases it may be necessary to 'flatten' a shot, or reduce the total contrast that appears in the shot, which may require more lighting to be used. Many people also believe that highlights are less visually pleasing with digital acquisition, because digital sensors tend to 'clip' them very sharply, whereas film produces a 'softer' roll-off effect with over-bright regions of the image. Some more recent digital cinema cameras attempt to more closely emulate the way film handles highlights, though how well they achieve this is a matter of some dispute. A few cinematographers have started deliberately using the 'harsh' look of digital highlights for aesthetic purposes. One notable example of such use is *Battlestar Galactica.*

Digital acquisition typically offers better performance than film in low-light conditions, allowing less lighting and in some cases completely natural or practical lighting to be used for shooting, even indoors. This low-light sensitivity also tends to bring out shadow detail. Some directors have tried a "best for the job" approach, using digital acquisition for indoor or night shoots, and traditional film for daylight exteriors.

Resolution

Substantive debate over the subject of film resolution *vs.* digital image resolution is clouded by the fact that it is difficult to meaningfully and objectively determine the resolution of either. Unlike a digital sensor, a film frame does not have a regular grid of discrete pixels. Rather, it has an irregular pattern of differently sized grains. As a film frame is scanned at higher and higher resolutions, image detail is increasingly masked by grain, but it is difficult to determine at what point there is no more useful detail to extract. Moreover, different film stocks have widely varying ability to resolve detail.

Determining resolution in digital acquisition seems straightforward, but is significantly complicated by the way digital camera sensors work in the real world. This is particularly true in the case of high-end digital cinematography cameras that use a single large bayer pattern CMOS sensor. A bayer pattern sensor does not sample full RGB data at every point; each pixel is biased toward red, green *or* blue, and a full colour image is assembled from this checkerboard of colour by processing the image through a demosaicing algorithm. Generally with a bayer pattern sensor, actual resolution will fall somewhere between the "native" value and half this figure, with different demosaicing algorithms producing different results. Additionally, most digital cameras (both bayer and three-chip designs) employ optical low-pass filters to avoid aliasing. Such filters reduce resolution.

In general, it is widely accepted that film exceeds the resolution of HDTV formats and the 2K digital cinema format, but there is still significant debate about whether 4K digital acquisition can match the results achieved by scanning 35 mm film at 4K, as well as whether 4K scanning actually extracts all the useful detail from 35 mm film in the first place. However, as of 2007 the majority of films that use a digital intermediate are done at 2K because of the costs associated with working at higher resolutions. Additionally, 2K projection is chosen for almost all permanent digital cinema installations, often even when 4K projection is available.

One important thing to note is that the process of optical duplication, used to produce theatrical release prints for movies that originate both on film and digitally, causes significant loss of resolution. If a 35 mm negative does capture more detail than 4K digital acquisition, ironically this may only be visible when a 35 mm movie is scanned and projected on a 4K digital projector.

Grain and Noise

Film has a characteristic grain structure, which many people view positively, either for aesthetic reasons or because it has become associated with the look of 'real' movies. Different film stocks have different grain, and cinematographers may use this for artistic effect. Digitally acquired footage lacks this grain structure. Electronic noise is sometimes visible in digitally acquired footage, particularly in dark areas of an image or when footage was shot in low lighting conditions and gain was used. Some people believe such noise is a workable aesthetic substitute for film grain, while others believe it has a harsher look that detracts from the image.

Well shot, well lit images from high-end digital cinematography cameras can look almost eerily clean. Some people believe this makes them look "plasticky" or computer generated, while others find it to be an interesting new look, and argue that film grain can be emulated in post-production if desired. Since most theatrical exhibition still occurs via film prints, the super-clean look of digital acquisition is often lost before moviegoers get to see it, because of the grain in the film stock of the release print.

Digital Intermediate Workflow

The process of using digital intermediate workflow, where movies are colour graded digitally instead of via traditional photochemical finishing techniques, has become common, largely because of the greater artistic control it provides to filmmakers. In 2007, all of the 10 most successful movies released used the digital intermediate process. In order to utilize digital intermediate workflow with film, the camera negative must be processed and then scanned. High quality film scanning is time consuming and expensive. With digital acquisition, this step can be skipped, and footage can go directly into a digital intermediate pipeline as digital data. Some filmmakers have years of experience achieving their artistic vision using the techniques available in a traditional photochemical workflow, and prefer that finishing process. While it would be theoretically possible to use such a process with digital acquisition by creating a film negative on a film recorder, in general digital acquisition is not a suitable choice if a traditional finishing process is desired.

Sound

Films are traditionally shot with dual-system recording, where picture is recorded on camera, and sync sound is recorded to a separate sound recording device. In post-production, picture and sound are synced up. Many cameras used for digital cinematography can record sound internally, already in sync with picture. This eliminates the need for syncing in post, which can lead to faster workflows. However, most sound recording is done by specialist operators, and the sound will likely be separated and further processed in post-production anyway. Also, recording sound to the camera may require running additional cables to the camera, which may be problematic in some shooting situations, particularly in shots where the camera is moving. Wireless transmission systems can eliminate this problem, but are not suitable for use in all circumstances.

Archiving

Many people feel there is significant value in having a film negative master for archival purposes. As long as the negative does not physically degrade, it will be possible to recover the image from it in the future, regardless of changes in technology. In contrast, even if digital data is stored on a medium that will preserve its integrity, changes in technology may render the format unreadable or expensive to recover over time. For this reason, film studios distributing digitally-originated films often make film-based separation masters of them for archival purposes.

Economics

Low-budget/Independent Filmmaking

For the last 25 years, many respected filmmakers like George Lucas have predicted that electronic or digital cinematography would bring about a revolution in filmmaking, by dramatically lowering costs. For low-budget and so-called "no-budget" productions, digital cinematography on prosumer cameras clearly has cost benefits over shooting on 35 mm or even 16 mm film. The cost of film stock, processing, telecine, negative cutting, and titling for a feature film can run to tens of thousands of dollars according to *From Reel to Deal*, a book on independent film production by Dov S-S Simens. Costs directly attributable to shooting a low-budget feature on 35 mm film could be $50,000 on the low side, and over twice that on the high side. In contrast, obtaining a high-definition prosumer camera and sufficient tape stock to shoot a feature can easily be done for under $10,000, or significantly less if, as is typically the case with 35 mm shoots, the camera is rented.

If a 35 mm print of the film is required, an April 2003 article in American Cinematographer found the costs between shooting film and video are roughly the same. The benefit to shooting video is that the cost of a film-out is only necessary should the film find a distributor to pick up the cost. When shooting film, the costs are upfront and cannot be deferred in such a manner. On the other hand, the same article found 16 mm film to deliver better image quality in terms of resolution and dynamic range. Given the progress digital acquisition, film recording, and related technologies have seen in the last few years, it is unclear how relevant this article is today.

Most extremely low-budget movies never receive wide distribution, so the impact of low-budget video acquisition on the industry remains to be seen. It is possible that as a result of new distribution methods and the long tail effects they may bring into play, more such productions may find profitable distribution in the future. Traditional distributors may also begin to acquire more low-budget movies as better affordable digital acquisition eliminates the liability of low picture quality, and as they look for a means to escape the increasingly drastic "boom and bust" financial situation created by spending huge amounts of money on a relatively small number of very large movies, not all of which succeed.

Hollywood

On higher budget productions, the cost advantages of digital cinematography are not as significant, primarily because the costs imposed by working with film are simply not major expenses for such productions. Two recent films, *Sin City* and *Superman Returns*, both shot on digital tape, had budgets of $40 million and close to $200 million respectively. The cost savings, though probably in the range of several hundred thousand to over a million dollars, were negligible as a percentage of the total production budgets in these cases.

Rick McCallum, a producer on *Attack of the Clones*, has commented that the production spent $16,000 for 220 hours of digital tape, where a comparable amount of film would have cost $1.8 million. However, this does not necessarily indicate the actual cost savings. The low incremental cost of shooting additional footage may encourage filmmakers to use far higher shooting ratios with digital. The lower shooting ratios typical with film may save time in editing, lowering post-production costs somewhat.

Shooting in digital requires a digital intermediate workflow, which is more expensive than a photochemical finish. However, a digital intermediate may be desirable even with film acquisition because of the creative possibilities it provides, or a film may have a large number of effects shots which would require digital processing anyway. Digital intermediate workflow is coming down in price, and is quickly becoming standard procedure for high-budget Hollywood movies.

Industry Acceptance of Digital Cinematography

For over a century, virtually all movies have been shot on film and nearly every film student learns about how to handle 16 mm and 35 mm film.

Today, digital acquisition accounts for the vast majority of moving image acquisition, as most content for broadcast is shot on digital formats. Most movies destined for theatrical release are still shot on film, however, as are many dramatic TV series and some high-budget commercials. High-end digital cinematography cameras suitable for acquiring footage intended for theatrical release are on the market since 1999/2000, and have meanwhile gained widespread adoption.

Some notable high-profile directors that have shot with digital equipment include:

- Robert Altman—*A Prairie Home Companion*
- Jean-Jacques Annaud—*Two Brothers*
- Spike Lee—*Bamboozled*
- Tim Burton—*Corpse Bride*
- James Cameron—Ghosts of the Abyss, Aliens of the Deep
- Francis Ford Coppola—*Youth without Youth*
- David Fincher—*Zodiac*
- Mel Gibson—*Apocalypto*
- Alex Proyas—*Knowing*
- Anthony Hopkins—*Slipstream*
- Peter Jackson—Crossing the Line
- George Lucas—Episodes *II* and *III* of *Star Wars*
- Sidney Lumet—*Before the Devil Knows You're Dead*
- David Lynch—*Inland Empire*
- Michael Mann—*Miami Vice, Collateral*
- Rob Minkoff—*The Forbidden Kingdom*
- Michael Moore—*Bowling for Columbine*
- Greg Mottola—*Superbad*
- Doug Liman—*Jumper*
- Peter Greenaway—Nightwatching
- Martin Scorsese—Shine a Light
- Robert Rodriguez—*Sin City, Grindhouse*
- Tony Scott—*Déjà Vu*
- Bryan Singer—*Superman Returns*
- Steven Soderbergh—*Guerrilla*
- Sylvester Stallone—*Rocky Balboa*
- Lee Tamahori—*Next*

- Lars von Trier—*Dogville, Manderlay*
- Andy Wachowski and Larry Wachowski—*Speed Racer*
- David Zucker—*Scary Movie 4*

Some of these directors are strong supporters of the change from film to digital, some of them declare that it depends on the particular movie. Directors Steven Spielberg, M. Night Shyamalan, Oliver Stone and Paul Thomas Anderson belong to the opposing camp, and have vowed to continue to shoot on film. Some directors have expressed an openness for either format, such as Jean-Jacques Annaud who used 35 mm and HDCAM together for Two Brothers, or Quentin Tarantino, who, while he ended up shooting his contribution on film, expressed an interest in digital acquisition for Grindhouse.

Lower-budget and limited-release movies have adopted digital cinematography at a somewhat faster pace, although some filmmakers still choose to shoot such productions on 16 mm film, the traditional medium for that market segment. As the digital intermediate process gains wider use, even for finishing movies shot on film, and as digital acquisition technology continues to improve, it seems likely digital cinematography will continue to gain wider acceptance.

Digital technology has eclipsed analogue alternatives in many other content creation and distribution markets. On the content creation side, digital photo cameras significantly outsell film photo cameras, digital video tape formats like MiniDV have superseded analogue tape formats, digital audio workstations have almost entirely replaced multi-track tape recorders, digital non-linear editing systems have displaced Moviola/Steenbeck equipment as the standard means of editing movies, and page layout software running on desktop computers has come to dominate the graphic design industry. On the distribution side, CDs have largely replaced LPs, DVDs have largely replaced VHS tapes, and digital cable systems are displacing analogue cable systems. It seems likely that despite current resistance on the part of some in the industry, digital technology will eventually be similarly successful in the feature film acquisition and theatrical exhibition markets.

List of Major Films Shot in Digital

In the last decade a large number of films have been shot digitally.

Some of them are independent, low-budget productions, while others are major Hollywood- and Europe-based productions.

Sony HDCAM/cinealta (750/900/F23)

- *Star Wars Episode II: Attack of the Clones* (2002)
- *Collateral* (2004) (exterior night scenes)
- *Two Brothers* (2004) (tiger shots)
- *Star Wars Episode III: Revenge of the Sith* (2005)
- *Sin City* (2005)
- *Me and You and Everyone We Know (2005)*
- *Speed Racer* (2008)
- *Cloverfield* (2008) (segments, other shots include the Panasonic HVX-200, as well as the Thompson Viper)
- *Genghis Khan* (2005, BBC History)

Panasonic SDX-900

- *Space Race (TV series)* (2005)
- *Rome (TV series)* (2006)
- *If*
- *Impressionists*

Thomson Viper

- *Collateral* (2004) (exterior night scenes)
- *Zodiac* (2007)
- *Chemical Wedding* (2008)
- *Cloverfield* (2008) (segments, other shots include the Panasonic HVX-200, as well as one of Sony's CineAlta cameras, the F23)
- *The Curious Case of Benjamin Button* (2008)
- *Surviving Evil*

Panavision Genesis

- *Flyboys* (2006)
- *Superman Returns* (2006)
- *Click* (2006)
- *Apocalypto* (2006)
- *Balls of Fury* (2007)
- *I Now Pronounce You Chuck and Larry* (2007)
- *Next* (2007)

- *Reign Over Me* (2007)

Red One

- *Jumper* (2008) (some 2nd unit)
- *The Argentine* (2008)
- *Guerrilla* (2008)
- *Game* (2008)
- *Knowing* (2008)
- *The Informant* (2009)

4

Telephony: A Brief Overview

TELEPHONY

In telecommunication, telephony (pronounced teh-LEH-fuh-nee) encompasses the general use of equipment to provide voice communication over distances, specifically by connecting telephones to each other. Telephones originally were connected directly together in pairs. Each user had separate telephones wired to the various places he might wish to reach. This became inconvenient when people wanted to talk to many other telephones, so the telephone exchange was invented. Each telephone could then be connected to other local ones, thus inventing the local loop and the telephone call. Soon, nearby exchanges were connected by trunk lines, and eventually distant ones were as well. In modern times, most telephones are plugged into telephone jacks. Each jack is connected by inside wiring to a drop wire and then to a cable with other wires. Cables usually bring a large number of wires from all over a district access network to one wire centre or telephone exchange. When the user of a telephone wants to make a telephone call, equipment at the exchange examines the dialed telephone number and connects that telephone line to another in the same wire centre, or to a trunk to a distant exchange. Most of the exchanges in the world are connected to each other, forming the Public Switched Telephone Network or PSTN. By the end of the 20th century almost all were Stored programme Control exchanges.

Digital telephony is the use of digital technology in the provision of telephone services and systems. Almost all telephone calls are provided this way, but sometimes the term is restricted to cases in which the last mile is digital, or where the conversion between digital and analogue signals takes place inside the telephone. Telephony was digitized to cut the cost and improve the quality of voice services, but digital telephony was then found useful for new network services (ISDN) to transfer data speedily over telephone lines.

IP Telephony is a modern form of telephony which uses the TCP/IP protocol popularized by the internet to transmit digitized voice data. Contrast this with the operation of POTS (an acronym for "Plain Old Telephone Service").

Computer Telephony Integration (CTI) enables computers to know about and control phone functions such as making and receiving voice, fax, and data calls with telephone directory services and caller identification. The integration of telephone software and computer systems is a major development in the evolution of the automated office.

CTI is not a new concept. Such links have been used in the past in large telephone networks but only dedicated call centres could justify the costs of the required equipment installation. Primary telephone service providers are offering information services such as Automatic Number Identification and Dialed Number Identification Service on a scale wide enough for its implementation to bring real value to business or residential telephone usage. A new generation of applications (middleware) is being developed as a result of standardization and availability of low cost computer telephony links.

The telephone [from the Greek words tele (τηλε) = far and phone (φωϖη) = voice] is a telecommunications device that is used to transmit and receive sound (most commonly speech), usually two people conversing but occasionally three or more. It is one of the most common household appliances in the world today. Most telephones operate through transmission of electric signals over a complex telephone network which allows almost any phone user to communicate with almost anyone.

Basic Principle

A traditional landline telephone system, also known as "plain old telephone service" (POTS), commonly handles both signalling and audio information on the same twisted pair of insulated wires: the telephone line. Although originally designed for voice communication, the system has been adapted for data communication such as Telex, Fax and Internet communication.

The signalling equipment consists of a bell, beeper, light or other device to alert the user to incoming calls, and number buttons or a rotary dial to enter a telephone number for outgoing calls. A twisted pair line is preferred as it is more effective at rejecting electromagnetic interference (EMI) and crosstalk than an untwisted pair.

A calling party wishing to speak to another party will pick up the telephone's handset, thus operating a button switch or "switchhook", which puts the telephone into an active state or "off hook" by connecting the transmitter (microphone), receiver (speaker) and related audio components to the line. This circuitry has a low resistance (less than 300 Ohms) which causes DC current (48 volts, nominal) from the telephone exchange to flow through the line. The exchange detects this DC current, attaches a digit receiver circuit to the line, and sends a dial tone to indicate readiness. On a modern telephone, the calling party then presses the number buttons in a sequence corresponding to the telephone number of the called party. The buttons are connected to a tone generator that produces DTMF tones which are sent to the exchange. A rotary dial telephone employs pulse dialing, sending electrical pulses corresponding to the telephone number to the exchange. (Most exchanges are still equipped to handle pulse dialing.) Provided the called party's line is not already active or "busy", the exchange sends an intermittent ringing signal (generally over 100 volts AC) to alert the called party to an incoming call. If the called party's line is active, the exchange sends a busy signal to the calling party. However, if the called party's line is active but has call waiting installed, the exchange sends an intermittent audible tone to the called party to indicate an incoming call.

When a landline phone is inactive or "on hook", its alerting device is connected across the line through a capacitor, which prevents DC current from flowing through the line. The circuitry at the telephone exchange detects the absence of DC current flow and thus that the phone is on hook with only the alerting device electrically connected to the line. When a party initiates a call to this line, the ringing signal transmitted by the telephone exchange activates the alerting device on the line. When the called party picks up the handset, the switchhook disconnects the alerting device and connects the audio circuitry to the line. The resulting low resistance now causes DC current to flow through this line, confirming that the called phone is now active. Both phones being active and connected through the exchange, the parties may now converse as long as both phones remain off hook. When a party "hangs up", placing the handset back on the cradle or hook, DC current ceases to flow in that line, signalling the exchange to disconnect the call. Calls to parties beyond the local exchange are carried over "trunk" lines which establish connections between exchanges. In modern telephone networks, fiber-optic cable and digital technology are often employed in such connections. Satellite technology may be used for communication over very long distances.

In most telephones, the transmitter and receiver (microphone and speaker) are located in the handset, although in a speakerphone these components may be located in the base or in a separate enclosure. Powered by the line, the transmitter produces an electric current whose voltage varies in response to the sound waves arriving at its diaphragm. The resulting current is transmitted along the telephone line to the local exchange then on to the other phone (via the local exchange or a larger network), where it passes through the coil of the receiver. The varying voltage in the coil produces a corresponding movement of the receiver's diaphragm, reproducing the sound waves present at the transmitter. A Lineman's handset is a telephone designed for testing the telephone network, and may be attached directly to aerial lines and other infrastructure components.

History

Credit for inventing the electric telephone remains in dispute. As with other great inventions such as radio, television, light bulb, and computer, there were several inventors who did pioneer experimental work on voice transmission over a wire and improved on each other's ideas. Innocenzo Manzetti, Antonio Meucci, Johann Philipp Reis, Elisha Gray, Alexander Graham Bell, and Thomas Edison, among others, have all been credited with pioneer work on the telephone.

The early history of the telephone is a confusing morass of claim and counterclaim, which was not clarified by the huge mass of lawsuits which hoped to resolve the patent claims of individuals.

The Bell and Edison patents, however, were forensically victorious and commercially decisive.

Early Development

- 1844—Innocenzo Manzetti first mooted the idea of a "speaking telegraph" (telephone).
- 26 August 1854—Charles Bourseul publishes an article in a magazine L'Illustration (Paris): "Transmission électrique de la parole".
- 22 August 1865, La Feuille d'Aoste reported "It is rumored that English technicians to whom Mr. Manzetti illustrated his method for transmitting spoken words on the telegraph wire intend to apply said invention in England on several private telegraph lines."
- 28 December 1871—Antonio Meucci files a patent caveat (n.3335) in the U.S. Patent Office titled "Sound Telegraph", describing communication of voice between two people by wire.
- 1874—Meucci, after having renewed the caveat for two years, fails to find the money to renew it. The caveat lapses.
- 6 April 1875—Bell's U.S. Patent 161,739 "Transmitters and Receivers for Electric Telegraphs" is granted. This uses multiple vibrating steel reeds in make-break circuits.
- 11 February 1876—Gray invents a liquid transmitter for use with a telephone but does not build one.
- 14 February 1876—Elisha Gray files a patent caveat for transmitting the human voice through a telegraphic circuit.
- 14 February 1876—Alexander Bell applies for the patent "Improvements in Telegraphy", for electromagnetic telephones using undulating currents.
- 19 February 1876—Gray is notified by the U.S. Patent Office of an interference between his caveat and Bell's patent application. Gray decides to abandon his caveat.
- 7 March 1876—Bell's U.S. patent 174,465 "Improvement in Telegraphy" is granted, covering "the method of, and apparatus for, transmitting vocal or other sounds telegraphically ... by causing electrical undulations, similar in form to the vibrations of the air accompanying the said vocal or other sound."

- 10 March 1876—The first successful telephone transmission of clear speech using a liquid transmitter when Bell spoke into his device, "Mr. Watson, come here, I want to see you." and Watson heard each word distinctly.
- 30 January 1877—Bell's U.S. patent 186,787 is granted for an electromagnetic telephone using permanent magnets, iron diaphragms, and a call bell.
- 27 April 1877—Edison files for a patent on a carbon (graphite) transmitter. The patent 474,230 was granted 3 May 1892, after a 15 year delay because of litigation. Edison was granted patent 222,390 for a carbon granules transmitter in 1879.

Early Commercial Instruments

Early telephones were technically diverse. Some used a liquid transmitter, some had a metal diaphragm that induced current in an electromagnet wound around a permanent magnet, and some were "dynamic"—their diaphragm vibrated a coil of wire in the field of a permanent magnet or the coil vibrated the diaphragm. This dynamic kind survived in small numbers through the 20th century in military and maritime applications where its ability to create its own electrical power was crucial. Most, however, used the Edison/Berliner carbon transmitter, which was much louder than the other kinds, even though it required an induction coil, actually acting as an impedance matching transformer to make it compatible to the impedance of the line. The Edison patents kept the Bell monopoly viable into the 20th century, by which time the network was more important than the instrument.

Early telephones were locally powered, using either a dynamic transmitter or by the powering of a transmitter with a local battery. One of the jobs of outside plant personnel was to visit each telephone periodically to inspect the battery. During the 20th century, "common battery" operation came to dominate, powered by "talk battery" from the telephone exchange over the same wires that carried the voice signals. Late in the century, wireless handsets brought a revival of local battery power.

Early telephones had one wire for both transmitting and receiving of audio, with ground return as used in telegraphs. The earliest dynamic telephones also had only one opening for sound, and the user alternately listened and spoke (rather, shouted) into the same hole. Sometimes the instruments were operated in pairs at each end, making conversation more convenient but were more expensive. At first, the benefits of an exchange were not exploited. Telephones instead were leased in pairs to the subscriber, who had to arrange telegraph contractors to construct a line between them, for example between his home and his shop. Users who wanted the ability to speak to several different locations would need to obtain and set up three or four pairs of telephones. Western Union, already using telegraph exchanges, quickly extended the principle to its telephones in New York City and San Francisco, and Bell was not slow in appreciating the potential.

Signalling began in an appropriately primitive manner. The user alerted the other end, or the exchange operator, by whistling into the transmitter. Exchange operation soon resulted in telephones being equipped with a bell, first operated over a second wire and later with the same wire using a condenser (capacitor). Telephones connected to the earliest Strowger automatic exchanges had seven wires, one for the knife switch, one for each telegraph key, one for the bell, one for the push button and two for speaking.

Rural and other telephones that were not on a common battery exchange had a magneto or hand-cranked generator to produce a high voltage alternating signal to ring the bells of other telephones on the line and to alert the operator.

In the 1890s a new smaller style of telephone was introduced, packaged in three parts. The transmitter stood on a stand, known as a "candlestick" for its shape. When not in use, the receiver hung on a hook with a switch in it, known as a "switchhook." Previous telephones required the user to operate a separate switch to connect either the voice or the bell. With the new kind, the user was less likely to leave the phone "off the hook." In phones connected to magneto exchanges, the bell, induction coil, battery and magneto were in a separate "bell box." In phones connected to common battery exchanges, the bell box was installed under a desk, or other out of the way place, since it did not need a battery or magneto.

Cradle designs were also used at this time, having a handle with the receiver and transmitter attached, separate from the cradle base that housed the magneto crank and other parts. They were larger than the "candlestick" and more popular.

Disadvantages of single wire operation such as crosstalk and hum from nearby AC power wires had already led to the use of twisted pairs and, for long distance telephones, four-wire circuits. Users at the beginning of the 20th century did not place long distance calls from their own telephones but made an appointment to use a special sound proofed long distance telephone booth furnished with the latest technology.

What turned out to be the most popular and longest lasting physical style of telephone was introduced in the early 20th century, including Bell's Model 102. A carbon granule transmitter and electromagnetic receiver were united in a single molded plastic handle, which when not in use sat in a cradle in the base unit. The circuit diagram of the Model 102 shows the direct connection of the receiver to the line, while the transmitter was induction coupled, with energy supplied by a local battery. The coupling transformer, battery, and ringer were in a separate enclosure. The dial switch in the base interrupted the line current by repeatedly but very briefly disconnecting the line 1-10 times for each digit, and the hook switch (in the center of the circuit diagram) permanently disconnected the line and the transmitter battery while the handset was on the cradle.

After the 1930s, the base also enclosed the bell and induction coil, obviating the old separate bell box. Power was supplied to each subscriber line by central office batteries instead of a local battery, which required periodic service. For the next half century, the network behind the telephone became progressively larger and much more efficient, but after the dial was added the instrument itself changed little until touch tone replaced the dial in the 1960s.

Digital Telephony

The Public Switched Telephone Network (PSTN) has gradually evolved towards digital telephony which has improved the capacity and quality of the network. End-to-end analogue telephone networks were first modified in the early 1960s by upgrading transmission networks with T1 carrier systems. Later technologies such as SONET and fiber optic transmission methods further advanced digital transmission. Although analogue carrier systems existed, digital transmission made it possible to significantly increase the number of channels multiplexed on a single transmission medium. While today the end instrument remains analogue, the analogue signals reaching the aggregation point [Serving Area Interface (SAI) or the central office (CO)] are typically converted to digital signals. Digital loop carriers (DLC) are often used, placing the digital network ever closer to the customer premises, relegating the analogue local loop to legacy status.

IP Telephony

Internet Protocol (IP) telephony (also known as Internet telephony) is a service based on Voice over IP (VoIP), a disruptive technology that is rapidly gaining ground against traditional telephone network technologies. In Japan and South Korea up to 10 per cent of subscribers, as of January 2005, have switched to this digital telephone service. A January 2005 Newsweek article suggested that Internet telephony may be "the next big thing." As of 2006 many VoIP companies offer service to consumers and businesses.

IP telephony uses a broadband Internet connection and IP Phones to transmit conversations as data packets. In addition to replacing POTS (plain old telephone service), IP telephony is also competing with mobile phone networks by offering free or lower cost connections via WiFi hotspots. VoIP is also used on private wireless networks which may or may not have a connection to the outside telephone network.

IP telephony technology transforms many non-telephone electronics devices into unified communications devices which simulate telephone usage, such as adding telephone-like features to portable game devices, digital picture frames, or handheld GPS receivers, typically by incorporating a voice engine. When used on a personal computer, an IP telephone is referred to as a soft phone.

Usage

By the end of 2006, there were a total of nearly 4 billion mobile and fixed line subscribers and over 1 billion Internet users worldwide. This included 1.27 billion fixed line subscribers and 2.68 billion mobile subscribers.

Telephone Operating Companies

In some countries, many telephone operating companies (commonly abbreviated to *telco* in American English) are in competition to provide telephone services. Some of them are included in the following list. However, the list only includes facilities based providers and not companies which lease services from facilities based providers in order to serve their customers.

Patents

- US 174,465—*Telegraphy* (Bell's first telephone patent)—Alexander Graham Bell
- US 186,787—*Electric Telegraphy* (permanent magnet receiver)—Alexander Graham Bell
- US 474,230—*Speaking Telegraph* (graphite transmitter)—Thomas Edison
- US 203,016—*Speaking Telephone* (carbon button transmitter)—Thomas Edison
- US 222,390—*Carbon Telephone* (carbon granules transmitter)—Thomas Edison
- US 485,311—*Telephone* (solid back carbon transmitter)—Anthony C. White (Bell engineer) This design was used until 1925 and installed phones were used until the 1940s
- US 3,449,750—*Duplex Radio Communication and Signalling Appartus*—G.H. Sweigert
- US 3,663,762—*Cellular Mobile Communication System*—Amos Edward Joel (Bell Labs)
- US 3,906,166—*Radio Telephone System* (DynaTAC cell phone)—Martin Cooper *et al.* (Motorola).

DIGITAL TELEPHONY

Digital telephony is the use of digital electronics in the provision of digital telephone services and systems. Since the 1960s a digital core network has almost entirely replaced the old analog system, and much of the access network has also been digitized. Digital telephony was introduced to provide voice services at lower cost, but was then found to be of great value to new network services such as ISDN that could use digital facilities to transfer data speedily over telephone lines.

Milestones in Digital Telephony

- early experiments with pulse code modulation in telephony

- the 8-bit, 8kHz standard is developed; Nyquist's theorem and the standard 3.5kHz telephony bandwidth
- DS0 as the basic digital telephony bitstream standard
- non-linear quantization: A-law vs. ì-law, and transcoding between the two
- bit error rate and intelligibility
- first practical digital telephone systems put into service
- the U.S. T-carrier system and the European E-carrier system developed to carry digital telephony
- introduction of space-time switching in fully digital electronic switching systems
- replacement of tone signalling with digital signalling for trunks
- in-band signalling vs. out-of-band signalling
- the problem of bit-robbing
- development of SS7
- emergence of fiber optic networking allows greater reliability and call capacity
- transition from plesiochronous transmission to synchronous systems like SONET/SDH
- optical self-healing ring networks further increase reliability
- digital/optical systems revolutionize international long-distance networks, particularly undersea cables
- digital telephone exchanges eliminate moving parts, make exchange equipment much smaller and more reliable
- separation of exchange and concentrator functions
- roll-out of digital systems throughout the PSTN
- provision of intelligent network services
- digital speech coding and compression
- speech compression on international digital trunks
- phone tapping in the digital environment
- introduction of digital mobile telephony, specialized compression algorithms for high ite error rates
- direct digital termination to customers via ISDN; PRI catches on, BRI mostly does not, except in Germany
- the effects of digital telephony, and digital termination at the ISP, on modem performance

- voice over IP as a carrier strategy
- emergence of ADSL leads to voice over IP becoming a consumer product, and the slow demise of dial-up Internet access
- expected convergence of VoIP, mobile telephony, etc.
- flattening of telephony tariffs, increasing moves towards flat rate pricing as the marginal cost of telephony drops further and further.

5

Broadcasting: Special Focus on Digital Technology and Process

BROADCASTING

Broadcasting is the distribution of audio and/or video signals which transmit programmes to an audience. The audience may be the general public or a relatively large sub-audience, such as children or young adults. There are wide variety of broadcasting systems, all of which have different capabilities. The smallest broadcasting systems are institutional public address systems, which transmit verbal messages and music within a school or hospital, and low-powered broadcasting systems which transmit radio stations or television stations to a small area. National radio and television broadcasters have nationwide coverage, using retransmitter towers, satellite systems, and cable distribution. Satellite radio and television broadcasters can cover even wider areas, such as entire continents, and Internet channels can distribute text or streamed music worldwide.

The sequencing of content in a broadcast is called a schedule. As with all technological endeavours, a number of technical terms and slang have developed. A list of these terms can be found at list of broadcasting terms. Television and radio programmes are distributed through radio broadcasting or cable, often both simultaneously. By coding signals and having decoding equipment in homes, the latter also enables subscription-based channels and pay-per-view services.

The term "broadcast" was coined by early radio engineers from the mid-western United States. Broadcasting forms a very large segment of the mass media. Broadcasting to a very narrow range of audience is called narrowcasting.

Business Models of Broadcasting

There are several dominant business models of broadcasting. Each differs in the method by which stations are funded:

- in-kind donations of time and skills by volunteers (common with community broadcasters)
- direct government payments or operation of public broadcasters
- indirect government payments, such as radio and television licenses
- grants from foundations or business entities
- selling advertising or sponsorships
- public subscription or membership, and
- fees charged to all owners of TV sets or radios, regardless of whether they intend to receive that programme or not (an approach used in the UK)

Broadcasters may rely on a combination of these business models. For example, National Public Radio, a non-commercial network within the United States, receives grants from the Corporation for Public Broadcasting (which in turn receives funding from the U.S. Government), by public membership, and by selling "extended credits" to corporations.

Recorded Broadcasts and Live Broadcasts

One can distinguish between recorded and live broadcasts. The former allows correcting errors, and removing superfluous or undesired material, rearranging it, applying slow-motion and repetitions, and other techniques to enhance the programme. However some live events like sports telecasts can include some of the aspects including slow motion clips of important goals/hits etc in between the live telecast.

American radio network broadcasters habitually forbade pre-recorded broadcasts in the 1930s and 1940s, requiring radio programmes played for the Eastern and Central time zones to be repeated three hours later for the Pacific time zone. This restriction was dropped for special occasions, as in the case of the German dirigible airship *Hindenburg* at Lakehurst, New Jersey in 1937. During World War II, pre-recorded broadcasts from war correspondents were allowed on U.S. radio. In addition, American radio programmes were recorded for playback by Armed Forces Radio stations around the world.

A disadvantage of recording first is that the public may know the outcome of an event from another source, which may be a spoiler. In addition, prerecording prevents live announcers from deviating from an officially-approved script, as occurred with propaganda broadcasts from Germany in the 1940s and with Radio Moscow in the 1980s.

Many events are advertised as being live, although they are often "recorded live" (sometimes this is referred to as "live-to-tape"). This is particularly true of performances of musical artists on radio when they visit for an in-studio concert performance. This intentional blurring of the distinction between live and recorded media is viewed with chagrin among many music lovers. Similar situations have sometimes appeared in television (*The Cosby Show* is recorded in front of a live studio audience).

Distribution Methods

A broadcast may be distributed through several physical means. If coming directly from the studio at a single radio or TV station, it is simply sent through the air chain to the transmitter and thence from the antenna on the tower out to the world. Programming may also come through a communications satellite, played either live or recorded for later transmission. Networks of stations may simulcast the same programming at the same time, originally via microwave link, and now mostly by satellite.

Distribution to stations or networks may also be through physical media, such as analogue or digital videotape, CD, DVD, and sometimes other formats. Usually these are included in another broadcast, such as when electronic news gathering returns a story to the station for inclusion on a news programme.

The final leg of broadcast distribution is how the signal gets to the listener or viewer. It may come over the air as with a radio station or TV station to an antenna and receiver, or may come through cable TV or cable radio (or "wireless cable") via the station or directly from a network. The Internet may also bring either radio or TV to the recipient, especially with multicasting allowing the signal and bandwidth to be shared.

The term "broadcast network" is often used to distinguish networks that broadcast an over-the-air television signal that can be received using a television antenna from so-called networks that are broadcast only via cable or satellite television. The term "broadcast television" can refer to the programming of such networks.

DIGITAL VIDEO BROADCASTING

Digital Video Broadcasting (DVB) is a suite of internationally accepted open standards for digital television. DVB standards are maintained by the *DVB Project*, an industry consortium with more than 270 members, and they are published by a *Joint Technical Committee* (JTC) of European Telecommunications Standards Institute (ETSI), European Committee for Electrotechnical Standardization (CENELEC) and European Broadcasting Union (EBU). The interaction of the DVB sub-standards is described in the *DVB Cookbook*. Many aspects of DVB are patented, including elements of the MPEG video coding and audio coding.

Transmission

DVB systems distribute data using a variety of approaches, including by satellite (DVB-S, DVB-S2 and DVB-SH; also DVB-SMATV for distribution via SMATV); cable (DVB-C); terrestrial television (DVB-T, DVB-T2) and digital terrestrial television for handhelds (DVB-H, DVB-SH); and via microwave using DTT (DVB-MT), the MMDS (DVB-MC), and/or MVDS standards (DVB-MS).

These standards define the physical layer and data link layer of the distribution system. Devices interact with the physical layer via a synchronous parallel interface (SPI), synchronous serial interface (SSI), or asynchronous serial interface (ASI). All data is transmitted in MPEG-2 transport streams with some additional constraints (DVB-MPEG). A standard for temporally-compressed distribution to mobile devices (DVB-H) was published in November, 2004.

These distribution systems differ mainly in the modulation schemes used and error correcting codes used, due to the different technical constraints. DVB-S (SHF) uses QPSK, 8PSK or 16-QAM.

DVB-S2 uses QPSK, 8PSK, 16APSK or 32APSK, at the broadcasters decision. QPSK and 8PSK are the only versions regularly used. DVB-C (VHF/UHF) uses QAM: 16-QAM, 32-QAM, 64-QAM, 128-QAM or 256-QAM. Lastly, DVB-T (VHF/UHF) uses 16-QAM or 64-QAM (or QPSK) in combination with COFDM and can support hierarchical modulation.

The DVB-T2 standard is expected to be published at the end of June 2008 and is expected to be approved and submitted to ETSI during 2008.

The DVB-T2 standard will give more-robust TV reception and increase the possible bit-rate by over 30 per cent for single transmitters (as in the UK) and is expected to increase the max bit-rate by over 50 per cent in large single-frequency networks (as in Germany, Sweden).

Content

Besides audio and video transmission, DVB also defines data connections (DVB-DATA-EN 301 192) with return channels (DVB-RC) for several media (DECT, GSM, PSTN/ISDN, satellite etc.) and protocols (DVB-IPTV: Internet Protocol; DVB-NPI: network protocol independent).

Older technologies such as teletext (DVB-TXT) and vertical blanking interval data (DVB-VBI) are also supported by the standards to ease conversion. However for many applications more advanced alternatives like DVB-SUB for sub-titling are available.

Encryption and Metadata

The conditional access system (DVB-CA) defines a Common Scrambling Algorithm (DVB-CSA) and a physical Common Interface (DVB-CI) for accessing scrambled content. DVB-CA providers develop their wholly proprietary conditional access systems with reference to these specifications. Multiple simultaneous CA systems can be assigned to a scrambled DVB programme stream providing operational and commercial flexibility for the service provider.

DVB is also developing a Content Protection and Copy Management system for protecting content after it has been received (DVB-CPCM), which is intended to allow flexible use of recorded content on a home network or beyond, while preventing unconstrained sharing on the Internet. DVB-CPCM has been the source of much controversy in the popular press and it is said that CPCM is the DVB's answer to the failed American Broadcast Flag.

DVB transports include metadata called Service Information (DVB-SI, ETSI EN 300 468, ETSI TR 101 211) that links the various elementary streams into coherent programmes and provides human-readable descriptions for electronic programme guides as well as for automatic searching and filtering.

Recently, DVB has adopted a profile of the metadata defined by the TV-Anytime Forum (DVB-TVA, ETSI TS 102323). This is an XML Scheme based technology and the DVB profile is tailored for enhanced Personal Digital Recorders. DVB lately also started an activity to develop a service for IPTV (DVB-IPI, ETSI TR 102033, ETSI TS 102034, ETSI TS 102814) which also includes metadata definitions for a broadband content guide (DVB-BCG, ETSI TS 102 539).

Software Platform

The DVB Multimedia Home Platform (DVB-MHP) defines a Java-based platform for the development of consumer video system applications. In addition to providing abstractions for many DVB and MPEG-2 concepts, it provides interfaces for other features like network card control, application download, and layered graphics.

Return Channel

DVB has standardized a number of return channels that work together with DVB(-S/T/C) to create bi-directional communication. RCS is short for Return Channel Satellite, and specifies return channels in C, K_u and K_a frequency bands with return bandwidth of up to 2 Mbit/s. DVB-RCT is short for Return Channel Terrestrial, specified by ETSI EN 301958.

Adoption

DVB-S and DVB-C were ratified in 1994. DVB-T was ratified in early 1997. The first commercial DVB-T broadcasts were performed by the United Kingdom's Digital TV Group in late 1998. In 2003 Berlin, Germany was the first area to completely stop broadcasting analogue TV signals. Many European countries aim to be fully covered with digital television by 2010 and switch off PAL/SECAM services by then.

As of 2005, DVB-T television sets are not significantly more expensive than analogue television sets. Most popular in Europe are the set-top boxes that enable DVB-T to be received through an ordinary analogue television, with the price dropping remarkably in 2007.

In its origin Europe, in Australia, South Africa and India DVB is used throughout the areas it covers or is at least decided to be. This also holds true for cable and satellite in most Asian, African and many South American countries. Many of these have not yet selected a format for digital terrestrial broadcasts (DTTV) and a few (Canada, Mexico and South Korea) chose ATSC instead of DVB-T.

Hong Kong

In Hong Kong, several cable TV operators such as TVB Pay Vision and Cable TV have already started using DVB-S or DVB-C. The government however has adopted the DMB-T/H standard, developed in mainland China, for its digital terrestrial broadcasting services which has started since 31st December 2007.

Japan

With the exception of Sky PerfecTV!, Japan uses different formats in all areas (ISDB), which are however quite similar to their DVB counterparts. SkyPerfect is a satellite provider using DVB on their 124 and 128 degrees east satellites. Their satellite at 110 degrees east does not use DVB, however.

Malaysia

In Malaysia, a new Pay-TV station MiTV began service in September 2005 using IPTV over DVB-T technology while lone satellite programming provider ASTRO has been transmitting in DVB-S since its inception in 1996. Free-to-air DVB-T trials began in late 2006 with a simulcast of both RTM1 and RTM2 plus a new channel called RTM3/RTMi. In April 2007, RTM announced that the outcome of the test is favourable and expects DVB-T to go public by the end of 2007. As of 2008, the trial digital line-up has expanded to include a Music Television channel called Muzik Aktif, and a Sports channel called Arena, with a news channel called Berita Aktif planned for inclusion in the extended trials soon. Analogue shut-off date is also announced to be sometime in 2015.

Norway

In Norway, DVB broadcasting is marketed under RiksTV (encrypted pay channels) and NRK (unecrypted public channels). DVB-T broadcasting via the terrestrial network began in November 2007, and has subsequently been rolled out one part of the country at a time. The Norwegian implementation of DVB-T is different from most others, as it uses H.264 with HE-AAC audio encoding, while most other countries have adapted the less recent MPEG-2 standard. Notably most DVB software for PC have problems with this, though in late 2007 software compatible software has been released, like DVBViewer using the libfaad2 library. Sony has released several HDTVs (Bravia W3000, X3000, X3500) that support Norway's DVB-T implementation without use of a separate set-top box, and Sagem ITD91 HD, Grundig DTR 8720 STBs are others.

New Zealand

In New Zealand, DVB broadcasting is marketed under the Freeview brand name. SD MPEG-2 DVB-S broadcasts via satellite began on 2 May 2007 and DVB-T (terrestrial) broadcasts began April 2008 broadcasting in HD H.264 video with HE-AAC audio. Initially, consumers will be required to purchase set-top boxes, as DVB-capable TV sets are not yet available in New Zealand.

North America

In North America, DVB-S is often used in signal compression and encoding of digital satellite communications alongside Hughes DSS. Unlike Motorola's DigiCipher 2 standard, DVB has a wider adoption in terms of the number of manufacturers of receivers. Cable operators either use DVB-C or OpenCable. Terrestrial HDTV broadcasts use ATSC digital encoding with 8VSB modulation instead of DVB-T's COFDM.

Canada, Mexico and the United States have chosen ATSC instead of DVB-T.

DVB Compliant Productsm

Companies that manufacture a product which is compliant to one or more DVB standards have the option of registering a Declaration of Conformity for that product. Wherever the DVB trademark is used in relation to a product—be it a broadcast, a service, an application or equipment—the product must be registered with the DVB Project Office.

ISDB

Integrated Services Digital Broadcasting (ISDB) is a Japanese standard for digital television (DTV) and digital radio used by the county's radio and television stations. ISDB replaced the previously used MUSE *"Hi-vision"* analogue HDTV system.

Introduction

ISDB is maintained by the Japanese organization ARIB. The standards can be obtained for free at the Japanese organization DiBEG website and at ARIB.

The core standards of ISDB are ISDB-S (satellite television), ISDB-T(terrestrial), ISDB-C (cable) and 2.6GHz band mobile broadcasting which are all based on MPEG-2 video and audio coding as well as the transport stream described by the MPEG-2 standard, and are capable of high definition television (HDTV). ISDB-T and ISDB-Tsb are for mobile reception in TV bands. 1seg is the name of an ISDB-T service for reception on cell phones, laptop computers and vehicles. The concept was named for its similarity to ISDN, because both allow multiple channels of data to be transmitted together (a process called multiplexing). This is also much like another digital radio system, Eureka 147, which calls each group of stations on a transmitter an ensemble; this is very much like the multi-channel digital TV standard DVB-T. ISDB-T operates on unused TV channels, an approach taken by other countries for TV but never before for radio.

Video and Audio Compression

ISDB has adopted the MPEG-2 video and audio compression system. ATSC and DVB also adopted the same system. DVB and ISDB also provide for other video compression methods to be used, including JPEG and MPEG-4, although JPEG is only a required part of the MHEG standard.

Transmission

The various flavours of ISDB differ mainly in the modulations used, due to the requirements of different frequency bands. The 12 GHz band ISDB-S uses PSK modulation, 2.6 GHz band digital sound broadcasting uses CDM and ISDB-T (in VHF and/or UHF band) uses COFDM with PSK/QAM.

Interaction

Besides audio and video transmission, ISDB also defines data connections (Data broadcasting) with the internet as a return channel over several media (10Base-T/100Base-T, Telephone line modem, Mobile phone, Wireless LAN (IEEE 802.11) etc.) and with different protocols. This is used, for example, for interactive interfaces like data broadcasting (ARIB STD B-24) and electronic programme guides (EPG).

Interfaces and Encryption

The ISDB specification describes a lot of (network) interfaces, but most importantly the Common Interface for Conditional Access (ARIB STD-B25) with the Common Scrambling Algorithm (CAS) system called MULTI2 required for (de-)scrambling television.

The ISDB CAS system is operated by a company named *B-CAS* in Japan; the CAS card is called *B-CAS card*. The Japanese ISDB signal is always encrypted by the B-CAS system even if it is a free television programme. That is why it is commonly called "Pay per view system without charge." An interface for mobile reception is under consideration.

ISDB supports RMP (Rights management and protection). Since all digitial television (DTV) systems carry digital data content, a DVD or high-definition (HD) recorder could easily copy content losslessly. Hollywood requested copy protection; this was the main reason for RMP being mandated. The content has three modes: "copy once", "copy free" and "copy never." In "copy once" mode, a programme can be stored on a hard disc recorder, but cannot be further copied; only moved to another copy-protected media—and this move operation will mark the content "copy one generation", which is mandated to permanently prevent further copying. "Copy never" programming may only be timeshifted and cannot be permanently stored. Currently, the Japanese government is evaluating using the Digital Transmission Content Protection (DTCP) "Encryption plus Non-Assertion" mechanism, to allow making multiple copies of digital content between compliant devices.

Receiver

There are two types of ISDB receiver: TV and STB (Set top box). The aspect ratio of ISDB television is 16:9; televisions fulfilling these specs are called Hi-vision TVs. There are three TV types: CRT (Cathode ray tube), PDP (Plasma display panel) and LCD (Liquid crystal display), with LCD being the most popular Hi-Vision format on the Japanese market right now.

LCD share as measured by JEITA in November 2004 was about 60 per cent. While PDP set occupies the high end market with units that are over 50 inches (1270 mm), PDP and CRT set shares are about 20 per cent each. CRT set are considered low end for Hi-Vision. STB is sometimes referred to as digital tuner. High-end ISDB STB have several interfaces:

- F connector(s) for RF input.
- D4 connector for HDTV monitor in home cinema.
- Optical digital audio interface for audio amplifier and speakers for 5.1 surround audio in a home cinema.
- IEEE 1394 (aka FireWire) interface for digital data recorders (like DVD recorders) in a home cinema.
- RCA video jack provides SDTV signal that is sampled down from the HDTV signal for analogue CRT television sets or VCRs.
- RCA audio jacks provide stereo audio for analogue CRT television sets or VCRs.
- S video are for VCRs or analogue CRT television sets.
- 10BASE-T/100BASE-T and modular jack telephone line modem interfaces for an internet connection.
- B-CAS card interface to de-scramble.
- IR interface jack for controlling a VHS or DVD player.

Problems

Though ISDB is a feature-rich system, many problems have surfaced recently.

Copy Protection Technology

Every TV broadcast (including free TV) is encrypted with "Copy-Once", which allows users to record to a digital media (D-VHS, DVD, HDD, etc.) but does not allow dubbing to another digital media. On the other hand, the "Copy-Once" technology does not prohibit all types of dubbing. It is possible to dub to an analogue media (such as standard VHS) and if recorded to an HDD, it will allow users to "Move" the contents to a D-VHS, but not copy. In contrast, 1seg digital broadcasts which are for low-bandwidth mobile reception and occupy 1/13th of a digital channel, are transmitted 'in the clear' and do not carry copy protection information.

Many users are also very worried about the recent news of severe protection in the future. There are modes in ISDB to not allow the output of signal from an Analogue connector (D-connector, Component, Composite, S-Video, etc.). There are already plans to not allow analogue output for "Copyright Protection" reasons. (Same as Blu-ray and HD DVD). This will make all currently sold STB Tuners, and the majority of LCD/ Plasma TVs without HDMI inputs unusable. Plus all analogue VHS, D-VHS that can only record via analogue input, and all DVD players will also become unusable. These more limiting copy protection technologies will all start after analogue broadcasting ends (when there won't be any choice for viewers). Currently, no financial assistance schemes have been announced, and viewers without proper devices will be forced to buy a new compatible TV or set top box in order to view ISDB broadcasts. Though not clear, it is said that there are also plans to protect all programmes with "Copy-Never."

The copy protection on ISDB broadcasts can be circumvented with the proper hardware and software.

B-CAS Card

The B-CAS card is required to decode all broadcasts. These cards are included with every digital TV or Tuner at no charge. To use this card, you must agree to the statement written on the registration card. Despite the fact that the card must be inserted to watch TV, if you don't agree to the statement, then the user cannot watch digital broadcasts. Essentially, users are "forced" to agree with the statement. Though registration is not required, it is recommended to fully enjoy interactive programmes. Unregistered B-CAS card displays a watermark in a corner of the screen, suggesting the user to register. However, many viewers worry about the leaking of personal information, and the power/rights the TV stations have to access personal information for almost every citizen in Japan. In case of loss or destruction, new B-CAS card of the same number can be issued for a fee of 2,000 yen.

Services

1. One HDTV or up to three SDTV services within one channel.
2. Provides Data broadcasting.
3. Interactive services such as games or shopping, via telephone line or broadband internet.
4. EPG (Electronic Programme Guide)
5. Ability to send firmware patches for the TV/tuner over the air.

ISDB-S

History

Japan started digital broadcasting using the DVB-S standard by PerfecTV in October/1996, and DirecTV in December/1997, with communication satellites. Still, DVB-S did not satisfy the requirements of Japanese broadcasters, such as NHK, key commercial broadcasting stations like , TBS, Fuji Television, TV Asahi, TV Tokyo, and WOWOW (Movie-only Pay-TV broadcasting). Consequently, ARIB developed the ISDB-S standards. The requirements were HDTV capability, interactive services, network access and effective frequency utilization, and other technical requirements. The DVB-S standard allows the transmission of a bit stream of roughly 34 Mbit/s with a satellite transponder, which means the transponder can send one HDTV channel. Unfortunately, the NHK broadcasting satellite had only four vacant transponders, which led ARIB and NHK to develop ISDB-S: The new standard could transmit at 51 Mbit/s with a single transponder, which means that ISDB-S is 1.5 times more efficient than DVB-S and that one transponder can transmit two HDTV channels, along with other independent audio and data. Digital satellite broadcasting (BS digital) was started by NHK and followed commercial broadcasting stations on 1 December 2000. Today, SKY PerfecTV!, successor of Skyport TV, and Sky D, CS burn, Platone, EP, DirecTV, J Sky B, and PerfecTV!, adopted the ISDB-S system for use on the 110 degree (east longitude) wide-band communication satellite.

Technical Specification

Summary of ISDB-S (Satellite digital broadcasting).

Transmission channel coding	*Modulation*	TC8PSK, QPSK, BPSK (Hierarchical transmission)	
	Error correction coding	Inner coding	Trellis [TC8PSK] and Convolution
		Outer coding	RS(204,188)
		TMCC	Convolution coding+RS
	Time domain multiplexing	TMCC	
Conditional Access		Multi-2	
Data broadcasting		ARIB STD B-24 (BML, ECMA script)	
Service information		ARIB STD B-10	
Multiplexing		MPEG-2 Systems	
Audio coding		MPEG-2 Audio(AAC)	
Video coding		MPEG-2 Video	

Channel

Frequency and channel specification of Japanese Satellites using ISDB-S.

Method	*BS digital broadcasting*	*Wide band CS digital broadcasting*
Frequency band	11.7 to 12.2 GHz	12.2 to 12.75 GHz
Transmission bit rate	51 Mbit/s (TC8PSK)	40 Mbit/s (QPSK)
Transmission band width	34.5 MHz*	34.5 MHz

Note: *Compatible with 27 MHz band satellite transponder for analogue FM broadcasting.

ISDB-T

History

HDTV was invented at NHK STRL (Japan Broadcasting

Corporation's Science and Technical Research Laboratories). The research of HDTV started as early as in the 1960s, though only in 1973 a standard was proposed to the ITU-R (CCIR). In the 1980s, the television camera, high definition cathode-ray tube, video tape recorder and editing equipment among others were developed. In 1982 NHK developed MUSE (Multiple sub-nyquist sampling Encoding), the first HDTV video compression and transmission system. MUSE adopted digital video compression system, but for transmission frequency modulation had been adopted after a digital-to-analogue converter converted the digital signal. In 1987, NHK made demonstration of MUSE in the Washington D.C. and NAB. The demonstration made great impression on the U.S. As a result of this, the U.S. developed ATSC, a terrestrial digital DTV system. Europe also developed their own DTV system, DVB. Japan started R&D of a completely digital system in the 1980s that led to ISDB. Japan started terrestrial digital broadcasting using ISDB-T standard by NHK and commercial broadcasting stations on the 1 December 2003.

Feature

ISDB-T is characterized by the following features:

- ISDB-T (Integrated Services Digital Broadcasting-Terrestrial) use UHF470 MHz-770 MHz, bandwidth of 300 MHz, allocate 50 channels, namely ch.13-ch.62, each channel is 6 MHz width (actually 5.572 MHz effective bandwidth and 430 kHz guard band between channels).
- These 50 channels, ch.13-ch.62, are called "physical channel".
- ISDB-T single channel bandwidths 5.572 MHz has number of carriers 5,617 with interval of 0.99206 kHz.
- ISDB-T allows to switch to two or three SDTV channels instead of one HDTV channel (multiplexing SDTV channels).
- Each channel is further divided into 13 segments. 1seg uses only single segment, and the remainder can be allocated as (1) one 12-segments HDTV programme, (2) three 4-segments SDTV programmes, or (3) one 8-segments (Medium Definition) programme and one 4-segments SDTV programme, broadcasted from a single

TV station as the *multiple-programme arrangement Maruchi hensei?*) in simultaneous broadcasting.

- ◆ The single segment for 1seg is further divided and broadcasting as *multiple-programme arrangement*.

- The combination of these services (1), (2) or (3) can be changed at anytime. Mostly NHK Educational TV and Open University of Japan broadcasts with these 3 modes appropriately.
- ISDB-T transmits a HDTV channel and a mobile TV channel 1seg within the 6 MHz bandwidth.
- ISDB-T provides interactive services with data broadcasting.
- ISDB-T provides EPG (Electronic Programme Guides).
- ISDB-T supports internet access as a return channel that works to support the data broadcasting. Internet access is also provided on mobile phones.
- ISDB-T provides SFN (Single Frequency Network) and on-channel repeater technology. SFN makes efficient utilization of the frequency resource (spectrum).
- ISDB-T can be received indoors with a simple indoor antenna.
- ISDB-T provides robustness to multipath interference ("ghosting").
- ISDB-T provides robustness to co-channel analogue television interference.
- ISDB-T provides robustness to electromagnetic interferences that come from motor vehicles and power lines in urban environments.
- ISDB-T is claimed to allow HDTV to be received on moving vehicles at over 100 km/h (this has not yet been proven in real-world operation); DVB-T can only receive SDTV on moving vehicles, and it is claimed that ATSC cannot be received on moving vehicles at all (however, in early 2007 there were reports of successful reception of ATSC on laptops using USB tuners in moving vehicles).
- 1seg is a mobile terrestrial digital audio/video broadcasting service in Japan. Although 1seg is designed for mobile usage, reception has proved problematic in moving vehicles. Because of reception on high speed

vehicle, UHF transmission is shaded by buildings and hills frequently, but reported well receiving in Shinkansen as far as run in flat or rural area.

Adoption

ISDB-T was adopted for commercial transmissions in Japan in December 2003. It currently comprises a market of about 100 million television sets. ISDB-T had 10 million subscribers by the end of April 2005. Along with the wide use of ISDB-T, the price of STB is getting low. The price of ISDB-T STB in the lower end of the market is ¥19800 as of 19 April 2006. (Japanese) uniden. By November 2007 only a few older, low-end STB models could be found in the Japanese market (average price U$180,-) showing a tendency towards replacement by high end equipment like PVRs and TV sets with inbuilt tuners. The Dibeg web page (http://www.dibeg.org/news/news-5/news-e5.htm#dn068e) confirms this tendency by showing low significance of the digital tuner STB market in Japan.

Brazil, which currently uses an analogue TV system (PAL-M) that slightly differs from any other countries, has chosen ISDB-T modulation for its DTV format, calling it SBTVD-T (*Sistema Brasileiro de Televisão Digital-Terrestre*). SBTVD-T differs from ISDB-T in that it uses the H.264 video codec instead of ISDB-T's MPEG2 and an improved tuner. Other than Brazil, there are a few countries, mainly from Mercosur, such as Argentina, Chile and Venezuela are considering ISDB-T-based SBTVD which could provide common market benefits from the regional South American development of the technology instead of importing it, as is the case with the other standards. Also, it seems to have an advantage over ATSC and DVB-T in reception tests. Nevertheless, in August 2007 Uruguay officially chose DVB-T + DVB-H as its DTV standard. Chile, which was set to make an official decision on late December 2007 later delayed its decision until March 2008.

The ABERT/SET group in Brazil did system comparison tests of DTV under the supervision of the CPqD foundation. The comparison tests were done under the direction of a work group of SET (the Brazilian Television Engineering Society) and ABERT (the Brazilian Association of Radio and Television Broadcasters). The ABERT/SET group selected ISDB-T as the best choice in digital broadcasting modulation systems among ATSC, DVB-T and ISDB-T. ISDB-T was singled out as the most flexible of all for meeting the needs of mobility and portability. It is most efficient for mobile and portable reception. In June 29, 2006, Brazil announced ISDB-T-based SBTVD as the chosen standard for Digital TV transmissions, to be fully implemented by 2016. By November 2007 (one month prior DTTV launch), a few suppliers started to announce zapper STBs of the new Nippon-Brazilian SBTVD-T Standard, at that time without interactivity.

The implementation rollout at Brazil is proceeding successfully although some say the implementation could be more accelerated. It terms of broadcasting, the implementation plan seems to be on target once in only 8 months since the start the digital signal is present in 4 state capitals and till end of 2008 other 3 capitals will receive the signal. In terms of end-customers the implementation could be better once till the moment it is estimated only 20,000 set-top boxes sold. Part of this low sales number can be explained by the prices that in the beginning ranged from BRL 600 to BRL 1,100. However recently new set-top boxes were launched in market at R$300 (aprox US$ 150); that will probably increase set-top box sales. Other reason to explain low sales level is the interactivity service not available yet. That is because the "middleware" developed by Brazilian universities (PUC Rio and Federal Univerity of Paraiba) will be finished only on October/2008. Once finished it is expected the interactivity will be a strong appeal bringing more and more people to Digital TV world. Addidionally mobile TV was started with success with Samsung and Toshiba cell phones, presenting very high quality and the best: Digital TV service for free! That is very impressive conquest once in a short period since launched Brazil is already offering digital mobile TV for free. In other countries such accomplishment occoured years later, and in some countries like USA and European countries this reality is far from reality and probably would not be for free.

Now Argentina is studying the adoption of ISDB-T. The idea is to implement ISDB-T to the whole Mercosur players (exception of Uruguay) with obvious gains in scale. Other countries testing/ studying ISDB-T standard: Chile, Venezuela and Peru.

Technical Specification

Segment Structure

ARIB has developed a segment structure called BST-OFDM. ISDB-T divides the frequency band of one channel into thirteen segments.

The broadcaster can select which combination of segments to use; this choice of segment structure allows for service flexibility. For example, ISDB-T can transmit both LDTV and HDTV using one TV channel or change to 3 SDTV, a switch that can be performed at any time. ISDB-T can also change the modulation scheme at the same time.

s11	s 9	s 7	s 5	s 3	s 1	s 0	s 2	s 4	s 6	s 8	s10	s12

Fig.5.1: Spectrum of 13 segments structure of ISDB-T (s0 is generally used for 1seg, s1-s12 are used for one HDTV or three SDTVs)

Summary of ISDB-T

Transmission channel coding	Modulation	64QAM-OFDM, 16QAM-OFDM, QPSK-OFDM, DQPSK-OFDM (Hierarchical transmission)
	Error correction coding	Inner coding, Convolution 7/8,3/4,2/3,1/2 Outer coding: RS(204,188)
	Guard interval	1/16,1/8,1/4
	Interleaving	Time, Frequency, bit, byte
	Frequency domain multiplexing	BST-OFDM (Segmented structure OFDM)
	Conditional Access	Multi-2
	Data broadcasting	ARIB STD B-24 (BML, ECMA script)
	Service information	ARIB STD B-10
	Multiplexing	MPEG-2 Systems
	Audio coding	MPEG-2 Audio (AAC)
	Video coding	MPEG-2 Video | MPEG-4 AVC/H.264*

Note: * H.264 used in one segment (1seg) broadcasting for portables and Mobile phone.

Channel

Specification of Japanese terrestrial digital broadcasting using ISDB-T.

Method	terrestrial digital broadcasting
Frequency band	VHF/UHF, Super high band
Transmission bit rate	19 Mbit/s(64QAM)
Transmission band width	5.6 MHz*

Note: * Compatible to 6 MHz band terrestrial analogue TV broadcasting.

2.6 GHz Mobile Satellite Digital Audio/Video Broadcasting

MobaHo! is the name of the services that uses the Mobile satellite digital audio broadcasting specifications. MobaHo! started its service on 20 October, 2004.

ISDB-Tsb

ISDB-Tsb is the terrestrial digital sound broadcasting specification. The technical specification is the same as ISDB-T. ISDB-Tsb supports the coded transmission of OFDM signals.

ISDB-C

ISDB-C is cable digital broadcasting specification. The technical specification is developed by JCTEA.

ISDB-Tmm

ISDB-Tmm (Terrestrial mobile multi-media) will use suitable number of segments by station with video coding MPEG-4 AVC/ H.264. With multiple channel, ISDB-Tmm will serve for dedicating contents such as sport, movie, music channel and other with CD quality sound.This service will use VHF band, 170-222 MHz after analogue television close down in July 2011.

Standards

ARIB and JCTEA developed the following standards has been given Table 5.1.

Table of Terrestrial HDTV Transmission Systems

HDTV Transmission Systems has been given in Table 5.2.

Countries and territories using ISDB-T

Asia/Pacific

- Japan
- Philippines (experimental)

Americas

- Brazil (MPEG-4 and AAC)
- Argentina (Experimental)

Table 5.1: ARIB and JCTEA Developed Standards

Channel	*Communication Satellite television digital broadcasting*	*Broadcasting/ Communication Satellite television digital broadcasting*	*Terrestrial television digital broadcasting*	*Satellite Sound digital broadcasting*	*Terrestrial Sound digital broadcasting*	*Cable television digital broadcasting*
Nick name	—	ISDB-S	ISDB-T	2.6 GHz mobile broadcasting	ISDB-Tsb	64QAM, Trans-modulation (ISDB-C)
Transmission	DVB-S	ARIB STD-B20, ITU-R BO.1408	ARIB STD-B31, ITU-R BT.1306-1	ARIB STD-B41	ARIB STD-B29, ITU-R BS.1114	ITU-T J.83 Annex C, J.183
Receiver	ARIB STD-B16	ARIB STD-B21		ARIB STD-B42	ARIB STD-B30	JCTEA STD-004, STD-007
Server type broadcasting	—	ARIB STD-B38				—
Conditional access	—	ARIB STD-B25 (Multi-2)				JCTEA STD-001
Service information	—	ARIB STD-B10				JCTEA STD-003
Data broadcasting	—	ARIB STD-B24 (BML), ARIB STD-B23 (EE or MHP like)				—
Video/Audio compression and multiplexing	MPEG-2	ARIB STD-B32 (MPEG)				—
Technical report	—	ARIB TR-B13	ARIB TR-B14	—	—	—

Table 5.2: Main Characteristics of Three DTTB Systems

Systems	*ATSC 8-VSB*	*DVB COFDM*	*ISDB BST-COFDM*
Source coding			
Video	Main profile syntax of ISO/IEC 13818-2 (MPEG-2 video)		
Audio	ATSC Standard A/52 (Dolby AC-3)	ISO/IEC 13818-2 (MPEG-2 layer II audio) and Dolby AC-3	ISO/IEC 13818-7 (MPEG-2 AAC audio)
Transmission system			
Channel coding		—	
Outer coding	R-S (207, 187, t = 10)	R-S (204, 188, t = 8)	
Outer interleaver	52 R-S block interleaver	12 R-S block interleaver	
Inner coding	Rate 2/3 trellis code	Punctured convolution code: Rate 1/2, 2/3,3/4, 5/6, 7/8 Constraint length = 7, Polynomials (octal) = 171, 133	
Inner interleaver	12 to 1 trellis code interleaver	Bit-wise interleaving and frequency interleaving	Bit-wise interleaving, frequency interleaving and selectable time interleaving
Data randomization		16-bit PRBS	
Modulation	8-VSB and 16-VSB	COFDM QPSK, 16QAM and 64QAM Hierarchical modulation: multi-resolution constellation (16QAM and 64 QAM) Guard interval: 1/32, 1/16, 1/8 & 1/4 of OFDM symbol 2 modes: 2k and 8k FFT	BST-COFDM with 13 frequency segments DQPSK, QPSK, 16QAM and 64QAM Hierarchical modulation: choice of three different modulations on each segment Guard interval: 1/32, 1/16, 1/8 & 1/4 of OFDM symbol 3 modes: 2k, 4k and 8k FFT

- Ecuador (Experimental)
- Bolivia (Experimental)
- Chile (Experimental)
- Peru (Experimental)
- Venezuela (Experimental).

6

Wireless Communication System: Kinds, Tools and Techniques

WIRELESS

Wireless communication is the transfer of *information* over a distance without the use of electrical conductors or "wires." The distances involved may be short (a few meters as in television remote control) or very long (thousands or even millions of kilometers for radio communications). When the context is clear the term is often simply shortened to "wireless." Wireless communications is generally considered to be a branch of telecommunications.

It encompasses various types of fixed, mobile, and portable two way radios, cellular telephones, personal digital assistants (PDAs), and wireless networking. Other examples of *wireless technology* include GPS units, garage door openers and/or garage doors, wireless computer mice, keyboards and headsets, satellite television and cordless telephones.

Introduction

Wireless operations permits services, such as long range communications, that are impossible or impractical to implement with the use of wires. The term is commonly used in the telecommunications industry to refer to telecommunications systems (e.g., radio transmitters and receivers, remote controls, computer networks, network terminals, etc.) which use some form of energy (e.g. radio frequency (RF), infrared light, laser light, visible light, acoustic energy, etc.) to transfer information without the use of wires. Information is transferred in this manner over both short and long distances.

Communication

The term "wireless" has become a generic and all-encompassing word used to describe communications in which electromagnetic waves or RF (rather than some form of wire) carry a signal over part or the entire communication path. Common examples of wireless equipment in use today include:

- Professional LMR (Land Mobile Radio) and SMR (Specialized Mobile Radio) typically used by business, industrial and Public Safety entities.
- Consumer Two Way Radio including FRS (Family Radio Service), GMRS (General Mobile Radio Service) and Citizens band ("CB") radios.
- The Amateur Radio Service (*Ham radio*).
- Consumer and professional Marine VHF radios.
- *Cellular telephones and pagers*: provide connectivity for portable and mobile applications, both personal and business.
- *Global Positioning System* (GPS): allows drivers of cars and trucks, captains of boats and ships, and pilots of aircraft to ascertain their location anywhere on earth.
- *Cordless computer peripherals*: the cordless mouse is a common example; keyboards and printers can also be linked to a computer via wireless.
- *Cordless telephone sets*: these are limited-range devices, not to be confused with cell phones.
- *Satellite television*: allows viewers in almost any location to select from hundreds of channels.

Wireless networking (i.e. the various flavours of unlicensed 2.4 GHz WiFi devices) is used to meet a variety of needs. Perhaps the most common use is to connect laptop users who travel from location to location. Another common use is for mobile networks that connect via satellite. A wireless transmission method is a logical choice to network a LAN segment that must frequently change locations. The following situations justify the use of wireless technology:

- To span a distance beyond the capabilities of typical cabling,

- To avoid obstacles such as physical structures, EMI, or RFI,
- To provide a backup communications link in case of normal network failure,
- To link portable or temporary workstations,
- To overcome situations where normal cabling is difficult or financially impractical, or
- To remotely connect mobile users or networks.

Wireless communication may be via:

- radio frequency communication,
- microwave communication, for example long-range line-of-sight via highly directional antennas, or short-range communication, or
- infrared (IR) short-range communication, for example from remote controls or via IRDA.

Applications may involve point-to-point communication, point-to-multipoint communication, broadcasting, cellular networks and other wireless networks. The term "wireless" should not be confused with the term "cordless", which is generally used to refer to powered electrical or electronic devices that are able to operate from a portable power source (e.g., a battery pack) without any cable or *cord* to limit the mobility of the cordless device through a connection to the main power supply. Some cordless devices, such as cordless telephones, are also wireless in the sense that information is transferred from the cordless telephone to the telephone's base unit via some type of wireless communications link. This has caused some disparity in the usage of the term "cordless", for example in Digital Enhanced Cordless Telecommunications.

In the last 50 years, wireless communications industry experienced drastic changes driven by many technology innovations.

History

The term "Wireless" came into public use to refer to a radio receiver or transceiver (a dual purpose receiver and transmitter device), establishing its usage in the field of wireless telegraphy early on; now the term is used to describe modern wireless connections such as in cellular networks and wireless broadband Internet. It is also used in a general sense to refer to any type of operation that is implemented without the use of wires, such as "wireless remote control", "wireless energy transfer", etc. regardless of the specific technology (e.g., radio, infrared, ultrasonic, etc.) that is used to accomplish the operation.

Early Wireless Work

David E. Hughes, eight years before Hertz's experiments, induced electromagnetic waves in a signalling system. Hughes transmitted Morse code by an induction apparatus. In 1878, Hughes's induction transmission method utilized a "clockwork transmitter" to transmit signals. In 1885, T.A. Edison used a vibrator magnet for induction transmission. In 1888, Edison deploys a system of signalling on the Lehigh Valley Railroad. In 1891, Edison attains the wireless patent for this method using inductance (U.S. Patent 465,971).

In the history of wireless technology, the demonstration of the theory of electromagnetic waves by Heinrich Rudolf Hertz in 1888 was important. The theory of electromagnetic waves were predicted from the research of James Clerk Maxwell and Michael Faraday. Hertz demonstrated that electromagnetic waves could be transmitted and caused to travel through space at straight lines and that they were able to be received by an experimental apparatus. The experiments were not followed up by Hertz and the practical applications of the wireless communication and remote control technology would be implemented by Nikola Tesla.

Further Information: Invention of Radio

Electromagnetic Spectrum

Light, colours, AM and FM radio, and electronic devices make use of the electromagnetic spectrum. In the US the frequencies that are available for use for communication are treated as a public resource and are regulated by the Federal Communications Commission. This determines which frequency ranges can be used for what purpose and by whom. In the absence of such control or alternative arrangements such as a privatized electromagnetic spectrum, chaos might result if, for example, airlines did not have specific frequencies to work under and an amateur radio operator was interfering with the pilot's ability to land an airplane. Wireless communication spans the spectrum from 9 kHz to 300 GHz.

Applications of Wireless Technology

Security Systems

- Wireless technology may supplement or replace hard wired implementations in security systems for homes or office buildings.

Television Remote Control

- Modern televisions use wireless (generally infrared) remote control units. Now we also use radio waves.

Cellular Telephony (phones and modems)

Perhaps the best known example of wireless technology is the cellular telephone and modems. These instruments use radio waves to enable the operator to make phone calls from many locations world-wide. They can be used anywhere that there is a cellular telephone site to house the equipment that is required to transmit and receive the signal that is used to transfer both voice and data to and from these instruments.

Categories of Wireless Implementations, Devices and Standards

- Radio communication system.
- Broadcasting.
- Amateur radio.
- Communication radio.
- Cordless telephony: DECT (Digital Enhanced Cordless Telecommunications).
- Cellular systems: 0G, 1G, 2G, 3G, Beyond 3G (4G), Future wireless.
- List of emerging technologies.
- Short-range point-to-point communication: Wireless microphones, Remote controls, IrDA, RFID (Radio Frequency Identification), Wireless USB, DSRC (Dedicated Short Range Communications), EnOcean, Near Field Communication.

- Wireless sensor networks: ZigBee, EnOcean; Personal area networks, Bluetooth, Ultra-wideband (UWB from WiMedia Alliance).
- Wireless computer networks: Wireless Local Area Networks (WLAN), (IEEE 802.11 branded as WiFi and HiperLAN), Wireless Metropolitan Area Networks (WMAN) and Broadband Fixed Access (BWA) (LMDS, WiMAX, WANKA and HiperMAN).

WIRELESS LOCAL LOOP

Wireless local loop (WLL), is a term for the use of a wireless communications link as the "last mile/first mile" connection for delivering plain old telephone service (POTS) and/or broadband Internet to telecommunications customers. Various types of WLL systems and technologies exist.

Other terms for this type of access include Broadband Wireless Access (BWA), Radio In The Loop (RITL), Fixed-Radio Access (FRA) and Fixed Wireless Access (FWA).

Definition of Fixed Wireless Service

Fixed Wireless Terminal (FWT) units differ from conventional mobile terminal units operating within cellular networks such as GSM in that a fixed wireless terminal or desk phone will be limited to an almost permanent location with almost no roaming abilities.

WLL and FWTs are generic terms for radio based telecommunications technologies and the respective devices which can be implemented using a number of different wireless and radio technologies.

Wireless Local Loop service is segmented into a number of broad market and deployment groups. Services are split between Licensed—commonly used by Carriers and Telcos—and Unlicensed services more commonly deployed by home users and Wireless ISPs (WISPs).

Licensed Point to Point Microwave Service

Licensed Microwave service has been used since the 1960s to transmit very large amounts of data. The AT&T Long Lines coast to coast backbone in the USA was largely carried over a chain of microwave towers. These systems have been largely using 3700-4200 MHz and 5000-6200 MHz. The 5 GHz band was even known as the "common carrier" band. This service typically was prohibitively expensive to be used for Local Loop, and was used for backbone networks. In the 1980s and 1990s it flourished under the growth of cell towers. This growth spurred research in this area, and as the cost continues to decline, it is being used as an alternative to T-1, T-3, and fiber connectivity.

Licensed Point to Multi Point Microwave Service

Multipoint microwave licenses are generally more expensive than point to point licenses. A single point to point system could be installed and licensed for 50,000 to 200,000 USD. A multipoint license would start in the millions of dollars. Multichannel Multipoint Distribution Service (MMDS) and Local Multipoint Distribution Service (LMDS) were the first true multi point services for wireless local loop. While Europe and the rest of the world developed the 3500 MHz band for affordable broadband fixed wireless, the U.S. provided LMDS and MMDS, and most implementations in the United States were conducted at 2500 MHz. The largest was Sprint Broadband's deployment of Hybrid Networks equipment. Sprint was plagued with difficulties operating the network profitably, and service was often spotty, due to inadequate radio link quality.

Unlicensed Multi Point Wireless Service

Most of the growth in long range radio communications since 2002 has been in the license free bands (mostly 900 MHz, 2.4 GHz and 5.8 GHz). Global Pacific Internet and Innetix started wireless service in California in 1995 using Breezecom (Alvarion) frequency hopping radio which later became the standard 802.11. Few years later Terago Networks in Canada and NextWeb Networks of Fremont beginning deploying reliable license free service. For Nextweb they originally deployed 802.11b equipment and later switched to Axxcelera which uses propriety protocol.

1995-2004: License-Free Equipment

Most of the early vendors of license free fixed wireless equipment such as Adaptive Broadband (Axxcelera), Trango Broadband,

Motorola (Orthogon), Proxim Networks, RedLine and BreezeCom (Alvarion) used proprietary protocols and hardware, creating pressure on the industry to adopt a standard for unlicensed fixed wireless. These Mac Layers typically used a 15-20 MHz channel using Direct Sequence Spread Spectrum and BPSK, CCK and QPSK for modulation.

These devices all describe the customer premises wireless system as the Subscriber Unit "SU", and the operator transmitter delivering the last mile local loop services as the "Access Point" (AP). 802.11 uses the terms AP and STA (Station).

2002-2005: Wi-Fi Local Loop

Originally designed for short range mobile internet and local area network access, 802.11 has emerged as the *de facto* standard for unlicensed Wireless Local Loop. More 802.11 equipment is deployed for long range data service than any other technology. These systems have provided varying results, as the operators were often small and poorly trained in radio communications, additionally 802.11 was not intended to be used at long ranges and suffered from a number of problems, such as the hidden node problem. Many companies such as KarlNet began modifying the 802.11 MAC to attempt to deliver higher performance at long ranges.

2005 Present: Maturation of the Wireless ISP Market

In nearly every metropolitan area worldwide, operators and hobbyists deployed more and more unlicensed broadband point to multipoint systems. Providers that had rave reviews when they started faced the prospect of seeing their networks degrade in performance, as more and more devices were deployed using the license free U-NII (5.3/5.4 GHz) and ISM (2.4 and 5.8 GHz) bands and competitors sprung up around them.

The Growing Interference Problem

Interference caused the majority of unlicensed wireless services to have much higher error rates and interruptions than equivalent wired or licensed wireless networks, such as the copper telephone network, and the coaxial cable network. This caused growth to slow, customers to cancel, and many operators to rethink their business model.

There were several responses to these problems.

2003: Voluntary Frequency Coordination (USA)

NextWeb, Etheric Networks, GateSpeed and a handful of other companies founded the first voluntary spectrum coordination body—working entirely independently of government regulators. This organization was founded in March 2003 as BANC, "Bay Area Network Coordination." By maintaining frequencies used in an interoperator database, disruptions between coordinating parties were minimized, as well as the cost of identifying new or changing transmission sources, by using the frequency database to determine what bands were in use. Because the parties in BANC comprised the majority of operators in the Bay Area, they used peer pressure to imply that operators who did not play nice would be collectively punished by the group, through interfering with the non cooperative, while striving not to interfere with the cooperative. BANC was then deployed in Los Angeles. Companies such as Deutsche Telekom joined. It looked like the idea had promise.

2005: Operators Flee Unlicensed for Licensed

The better capitalized operators began reducing their focus on unlicensed and instead focused on licensed systems, as the constant fluctuations in signal quality caused them to have very high maintenance costs. NextWeb, acquired by Covad for a very small premium over the capital invested in it, is one operator who focused on licensed service, as did WiLine. This led to fewer of the more responsible and significant operators actually using the BANC system. Without its founders active involvement, the system languished.

2005 to Present: Operators Develop Adaptive Network Technology

Operators began to apply the principles of self healing networks. Etheric Networks followed this path. Etheric Networks focused on improving performance by developing dynamic interference and fault detection and reconfiguration. As well as optimizing quality based routing software, such as MANET and using multiple paths to deliver service to customers. This approach is generally called "Mesh Networking" which relies on Ad-hoc Networking Protocols, however Mesh and ad-hoc networking protocols have yet to deliver high speed low latency business class end to end reliable local loop service, as the paths can sometimes traverse exponentially more radio links than a traditional star (AP->SU) topology.

Adaptive network management actively monitors the local loop quality and behaviour, using automation to reconfigure the network and its traffic flows, to avoid interference and other failures.

2006-2008: The Next Technology—WiMAX (or IEEE 802.16)

Currently more operators are running on the 802.11 MAC at 2 and 5 GHz. 802.16 is unlikely to outperform 802.11 until unlicensed 802.16 equipment becomes available. It may become the dominant medium for wireless local loop. Intel is promoting this standard, while Atheros and Broadcom are still focused largely on 802.11. Atheros, using its highly successful 802.11 OFDM chipsets, will likely be able to deliver comparable service levels to Intel's 802.16 TDM OFDM chipsets for the foreseeable future.

Mobile Technologies

These are available in Code Division Multiple Access (CDMA), Digital Enhanced Cordless Telecommunications—DECT (TDMA/DCA) (See ETSI 6 EN 300 765-1 V1.3.1 (2001-04) -"Digital Enhanced Cordless Telecommunications (DECT); Radio in the Local Loop (RLL); Access Profile (RAP); Part 1: Basic telephony services"), Global System for Mobile Communications (GSM), IS136 Time Division Multiple Access (TDMA) as well as analogue access technologies such as Advanced Mobile Phone System (AMPS), for which there will be independent standards defining every aspect of modulation, protocols, error handling, etc.

Deployment

The Wireless Local Loop market is currently an extremely high growth market, offering Internet Service Providers immediate access to customer markets without having to either lay cable through a metropolitan area MTA, or work through the ILECs, reselling the telephone, cable or satellite networks, owned by companies that prefer to largely sell direct.

This trend revived the prospects for local and regional ISPs, as those willing to deploy fixed wireless networks were not at the mercy of the large telecommunication monopolies. They were at the mercy of unregulated re-use of unlicensed frequencies upon which they communicate.

Due to the enormous quantity of 802.11 "Wi-Fi" equipment and software, coupled with the fact that spectrum licenses are not required in the ISM and U-NII bands, the industry has moved well ahead of the regulators and the standards bodies.

Sprint and ClearWire were preparing to roll out massive WiMAX networks in the United States, but those talks may be stalled pending new investment.

Wireless Local Loop (WLL) Standards

(*i*) *Mobile*:

- CDMA (USA).
- TDMA (USA).
- GSM (ITU—Worldwide).
- UMTS 3rd Generation (World).
- Personal Handy-phone System (PHS in Japan, PAS/ Xiaolingtong in China).

(*ii*) *Fixed or local area network*:

- DECT, for local loop.
- LMDS.
- 802.11, originally designed for short range mobile internet and network access service, it has emerged as the facto standard for Wireless Local Loop.
- WiMAX or IEEE 802.16 may become the dominant medium for wireless local loop. Currently more operators are running on the 802.11 MAC at 2 and 5 GHz. 802.16 is unlikely to outperform 802.11 until at least late 2008. Intel is promoting this standard, while Atheros and Broadcom are still focused largely on 802.11.
- Satellite Internet for autonomous building.

Manufacturers

- Airspan

- SR Telecom
- Alvarion
- Alloyant
- Cambridge Broadband
- P-Com
- Sony-Ericsson

WI-FI

Wi-Fi is the trade name for the popular wireless technology used in home networks, mobile phones, video games and more. In particular, it covers the various IEEE 802.11 technologies (including 802.11n, 802.11b, 802.11g, and 802.11a).

Wi-Fi technologies are supported by nearly every modern personal computer operating system, most advanced game consoles and Laptops, and many printers, and other peripherals.

Purpose

The purpose of Wi-Fi is to hide complexity by enabling wireless access to applications and data, media and streams. The main aims of Wi-Fi are the following:

- make access to information easier,
- ensure compatibility and co-existence of devices,
- eliminate cabling and wiring, and
- eliminate switches, adapters, plugs, pins and connectors.

Uses

A Wi-Fi enabled device such as a PC, game console, mobile phone, MP3 player or PDA can connect to the Internet when within range of a wireless network connected to the Internet. The coverage of one or more interconnected access points called a hotspot can comprise an area as small as a single room with wireless-opaque walls or as large as many square miles covered by overlapping access points. Wi-Fi technology has served to set up mesh networks, for example, in London. Both architectures can operate in community networks.

In addition to restricted use in homes and offices, Wi-Fi can make access publicly available at Wi-Fi hotspots provided either free of charge or to subscribers to various providers. Organizations and businesses such as airports, hotels and restaurants often provide free hotspots to attract or assist clients. Enthusiasts or authorities who wish to provide services or even to promote business in a given area sometimes provide free Wi-Fi access. Metropolitan-wide Wi-Fi (Muni-Fi) already has more than 300 projects in process. There were 879 Wi-Fi based Wireless Internet service providers in the Czech Republic as of May 2008.

Wi-Fi also allows connectivity in peer-to-peer (wireless ad-hoc network) mode, which enables devices to connect directly with each other. This connectivity mode can prove useful in consumer electronics and gaming applications.

When wireless networking technology first entered the market many problems ensued for consumers who could not rely on products from different vendors working together. The Wi-Fi Alliance began as a community to solve this issue—aiming to address the needs of the end-user and to allow the technology to mature. The Alliance created the branding *Wi-Fi CERTIFIED* to reassure consumers that products will interoperate with other products displaying the same branding.

Many consumer devices use Wi-Fi. Amongst others, personal computers can network to each other and connect to the Internet, mobile computers can connect to the Internet from any Wi-Fi hotspot, and digital cameras can transfer images wirelessly.

Routers which incorporate a DSL-modem or a cable-modem and a Wi-Fi access point, often set up in homes and other premises, provide Internet-access and internetworking to all devices connected (wirelessly or by cable) to them. One can also connect Wi-Fi devices in ad-hoc mode for client-to-client connections without a router.

As of 2007 Wi-Fi technology had spread widely within business and industrial sites. In business environments, just like other environments, increasing the number of Wi-Fi access-points provides redundancy, support for fast roaming and increased overall network-capacity by using more channels or by defining smaller cells. Wi-Fi enables wireless voice-applications (VoWLAN or WVOIP). Over the years, Wi-Fi implementations have moved toward "thin" access-points, with more of the network intelligence housed in a centralized network appliance, relegating individual access-points to the role of mere "dumb" radios. Outdoor applications may utilize true mesh topologies. As of 2007 Wi-Fi installations can provide a secure computer networking gateway, firewall, DHCP server, intrusion detection system, and other functions.

Advantages and Challenges

Operational Advantages

Wi-Fi allows LANs (Local Area Networks) to be deployed without cabling for client devices, typically reducing the costs of network deployment and expansion. Spaces where cables cannot be run, such as outdoor areas and historical buildings, can host wireless LANs. In 2008, wireless network adapters are built into most modern laptops. The price of chipsets for Wi-Fi continues to drop, making it an economical networking option included in even more devices. Wi-Fi has become widespread in corporate infrastructures.

Different competitive brands of access points and client network interfaces are inter-operable at a basic level of service. Products designated as "Wi-Fi Certified" by the Wi-Fi Alliance are backwards compatible. Wi-Fi is a global set of standards. Unlike mobile telephones, any standard Wi-Fi device will work anywhere in the world.

Wi-Fi is widely available in more than 220,000 public hotspots and tens of millions of homes and corporate and university campuses worldwide. WPA is not easily cracked if strong passwords are used and encryption has no known weaknesses. New protocols for Quality of Service (WMM) make Wi-Fi more suitable for latency-sensitive applications (such as voice and video), and power saving mechanisms (WMM Power Save) improve battery operation.

Limitations

Spectrum assignments and operational limitations are not consistent worldwide. Most of Europe allows for an additional 2 channels beyond those permitted in the U.S. for the 2.4 GHz band. (1–13 *vs.* 1–11); Japan has one more on top of that (1–14). Europe, as of 2007, was essentially homogeneous in this respect. A very confusing aspect is the fact that a Wi-Fi signal actually occupies five channels in the 2.4 GHz band resulting in only three non-overlapped channels in the U.S.: 1, 6, 11, and three or four in Europe: 1, 5, 9, 13 can be used if all the equipment on a specific area can be granted not to use 802.11b at all, even as fallback or beacon. Equivalent isotropically radiated power (EIRP) in the EU is limited to 20 dBm (0.1 W).

Reach

Due to reach requirements for wireless LAN applications, power consumption is fairly high compared to some other low-bandwidth standards. Especially Zigbee and Bluetooth supporting wireless PAN applications refer to much lesser propagation range of <10 m (ref. e.g. IEEE Std. 802.15.4 section 1.2 scope). Range is always making battery life a concern.

Wi-Fi networks have limited range. A typical Wi-Fi home router using 802.11b or 802.11g with a stock antenna might have a range of 32 m (120 ft) indoors and 95 m (300 ft) outdoors. Range also varies with frequency band. Wi-Fi in the 2.4 GHz frequency block has slightly better range than Wi-Fi in the 5 GHz frequency block. Outdoor range with improved (directional) antennas can be several kilometres or more with line-of-sight.

Wi-Fi performance decreases roughly quadratically as the range increases at constant radiation levels.

Mobility

Because of the very limited practical range of Wi-Fi, mobile use is essentially confined to such applications as inventory taking machines in warehouses or retail spaces, reading devices at check-out stands or receiving/shipping stations. Mobile use of Wi-Fi over wider ranges is limited to move, use, move, as for instance in an automobile moving from one hotspot to another.

Threats to security

The most common wireless encryption standard, Wired Equivalent Privacy or WEP, has been shown to be easily breakable even when correctly configured. Wi-Fi Protected Access (WPA and WPA2), which began shipping in 2003, aims to solve this problem and is now available on most products. Wi-Fi Access Points typically default to an "open" (encryption-free) mode. Novice users benefit from a zero-configuration device that works out of the box, but this default is without any wireless security enabled, providing open wireless access to their LAN. To turn security on requires the user to configure the device, usually via a software graphical user interface (GUI). Wi-Fi networks that are open (unencrypted) can be monitored and used to read and copy data (including personal information) transmitted over the network, unless another security method is used to secure the data, such as a VPN or a secure web page.

Population

Many 2.4 GHz 802.11b and 802.11g Access points default to the same channel on initial startup, contributing to congestion on certain channels. To change the channel of operation for an access point requires the user to configure the device. Yet, this default use of channels 1, 6 and 11 gives better performance than "advanced" users choosing channels 2, 5, 7 and 9 as "unused, free".

Channel Pollution

Standardization is a process driven by market forces. Interoperability issues between non-Wi-Fi brands or proprietary deviations from the standard can still disrupt connections or lower throughput speeds on all user's devices that are within range, to include the non-Wi-Fi or proprietary product. Moreover, the usage of the ISM band in the 2.45 GHz range is also common to Bluetooth, WPAN-CSS, ZigBee and any new system will take its share.

Wi-Fi pollution, or an excessive number of access points in the area, especially on the same or neighbouring channel, can prevent access and interfere with the use of other access points by others, caused by overlapping channels in the 802.11g/b spectrum, as well as with decreased signal-to-noise ratio (SNR) between access points. This can be a problem in high-density areas, such as large apartment complexes or office buildings with many Wi-Fi access points. Additionally, other devices use the 2.4 GHz band: microwave ovens, security cameras, Bluetooth devices and (in some countries) Amateur radio, video senders, cordless phones and baby monitors, all of which can cause significant additional interference. General guidance to those who suffer these forms of interference or network crowding is to migrate to a Wi-Fi 5 GHz product, (802.11a, or the newer 802.11n if it has 5 GHz support) as the 5 GHz band is relatively unused and there are many more channels available. This also requires users to set up the 5 GHz band to be the preferred network in the client and to configure each network band to a different name (SSID). It is also an issue when municipalities, or other large entities such as universities, seek to provide large area coverage. This openness is also important to the success and widespread use of 2.4 GHz Wi-Fi.

Hardwarm

Standard Devices

A wireless access point connects a group of wireless devices to an adjacent wired LAN. An access point is similar to a network hub, relaying data between connected wireless devices in addition to a (usually) single connected wired device, most often an ethernet hub or switch, allowing wireless devices to communicate with other wired devices.

Wireless adapters allow devices to connect to a wireless network. These adapters connect to devices using various external or internal interconnects such as PCI, miniPCI, USB, Express Card, Cardbus and PC card. Most newer laptop computers are equipped with internal adapters. Internal cards are generally more difficult to install. Wireless routers integrate a WAP, ethernet switch, and internal Router firmware application that provides IP Routing, NAT, and DNS forwarding through an integrated WAN interface. A wireless router allows wired and wireless ethernet LAN devices to connect to a (usually) single WAN device such as cable modem or DSL modem. A wireless router allows all three devices (mainly the access point and router) to be configured through one central utility. This utility is most usually an integrated web server which serves web pages to wired and wireless LAN clients and often optionally to WAN clients. This utility may also be an application that is run on a desktop computer such as Apple's AirPort.

Wireless network bridges connect a wired network to a wireless network. This is different from an access point in the sense that an access point connects wireless devices to a wired network at the data-link layer. Two wireless bridges may be used to connect two wired networks over a wireless link, useful in situations where a wired connection may be unavailable, such as between two separate homes. Wireless range extenders or wireless repeaters can extend the range of an existing wireless network. Range extenders can be strategically placed to elongate a signal area or allow for the signal area to reach around barriers such as those created in L-shaped corridors. Wireless devices connected through repeaters will suffer from an increased latency for each hop.

Additionally, a wireless device connected to any of the repeaters in the chain will have a throughput that is limited by the weakest link between the two nodes in the chain from which the connection originates to where the connection ends.

Distance Records

Distance records (using non-standard devices) include 382 km (237 mi) in June 2007, held by Ermanno Pietrosemoli and EsLaRed of Venezuela, transferring about 3 MB of data between mountain tops of El Aguila and Platillon. The Swedish Space Agency transferred data 310 km (193 mi), using 6 watt amplifiers to reach an overhead stratospheric balloon.

Wi-Fi availability in the home is on the increase. This extension of the Internet into the home space will increasingly be used for remote monitoring. Examples of remote monitoring include security systems and tele-medicine. In all these kinds of implementation, if the Wi-Fi provision is provided using a system running one of operating systems mentioned above, then it becomes unfeasible due to weight, power consumption and cost issues. Increasingly in the last few years (particularly as of early 2007), embedded Wi-Fi modules have become available which come with a real-time operating system and provide a simple means of wireless enabling any device which has and communicates via a serial port. This allows simple monitoring devices—for example, a portable ECG monitor hooked up to a patient in their home to be created. This Wi-Fi enabled device effectively becomes part of the internet cloud and can communicate with any other node on the internet. The data collected can hop via the home's Wi-Fi access point to anywhere on the internet.

These Wi-Fi modules are designed so that designers need minimal Wi-Fi knowledge to wireless-enable their products.

NETWORK SECURITY

During the early popular adoption of 802.11, providing open access points for anyone within range to use was encouraged to cultivate wireless community networks; particularly since people on average use only a fraction of their upstream bandwidth at any given time. Later, equipment manufacturers and mass-media advocated isolating users to a predetermined whitelist of authorized users referred to as "securing" the access point.

Measures to deter unauthorized users include suppressing the AP's SSID broadcast, allowing only computers with known MAC addresses to join the network, and various encryption standards. Suppressed SSID and MAC filtering are ineffective security methods as the SSID is broadcast in the open in response to a client SSID query and a MAC address can easily be spoofed. If the eavesdropper has the ability to change his MAC address, then he can potentially join the network by spoofing an authorized address.

WEP encryption can protect against casual snooping, but may also produce a misguided sense of security since freely available tools such as AirSnort or aircrack can quickly recover WEP encryption keys. Once it has seen 5-10 million encrypted packets, AirSnort can determine the encryption password in under a second; newer tools such as aircrack-ptw can use Klein's attack to crack a WEP key with a 50 per cent success rate using only 40,000 packets. The newer Wi-Fi Protected Access (WPA) and IEEE 802.11i (WPA2) encryption standards resolve most of the serious weaknesses of WEP encryption.

Attackers who have gained access to a Wi-Fi network can use DNS spoofing attacks very effectively against any other user of the network, because they can see the DNS requests made, and often respond with a spoofed answer before the queried DNS server has a chance to reply. One serious issue with wireless network security is not just encryption, but access to the network (signal reception). With wired networking it is necessary to get past either a firewall or the security guard and locked doors. With wireless it is only necessary to get reception and spend as long as you want, comfortably out of (easy) reach of the network owner. Most business networks protect sensitive data and systems by attempting to disallow external access. Thus being able to get wireless reception (and thus possibly break the encryption) becomes an attack vector on the network as well.

Recreational logging and mapping of other people's access points has become known as wardriving. It is also common for people to use open (unencrypted) Wi-Fi networks as a free service, termed piggybacking. Indeed, many access points are intentionally installed without security turned on so that they can be used as a free service. These activities do not result in sanctions in most jurisdictions, however legislation and case law differ considerably across the world. A proposal to leave graffiti describing available services was called warchalking. In a Florida court case, owner laziness was determined not to be a valid excuse.

Piggybacking is often unintentional. Most access points are configured without encryption by default, and operating systems such as Windows XP SP2 and Mac OS X may be configured to automatically connect to any available wireless network. A user who happens to start up a laptop in the vicinity of an access point may find the computer has joined the network without any visible indication. Moreover, a user intending to join one network may instead end up on another one if the latter's signal is stronger. In combination with automatic discovery of other network resources this could possibly lead wireless users to send sensitive data to the wrong middle man when seeking a destination. For example, a user could inadvertently use an insecure network to login to a website, thereby making the login credentials available to anyone listening, if the website is using an insecure protocol like HTTP, rather than a secure protocol like HTTPS.

History

Wi-Fi uses both single carrier direct-sequence spread spectrum radio technology (part of the larger family of spread spectrum systems) and multi-carrier OFDM (Orthogonal Frequency Division Multiplexing) radio technology. The regulations for unlicensed spread spectrum enabled the development of Wi-Fi, its onetime competitor HomeRF, Bluetooth, and many other products such as some types of cordless telephones.

Unlicensed spread spectrum was first made available in the US by the Federal Communications Commission in 1985 and these FCC regulations were later copied with some changes in many other countries enabling use of this technology in all major countries. The FCC action was proposed by Michael Marcus of the FCC staff in 1980 and the subsequent regulatory action took 5 more years. It was part of a broader proposal to allow civil use of spread spectrum technology and was opposed at the time by main stream equipment manufacturers and many radio system operators. The precursor to Wi-Fi was invented in 1991 by NCR Corporation/AT&T (later Lucent & Agere Systems) in Nieuwegein, the Netherlands. It was initially intended for cashier systems; the first wireless products were brought on the market under the name WaveLAN with speeds of 1 Mbit/s to 2 Mbit/s. Vic Hayes, who held the chair of IEEE 802.11 for 10 years and has been named the 'father of Wi-Fi,' was involved in designing standards such as IEEE 802.11b, and 802.11a.

City Wide Wi-Fi

Sunnyvale, California became the first city in the United States to offer city wide free Wi-Fi, Corpus Christi, Texas had offered free Wi-Fi until May 31, 2007 when the network was purchased by Earthlink. Philadelphia is also trying to save the Earthlink Wi-Fi for its city. New Orleans had free city wide Wi-Fi shortly after Hurricane Katrina. City wide Wi-Fi is available in nine cities in the UK, Newcastle Upon Tyne being the first UK city host, others include Leeds, Liverpool, Norwich and London. Other cities, such as the Minneapolis metro area, have a large number of Wi-Fi hotspots so you can receive good signals anywhere, even if from different sources. In Europe, the City of Luxembourg has a city-wide Wi-Fi network.

In Latin America, Mexico City downtown has a public Wi-Fi network. Also, many public squares in towns of Puerto Rico are offering Wi-Fi Internet access. As compared to Wireless Mesh, WiMax provides over 4 times the number of subcarriers over a variable bandwidth of 1 to 28 MHz. With more subcarriers and a variable length guard interval, the spectral efficiency has increased from 15 to 40 per cent compared to Wireless Mesh. The error vector magnitude of Wireless Mesh is higher than WiMax. This makes WiMax have a longer range. Wireless Mesh transmits and receives functions on the same channel where as WiMax transmits and receives functions at a different channel and at a different time. In Wireless Mesh the output power is virtually fixed however in WiMax the devices closer to the base stations emit less output power whereas the ones further away emit maximum output power. Wi-Fi can overpower WiMax if the city is meshed with hot spots. A very easy way to do it would be if mobile carriers integrate hot spots with their mobile base stations as WiMax chips are not as integrated as the Wi-Fi chips.

Origin and Meaning of the Term "Wi-Fi"

The term "Wi-Fi" suggests "Wireless Fidelity", comparing with the long-established audio recording term "High Fidelity" or "Hi-Fi", and "Wireless Fidelity" has often been used in an informal way, even by the Wi-Fi Alliance itself, but officially the term does not mean anything.

"Wi-Fi" was coined by a brand consulting firm called Interbrand Corporation that had been hired by the Alliance to determine a name that was "a little catchier than 'IEEE 802.11b Direct Sequence'." Interbrand invented "Wi-Fi" as simply a *play-on-words* with "Hi-Fi", as well as creating the yin yang style Wi-Fi logo.

The Wi-Fi Alliance initially complicated matters by stating that it *actually stood for* "Wireless Fidelity", as with the advertising slogan "The Standard for Wireless Fidelity", but later removed the phrase from their marketing. The Wi-Fi Alliance's early White Papers still held in their knowledge base: "... a promising market for wireless fidelity (Wi-Fi) network equipment." and "A Short History of WLANs." The yin yang logo indicates that a product had been certified for interoperability.

The Alliance has since downplayed the connection to "Hi-Fi." Their official position is that it is merely a brand name that stands for nothing in particular, and they now discourage the use of the term "Wireless Fidelity."

Wi-Fi Alliance

The Alliance promotes standards with the aim of improving the interoperability of wireless local area network products based on the IEEE 802.11 standards. The Wi-Fi Alliance, a consortium of separate and independent companies, agrees on a set of common interoperable products based on the family of IEEE 802.11 standards. The Wi-Fi Alliance certifies products via a set of defined test-procedures to establish interoperability. Those manufacturers with membership of Wi-Fi Alliance and whose products pass these interoperability tests can mark their products and product packaging with the Wi-Fi logo.

DIGITAL ENHANCED CORDLESS TELECOMMUNICATIONS

DECT or Digital Enhanced Cordless Telecommunications (formerly Digital European Cordless Telephone) is an ETSI standard for digital portable phones (cordless home telephones), commonly used for domestic or corporate purposes. DECT can also be used for wireless broadband data transfers. DECT is recognized by the ITU as fulfilling the IMT-2000 requirements and thus qualifies as a 3G system. Within the IMT-2000 group of technologies, DECT is referred to as IMT-FT (Frequency Time).

DECT was developed by ETSI but has since been adopted by many countries all over the world. The original DECT frequency band (1880 MHz–1900 MHz) is used in all countries in Europe. Outside Europe, it is used in most of Asia, Australia and South America. In the United States, the Federal Communications Commission in 2005 changed channelization and licensing costs in a nearby band (1920 MHz–1930 MHz, or 1.9 GHz), known as Unlicensed Personal Communications Services (UPCS), allowing DECT devices to be sold in the U.S. with only minimal changes. These channels are reserved exclusively for voice communication applications and therefore are less likely to experience interference from other wireless devices such as baby monitors and wireless networks. DECT devices made for use in the U.S. use the brand DECT 6.0 to distinguish them from both DECT devices used elsewhere and U.S. cordless equipment operating in the 900 MHz, 2.4 GHz and 5.8 GHz ISM bands. The "6.0" is a version number (as in software), not a spectrum band; the term "6.0 GHz" for DECT 6.0 phones is incorrect, since it operates at 1.9 GHz.

Application

The DECT standard fully specifies a means for a portable unit such as a cordless telephone to access a fixed telecoms network via radio, but unlike the GSM standards does not specify any internal aspects of the fixed network itself. Connectivity to the fixed network (which may be of many different kinds) is done through a base station or "Radio Fixed Part" to terminate the radio link, and a gateway to connect calls to the fixed network. In most cases the base station connection is to the public switched telephone network or telephone jack, although connectivity with newer technologies such as Voice over IP has become available. There are also other devices such as some baby monitors utilizing DECT, and in these devices there is no gateway functionality.

The DECT standard originally envisaged three major areas of application:

- Domestic cordless telephony, using a single base station to connect one or more handsets to the public telecoms network, which is now available.

- Enterprise premises cordless PABXs and wireless LANS, using many base stations for coverage. Calls continue as users move between different coverage cells, through a mechanism called handover. Traffic both within the system and to the public telecoms network.
- Public access, using large numbers of base stations to provide building or urban area coverage as part of a public telecoms network.

Of these, the domestic application (cordless home telephones) has been extremely successful. The enterprise PABX market had some success, and all the major PABX vendors have offered DECT access options. The public access application has not succeeded, since public cellular networks have fulfilled the need better. The one major application of DECT for public access, the Telecom Italia's FIDO network covering major cities in Italy, lasted about a year and was shut in 1997.

DECT has also been used for Fixed Wireless Access as a substitute for copper pairs in the "last mile" in countries such as India and South Africa. By using directional antenna and sacrificing some traffic capacity, cell coverage could extend to over 10 km. In Europe, the power limit laid down for use of the DECT spectrum (250 mW peak) was expressed in ERP, rather than the more commonly-used EIRP, thus permitting the use of powerful directional antenna to produce much higher EIRP and hence long ranges.

VoIP-IP-DECT. In business, DECT has become an essential part of many PABX installations with manufacturer's proprietary methods of supporting PABX features over the DECT standard. Since the onset of the migration from TDM PBXs to VoIP and VoIP hybrid solutions, manufacturers such as Phillips and Aastra have developed IP-DECT solutions where the backhaul from the base station is VoIP (H323 or SIP) but the handset loop is still DECT. These solutions are sometimes restricted by the cost of the base station and may be economic where the concentration of users is high. PBX networking vendors such as Cisco promote the adoption of WIFI-VoIP handsets as the replacement for DECT, but this imposes significant overhead on the design and complexity of the WIFI network in order to provide roaming, coverage and reservation of bandwidth, not to mention QOS. The question of Voice Mobility in commercial environments is still very open. DECT is robust but needs its own radio infrastructure. WIFI is deployed as an ad-hoc network environment. The new entrant into the field will be 3G-nano Cell technology where VoIP sessions would be supported as a private connection onto a 3G handset/PDA.

Features

Typical abilities of a domestic DECT Generic Access Profile (GAP) system include:

- Multiple handsets to one base station and one phone line socket. Which allows several cordless telephones to be placed around the house, all operating from the same telephone jack. Additional handsets usually have a battery charger station instead of a base station. The additional handsets do not require additional telephone sockets nor additional transceivers.
- Interference-free wireless operation to around 100 metres outdoors. Operates clearly in common congested domestic radio traffic situations. For instance, generally immune to interference from Wi-Fi networks or video senders, Bluetooth technology, baby monitors and other wireless devices.
- Ability to make internal (intercom) calls between handsets.
- An extended range between the telephone and base (allowing greater physical distance between the two devices).
- Extended battery talk-time, sometimes up to 24 hours.

Many DECT systems also include additional features such as Caller ID or a shared phonebook, but these are not standardized and may not work across different handset types. Some telephones also include a built-in digital answering machine and other features. A few of the telephones also allow users to utilize the DECT phone to retrieve wireless cell phone calls through Bluetooth technology. Additional features to look for include: handset ringers, headset jacks, redial, a "flash" button for answering call-waiting, speaker phone, and volume controls.

One final consideration is the type of battery it uses. Some telephones now utilize two rechargeable AA or AAA batteries, which are considerably less expensive than standard telephone batteries that, in some cases, can cost almost as much as purchasing a new telephone. The Consumer Reports 2008 Buying Guide offers an excellent explanation and evaluation of the various models that are currently available for sale in the United States.

Technical Details

Some DECT properties:

- *Audio codec*: G.726
- *Net bit rate*: 32 kbit/s
- *Frequency*: 1880 MHz–1900 MHz in Europe, 1920 MHz–1930 MHz in the US
- *Carriers*: 10 (1,728 kHz spacing) in Europe, 5 (1,728 kHz spacing) in the US
- *Time slots*: 2 × 12 (up and down stream)
- *Channel allocation*: dynamic
- *Average transmission power*: 10 mW (250 mW peak) in Europe, 4 mW (100 mW peak) in the US

The DECT physical layer uses:

- Frequency division multiple access (FDMA),
- Time division multiple access (TDMA), and
- Time division duplex (TDD).

This means that the radio spectrum is divided into physical channels in two dimensions: frequency and time. The maximum allowed power for portable equipment as well as base stations is 250 mW. A portable device radiates an average of about 10 mW during a call as it is only using one of 24 time slots to transmit.

The DECT media access control layer is the layer which controls the physical layer and provides connection oriented, connectionless and broadcast services to the higher layers. It also provides encryption services with the DECT Standard Cipher (DSC). The encryption is fairly weak, using a 35-bit initialization vector and encrypting the voice stream with 64-bit encryption. The DECT data link layer uses LAPC (Link Access Protocol Control), a specially designed variant of the ISDN data link protocol called LAPD. They are based on HDLC. The DECT network layer always contains the following protocol entities:

- Call Control (CC), and
- Mobility Management (MM).

Optionally it may also contain others:

- Call Independent Supplementary Services (CISS)
- Connection Oriented Message Service (COMS)
- Connectionless Message Service (CLMS)

All these communicate through a Link Control Entity (LCE).

The call control protocol is derived from ISDN DSS1, which is a Q.931 derived protocol. Many DECT-specific changes have been made. The mobility management protocol includes many elements similar to the GSM protocol, but also includes elements unique to DECT.

Unlike the GSM protocol, the DECT network specifications do not define cross-linkages between the operation of the entities (e.g. Mobility Management and Call Control). The architecture presumes that such linkages will be designed into the interworking unit that connects the DECT access network to whatever mobility-enabled fixed network is involved. By keeping the entities separate, the handset is capable of responding to any combination of entity traffic, and this creates great flexibility in fixed nework design without breaking full interoperability.

DECT GAP is an interoperability profile for DECT. The intent is that two different products from different manufacturers that both conform not only to the DECT standard, but also to the GAP profile defined within the DECT standard, are able to interoperate for basic calling. The DECT standard includes full testing suites for GAP, and GAP products on the market from different manufacturers are in practice interoperable for the basic functions.

DECT for Data Networks

Other interoperability profiles exist in the DECT suite of standards, and in particular the DPRS (DECT Packet Radio Services) bring together a number of prior interoperability profiles for the use of DECT as a wireless LAN and wireless internet access service. With good range (up to 200 m indoors and 6 km using directional antennae outdoors), dedicated spectrum, high interference immunity, open interoperability and data speeds of around 500 kbit/s, DECT appeared at one time to be a superior alternative to Wi-Fi. The protocol capabilities built into the DECT networking protocol standards were particularly good at supporting fast roaming in the public space, between hotspots operated by competing but connected providers. The first DECT product to reach the market, Olivetti's Net[3], was a wireless LAN, and German firms Dosch & Amand and Hoeft & Wessel built niche businesses on the supply of data transmission systems based on DECT.

However, the timing of the availability of DECT, in the mid-1990s, was too early to find wide application for wireless data outside niche industrial applications. Whilst contemporary providers of Wi-Fi struggled with the same issues, providers of DECT retreated to the more immediately lucrative market for cordless telephones. A key weakness was also the inaccessibility of the U.S. market, due to FCC spectrum restrictions at that time. By the time mass applications for wireless Internet had emerged, and the U.S. had opened up to DECT, well into the new century, the industry had moved far ahead in terms of performance and DECT's time as a wireless data transport was past.

Ironically, the failure of DECT as a data protocol became a strength when DECT 6.0 phones finally appeared in the U.S. in late 2005. By this time, the ISM bands had become crowded in the U.S., especially the 2.4 GHz band which is used by both the most common variants of Wi-Fi, 802.11b and 802.11g, and many cordless phones; thus interference between unlicensed devices has become common in these bands. However, because Wi-Fi does not operate in the UPCS band and DECT devices negotiate with each other for the available spectrum, not only are DECT 6.0 phones immune from this type of interference, their operation does not impair other nearby devices operating on the same frequency, which is a common issue with 2.4 GHz cordless phones.

IEEE 802.11

IEEE 802.11 is a set of standards for wireless local area network (WLAN) computer communication, developed by the IEEE LAN/MAN Standards Committee (IEEE 802) in the 5 GHz and 2.4 GHz public spectrum bands.

General Descriptionm

The 802.11 family includes over-the-air modulation techniques that use the same basic protocol. The most popular are those defined by the 802.11b and 802.11g protocols, and are amendments to the original standard. 802.11-1997 was the first wireless networking standard, but 802.11b was the first widely accepted one, followed by 802.11g and 802.11n. Security was originally purposefully weak due to export requirements of some governments, and was later enhanced via the 802.11i amendment after governmental and legislative changes. 802.11n is a new multi-streaming modulation technique that is still under draft development, but products based on its proprietary pre-draft versions are being sold. Other standards in the family (c–f, h, j) are service amendments and extensions or corrections to previous specifications.

802.11b and 802.11g use the 2.4 GHz ISM band, operating in the United States under Part 15 of the US Federal Communications Commission Rules and Regulations. Because of this choice of frequency band, 802.11b and g equipment may occasionally suffer interference from microwave ovens and cordless telephones. Bluetooth devices, while operating in the same band, in theory do not interfere with 802.11b/g because they use a frequency hopping spread spectrum signaling method (FHSS) while 802.11b/g uses a direct sequence spread spectrum signaling method (DSSS). 802.11a uses the 5 GHz U-NII band, which offers 8 non-overlapping channels rather than the 3 offered in the 2.4GHz ISM frequency band.

The segment of the radio frequency spectrum used varies between countries. In the US, 802.11a and 802.11g devices may be operated without a license, as explained in Part 15 of the FCC Rules and Regulations. Frequencies used by channels one through six (802.11b) fall within the 2.4 GHz amateur radio band. Licensed amateur radio operators may operate 802.11b/g devices under Part 97 of the FCC Rules and Regulations, allowing increased power output but not commercial content or encryption.

Protocols

Summary

Wireless local area network standards

802.11 Protocol	*Release*	*Freq. (GHz)*	*Typ through put (Mbit/s)*	*Max net bitrate (Mbit/s)*	*Mod.*	$r_{in.}$ *(m)*	$r_{out.}$ *(m)*
—	1997	2.4	0.9	2		~20	~100
a	1999	5	23	54	OFDM	~35	~120
b	1999	2.4	4.3	11	DSSS	~38	~140
g	2003	2.4	19	54	OFDM	~38	~140
n	2008	2.4, 5	74	248	OFDM	~70	~250
y	2008	3.7	23	0		~50	~5000

802.11-1997 (802.11 legacy)

The original version of the standard IEEE 802.11, released in 1997 and clarified in 1999, specified two raw net bit rates of 1 or 2 megabits per second (Mbit/s), plus forward error correction code, to be transmitted in Industrial Scientific Medical frequency band at 2.4 GHz.

Legacy 802.11 was rapidly supplemented (and popularized) by 802.11b.

802.11a

Release date	Op. Frequency	Net bit rate (Typ)	Net bit rate (Max)	Gross bit rate (Max)	Range (Indoor)
October 1999	5 GHz	23 Mbit/s	54 Mbit/s	72 Mbit/s	~35 m

The 802.11a standard uses the same data link layer protocol and frame format as the original standard, but an OFDM based air interface (physical layer). It operates in the 5 GHz band with a maximum net data rate of 54 Mbit/s, plus error correction code, which yields realistic net achievable throughput in the mid-20 Mbit/s.

Since the 2.4 GHz band is heavily used to the point of being crowded, using the relatively un-used 5 GHz band gives 802.11a a significant advantage. However, this high carrier frequency also brings a disadvantage: The effective overall range of 802.11a is less than that of 802.11b/g; 802.11a signals cannot penetrate as far as those for 802.11b because they are absorbed more readily by walls and other solid objects in their path.

802.11b

Release date	Frequency band	Data rate (typical)	Data rate (maximum)	Range (indoor)
October 1999	2.4 GHz	4.5 Mbit/s	11 Mbit/s	~38 m

802.11b has a maximum raw data rate of 11 Mbit/s and uses the same media access method defined in the original standard.

802.11b products appeared on the market in early 2000, since 802.11b is a direct extension of the modulation technique defined in the original standard. The dramatic increase in throughput of 802.11b (compared to the original standard) along with simultaneous substantial price reductions led to the rapid acceptance of 802.11b as the definitive wireless LAN technology.

802.11b devices suffer interference from other products operating in the 2.4 GHz band. Devices operating in the 2.4 GHz range include: microwave ovens, Bluetooth devices, baby monitors and cordless telephones.

802.11g

Release date	Op. Frequency	Net bit rate (Typ)	Net bit rate (Max)	Gross bit rate (Max)	Range (Indoor)
June 2003	2.4 GHz	19 Mbit/s	54 Mbit/s	72 Mbit/s	~38 m

In June 2003, a third modulation standard was ratified: 802.11g. This works in the 2.4 GHz band (like 802.11b), but uses the same OFDM based transmission scheme as 802.11a. It operates at a maximum physical layer bit rate of 54 Mbit/s exclusive of forward error correction codes, or about 19 Mbit/s average throughput. 802.11g hardware is fully backwards compatible with 802.11b hardware.

The then-proposed 802.11g standard was rapidly adopted by consumers starting in January 2003, well before ratification, due to the desire for higher speeds, and reductions in manufacturing costs. By summer 2003, most dual-band 802.11a/b products became dual-band/tri-mode, supporting a and b/g in a single mobile adapter card or access point. Details of making b and g work well together occupied much of the lingering technical process; in an 802.11g network, however, activity by a 802.11b participant will reduce the speed of the overall 802.11g network.

Like 802.11b, 802.11g devices suffer interference from other products operating in the 2.4 GHz band. Devices operating in the 2.4 GHz range include: microwave ovens, Bluetooth devices, baby monitors and cordless telephones.

802.11-2007

In 2003, task group TGma was authorized to "roll up" many of the amendments to the 1999 version of the 802.11 standard. REVma or 802.11ma, as it was called, created a single document that merged 8 amendments (802.11a,b,d,e,g,h,i, j) with the base standard. Upon approval on March 08, 2007, 802.11REVma was renamed to the current standard IEEE 802.11-2007. This is the single most modern 802.11 document available that contains cumulative changes from multiple sub-letter task groups.

802.11n

Release date	Op. Frequency	Data rate (Typ)	Data rate (Max)	Range (Indoor)
Pending	5 GHz and/or 2.4 GHz	74 Mbit/s	300 Mbit/s (2 streams)	~70 m

802.11n is a proposed amendment which improves upon the previous 802.11 standards by adding multiple-input multiple-output (MIMO) and many other newer features. Though there are already many products on the market based on Draft 2.0 of this proposal, the TGn workgroup is not expected to finalize the amendment until December 2009.

Channels and International Compatibility

802.11 divides each of the above-described bands into channels, analogously to how radio and TV broadcast bands are carved up but with greater channel width and overlap. For example the 2.4000-2.4835 GHz band is divided into 13 channels each of width 22 MHz but spaced only 5 MHz apart, with channel 1 centred on 2412 MHz and 13 on 2472, to which Japan adds a 14th channel 12 MHz above channel 13.

Availability of channels is regulated by country, constrained in part by how each country allocates radio spectrum to various services. At one extreme Japan permits the use of all 14 channels (with the exclusion of 802.11g/n from channel 14), while at the other Spain allowed only channels 10 and 11 (later all of the 14 channels have been allowed), to which France adds 12 and 13. Most other European countries are almost as liberal as Japan, disallowing only channel 14, while North America and some Central and South American countries further disallow 12 and 13. Besides specifying the centre frequency of each channel, 802.11

also specifies (in Clause 17) a spectral mask defining the permitted distribution of power across each channel. The mask requires that the signal be attenuated by at least 30 dB from its peak energy at ± 11 MHz from the centre frequency, the sense in which channels are effectively 22 MHz wide. One consequence is that stations can only use every fourth or fifth channel without overlap, typically 1, 6 and 11 in the Americas, 1, 5, 9 and 13 in Europe, etc. Another is that channels 1-13 effectively require the band 2401-2483 MHz, the actual allocations being for example 2400-2483.5 in the UK, 2402-2483.5 in the US, etc.

Since the spectral mask only defines power output restrictions up to ± 22 MHz from the center frequency to be attenuated by 50 dB, it is often assumed that the energy of the channel extends no further than these limits. It is more correct to say that, given the separation between channels 1, 6, and 11, the signal on any channel should be sufficiently attenuated to minimally interfere with a transmitter on any other channel. Due to the near-far problem a transmitter can impact a receiver on a "non-overlapping" channel, but only if it is close to the victim receiver (within a meter) or operating above allowed power levels.

Although the statement that channels 1, 6, and 11 are "non-overlapping" is limited to spacing or product density, the 1–6–11 guideline has merit. If transmitters are closer together than channels 1, 6, and 11 (for example, 1, 4, 7, and 10), overlap between the channels may cause unacceptable degradation of signal quality and throughput. However, overlapping channels may be used under certain circumstances. This way, more channels are available.

Standard and Amendments

Within the IEEE 802.11 Working Group, the following IEEE Standards Association Standard and Amendments exist:

- IEEE 802.11—THE WLAN STANDARD was original 1 Mbit/s and 2 Mbit/s, 2.4 GHz RF and IR standard (1997), all the others listed below are Amendments to this standard, except for Recommended Practices 802.11F and 802.11T.
- IEEE 802.11a—54 Mbit/s, 5 GHz standard (1999, shipping products in 2001).

- IEEE 802.11b—Enhancements to 802.11 to support 5.5 and 11 Mbit/s (1999).
- IEEE 802.11c—Bridge operation procedures; included in the IEEE 802.1D standard (2001).
- IEEE 802.11d—International (country-to-country) roaming extensions (2001).
- IEEE 802.11e—Enhancements: QoS, including packet bursting (2005).
- IEEE 802.11F—Inter-Access Point Protocol (2003) Withdrawn February 2006.
- IEEE 802.11g—54 Mbit/s, 2.4 GHz standard (backwards compatible with b) (2003).
- IEEE 802.11h—Spectrum Managed 802.11a (5 GHz) for European compatibility (2004).
- IEEE 802.11i—Enhanced security (2004).
- IEEE 802.11j—Extensions for Japan (2004).
- IEEE 802.11-2007—A new release of the standard that includes amendments a, b, d, e, g, h, i and j. (July 2007).
- IEEE 802.11k—Radio resource measurement enhancements (2008).
- IEEE 802.11l—(reserved and will not be used).
- IEEE 802.11m—Maintenance of the standard. Recent edits became 802.11-2007 (ongoing).
- IEEE 802.11n—Higher throughput improvements using MIMO (multiple input, multiple output antennas) (July 2009).
- IEEE 802.11o—(reserved and will not be used).
- IEEE 802.11p—WAVE—Wireless Access for the Vehicular Environment (such as ambulances and passenger cars) (working—2009).
- IEEE 802.11q—(reserved and will not be used, can be confused with 802.1Q VLAN trunking).
- IEEE 802.11r—Fast roaming Working "Task Group r"—(2008).
- IEEE 802.11s—ESS Extended Service Set Mesh Networking (working—2008).
- IEEE 802.11T—Wireless Performance Prediction (WPP)—test methods and metrics Recommendation (working—2008).

- IEEE 802.11u—Interworking with non-802 networks (for example, cellular) (proposal evaluation—).
- IEEE 802.11v—Wireless network management (early proposal stages—).
- IEEE 802.11w—Protected Management Frames (early proposal stages—2008).
- IEEE 802.11x—(reserved and will not be used, can be confused with 802.1x Network Access Control).
- IEEE 802.11y—3650-3700 MHz Operation in the U.S. (2008).
- IEEE 802.11z—Extensions to Direct Link Setup (DLS) (Aug. 2007—Dec. 2011).

There is no standard or task group named "802.11x." Rather, this term is used informally to denote any current or future 802.11 amendment, in cases where further precision is not necessary. (The IEEE 802.1x standard for port-based network access control is often mistakenly called "802.11x" when used in the context of wireless networks)

802.11F and 802.11T are recommended practices rather than standards, and are capitalized as such.

Standard or Amendment?

Both the terms "standard" and "amendment" are used when referring to the different variants of IEEE 802.11. As far as the IEEE Standards Association is concerned, there is only one current standard; it is denoted by IEEE 802.11 followed by the date that it was published. IEEE 802.11-2007 is the only version currently in publication. The standard is updated by means of amendments. Amendments are created by task groups (TG). Both the task group and their finished document are denoted by 802.11 followed by a non-capitalized letter. For example IEEE 802.11a and IEEE 802.11b. Updating 802.11 is the responsibility of task group m. In order to create a new version, TGm combines the previous version of the standard and all published amendments. TGm also provides clarification and interpretation to industry on published documents. New versions of the IEEE 802.11 were published in 1999 and 2007.

The working title of 802.11-2007 was 802.11-REVma. This denotes a third type of document, a "revision". The complexity of combining 802.11-1999 with 8 amendments made it necessary to revise already agreed upon text. As a result, additional guidelines associated with a revision had to be followed.

Nomenclature

Various terms in 802.11 are used to specify aspects of wireless local-area networking operation, and may be unfamiliar to some readers. For example, Time Unit (usually abbreviated TU) is used to indicate a unit of time equal to 1024 microseconds. Numerous time constants are defined in terms of TU (rather than the nearly-equal millisecond). Also the term "Portal" is used to describe an entity that is similar to an IEEE 802.1D bridge. A Portal provides access to the WLAN by non-802.11 LAN STAs.

Community Networks

With the proliferation of cable modems and DSL, there is an ever-increasing market of people who wish to establish small networks in their homes to share their high speed Internet connection.

Many hotspot or free networks frequently allow anyone within range, including passersby outside, to connect to the Internet. There are also efforts by volunteer groups to establish wireless community networks to provide free wireless connectivity to the public.

Security

In 2001, a group from the University of California, Berkeley presented a paper describing weaknesses in the 802.11 Wired Equivalent Privacy (WEP) security mechanism defined in the original standard; they were followed by Fluhrer, Mantin, and Shamir's paper entitled "Weaknesses in the Key Scheduling Algorithm of RC4". Not long after, Adam Stubblefield and AT&T publicly announced the first verification of the attack. In the attack they were able to intercept transmissions and gain unauthorized access to wireless networks.

The IEEE set up a dedicated task group to create a replacement security solution, 802.11i (previously this work was handled as part of a broader 802.11e effort to enhance the MAC layer). The Wi-Fi Alliance announced an interim specification called Wi-Fi Protected Access (WPA) based on a subset of the then current IEEE

802.11i draft. These started to appear in products in mid-2003. IEEE 802.11i (also known as WPA2) itself was ratified in June 2004, and uses government strength encryption in the Advanced Encryption Standard AES, instead of RC4, which was used in WEP. The modern recommended encryption for the home/consumer space is WPA2 (AES PreShared Key) and for the Enterprise space is WPA2 along with a radius server the strongest is EAP-TLS.

In January 2005, IEEE set up yet another task group, TGw, to protect management and broadcast frames, which previously were sent unsecured.

Non-Standard 802.11 Extensions and Equipment

Many companies implement wireless networking equipment with non-IEEE standard 802.11 extensions either by implementing proprietary or draft features. These changes may lead to incompatibilities between these extensions.

BLUETOOTH

Bluetooth is a wireless protocol utilizing short-range communications technology facilitating data transmission over short distances from fixed and/or mobile devices, creating wireless personal area networks (PANs). The intent behind the development of Bluetooth was the creation of a single digital wireless protocol, capable of connecting multiple devices and overcoming problems arising from synchronization of these devices. Bluetooth uses a radio technology called frequency hopping spread spectrum. It chops up the data being sent and transmits chunks of it on up to 75 different frequencies. In its basic mode, the modulation is Gaussian frequency shift keying (GFSK). It can achieve a gross data rate of 1 Mb/s. Bluetooth provides a way to connect and exchange information between devices such as mobile phones, telephones, laptops, personal computers, printers, GPS receivers, digital cameras, and video game consoles over a secure, globally unlicensed Industrial, Scientific, and Medical (ISM) 2.4 GHz short-range radio frequency bandwidth. The Bluetooth specifications are developed and licensed by the Bluetooth Special Interest Group (SIG). The Bluetooth SIG consists of companies in the areas of telecommunication, computing, networking, and consumer electronics.

Uses

Bluetooth is a standard and communications protocol primarily designed for low power consumption, with a short range (power-class-dependent: 1 meter, 10 meters, 100 meters) based on low-cost transceiver microchips in each device. Bluetooth enables these devices to communicate with each other when they are in range. The devices use a radio communications system, so they do not have to be in line of sight of each other, and can even be in other rooms, as long as the received transmission is powerful enough. Bluetooth device class indicates the type of device and the supported services of which the information is transmitted during the discovery process.

Class	*Maximum Permitted Power mW(dBm)*	*Range (approximate)*
Class 1	100 mW (20 dBm)	~100 meters
Class 2	2.5 mW (4 dBm)	~10 meters
Class 3	1 mW (0 dBm)	~1 meter

In most cases the effective range of Class 2 devices is extended if they connect to a Class 1 transceiver, compared to pure Class 2 network. This is accomplished by the higher sensitivity and transmission power of Class 1 devices.

Version	*Data Rate*
Version 1.2	1 Mbit/s
Version 2.0 + EDR	3 Mbit/s
WiMedia Alliance (proposed)	53—480 Mbit/s

Bluetooth Profiles

In order to use Bluetooth, a device must be compatible with certain Bluetooth profiles. These define the possible applications and uses of the technology.

List of Applications

More prevalent applications of Bluetooth include:

- Wireless control of and communication between a mobile

phone and a hands-free headset. This was one of the earliest applications to become popular.

- Wireless networking between PCs in a confined space and where little bandwidth is required.
- Wireless communications with PC input and output devices, the most common being the mouse, keyboard and printer.
- Transfer of files between devices with OBEX.
- Transfer of contact details, calendar appointments, and reminders between devices with OBEX.
- Replacement of traditional wired serial communications in test equipment, GPS receivers, medical equipment, bar code scanners, and traffic control devices.
- For controls where infrared was traditionally used.
- Sending small advertisements from Bluetooth enabled advertising hoardings to other, discoverable, Bluetooth devices.
- Two seventh-generation game consoles, Nintendo's Wii and Sony's PlayStation 3 use Bluetooth for their respective wireless controllers.
- Dial-up internet access on personal computer or PDA using a data-capable mobile phone as a modem.

Bluetooth vs. Wi-Fi in Networking

Bluetooth and Wi-Fi have different applications in today's offices, homes, and on the move: setting up networks, printing, or transferring presentations and files from PDAs to computers. Both are versions of unlicensed wireless technology. Wi-Fi differs from Bluetooth in that it provides higher throughput and covers greater distances, but requires more expensive hardware and may present higher power consumption.

They use the same frequency range, but employ different modulation techniques. While Bluetooth is a replacement for cabling in a variety of small-scale applications, Wi-Fi is a replacement for cabling for general local area network access. Bluetooth can be taken as replacement for USB or any other serial cable link, whereas Wi-Fi is wireless Ethernet communications according to the protocol architectures of IEEE 802.3 with TCP/IP. Both standards are operating at a specified bandwidth not identical with that of other networking standards; the mechanical plug compatibility problem known with cables is replaced by the compatibility requirement for an air interface and a protocol stack.

Bluetooth Devices

Bluetooth exists in many products, such as telephones, modems and headsets. The technology is useful when transferring information between two or more devices that are near each other in low-bandwidth situations. Bluetooth is commonly used to transfer sound data with telephones (i.e. with a Bluetooth headset) or byte data with hand-held computers (transferring files).

Bluetooth protocols simplify the discovery and setup of services between devices. Bluetooth devices can advertise all of the services they provide. This makes using services easier because more of the security, network address and permission configuration can be automated than with many other network types.

Wi-Fi

Wi-Fi is more like a traditional Ethernet network, and requires configuration to set up shared resources, transmit files, and to set up audio links (for example, headsets and hands-free devices). Technologies such as Zeroconf (e.g. Bonjour) and DHCP can automate some of this configuration, but not as much as Bluetooth. Wi-Fi uses the same radio frequencies as Bluetooth, but with higher power resulting in a stronger connection. Wi-Fi is sometimes called "wireless Ethernet." This description is accurate as it also provides an indication of its relative strengths and weaknesses. Wi-Fi requires more setup, but is better suited for operating full-scale networks it enables a faster connection, better range from the base station, and better security than Bluetooth.

Computer Requirements

A personal computer must have a Bluetooth adapter in order to communicate with other Bluetooth devices (such as mobile phones, mice and keyboards). While some desktop computers and most recent laptops come with a built-in Bluetooth adapter, others will require an external one in the form of a dongle.

Unlike its predecessor, IrDA, which requires a separate adapter for each device, Bluetooth allows multiple devices to communicate with a computer over a single adapter.

Operating System Support

Apple has supported Bluetooth since Mac OS X v10.2 which was released in 2002. For Microsoft platforms, Windows XP Service Pack 2 and later releases have native support for Bluetooth. Previous versions required users to install their Bluetooth adapter's own drivers, which were not directly supported by Microsoft. Microsoft's own Bluetooth dongles (packaged with their Bluetooth computer devices) have no external drivers and thus require at least Windows XP Service Pack 2.

Linux has two popular Bluetooth stacks, BlueZ and Affix. The BlueZ stack is included with most Linux kernels and it was originally developed by Qualcomm. The Affix stack was developed by Nokia. FreeBSD features Bluetooth support since its 5.0 release. NetBSD features Bluetooth support since its 4.0 release. Its Bluetooth stack has been ported to OpenBSD as well.

Mobile Phone Requirements

A mobile phone that is Bluetooth enabled is able to pair with many devices. To ensure the broadest support of feature functionality together with legacy device support, the OMTP forum has recently published a recommendations paper, entitled "Bluetooth Local Connectivity." This publication recommends two classes, Basic and Advanced, with requirements that cover imaging, printing, stereo audio and in car useage.

Specifications and Features

The Bluetooth specification was developed in 1994 by Jaap Haartsen and Sven Mattisson, who were working for Ericsson Mobile Platforms in Lund, Sweden. The specification is based on frequency-hopping spread spectrum technology.

The specifications were formalized by the Bluetooth Special Interest Group (SIG). The SIG was formally announced on May 20, 1998. Today it has a membership of over 11,000 companies worldwide. It was established by Ericsson, IBM, Intel, Toshiba, and Nokia, and later joined by many other companies.

Bluetooth 1.0 and 1.0B

Versions 1.0 and 1.0B had many problems, and manufacturers had difficulty making their products interoperable. Versions 1.0 and

1.0B also included mandatory Bluetooth hardware device address (BD_ADDR) transmission in the Connecting process (rendering anonymity impossible at the protocol level), which was a major setback for certain services planned for use in Bluetooth environments.

Bluetooth 1.1

- Ratified as IEEE Standard 802.15.1-2002.
- Many errors found in the 1.0B specifications were fixed.
- Added support for non-encrypted channels.
- Received Signal Strength Indicator (RSSI).

Bluetooth 1.2

This version is backward-compatible with 1.1 and the major enhancements include the following:

- Faster Connection and Discovery.
- *Adaptive frequency-hopping spread spectrum (AFH)*, which improves resistance to radio frequency interference by avoiding the use of crowded frequencies in the hopping sequence.
- Higher transmission speeds in practice, up to 721 kbit/s, as in 1.1.
- Extended Synchronous Connections (eSCO), which improve voice quality of audio links by allowing retransmissions of corrupted packets, and may optionally increase audio latency to provide better support for concurrent data transfer.
- Host Controller Interface (HCI) support for three-wire UART.
- Ratified as IEEE Standard 802.15.1-2005.

Bluetooth 2.0

This version of the Bluetooth specification was released on November 10, 2004. It is backward-compatible with the previous version 1.1. The main difference is the introduction of an Enhanced Data Rate (EDR) for faster data transfer. The nominal rate of EDR is about 3 megabits per second, although the practical data transfer rate is 2.1 megabits per second. The additional throughput is obtained by using a different radio technology for transmission of the data. Standard, or Basic Rate, transmission uses Gaussian Frequency Shift Keying (GFSK) modulation of the radio signal; EDR uses a combination of GFSK and Phase Shift Keying (PSK) modulation.

According to the 2.0 specification, EDR provides the following benefits:

- Three times faster transmission speed—up to 10 times (2.1 Mbit/s) in some cases.
- Reduced complexity of multiple simultaneous connections due to additional bandwidth.
- Lower power consumption through a reduced duty cycle.

The Bluetooth Special Interest Group (SIG) published the specification as "Bluetooth 2.0 + EDR" which implies that EDR is an optional feature. Aside from EDR, there are other minor improvements to the 2.0 specification, and products may claim compliance to "Bluetooth 2.0" without supporting the higher data rate. At least one commercial device, the HTC TyTN pocket PC phone, states "Bluetooth 2.0 without EDR" on its data sheet.

Bluetooth 2.1

Bluetooth Core Specification Version 2.1 is fully backward-compatible with 1.1, and was adopted by the Bluetooth SIG on July 26, 2007. This specification includes the following features:

- *Extended inquiry response*: provides more information during the inquiry procedure to allow better filtering of devices before connection. This information includes the name of the device, a list of services the device supports, plus other information like the time of day and pairing information.
- *Sniff subrating*: reduces the power consumption when devices are in the sniff low-power mode, especially on links with asymmetric data flows. Human interface devices (HID) are expected to benefit the most, with mouse and keyboard devices increasing the battery life by a factor of 3 to 10. It lets devices decide how long they will wait before sending keepalive messages to one another. Previous Bluetooth implementations featured keep alive

message frequencies of up to several times per second. In contrast, the 2.1 specification allows pairs of devices to negotiate this value between them to as infrequently as once every 5 or 10 seconds.

- *Encryption pause resume*: enables an encryption key to be refreshed, enabling much stronger encryption for connections that stay up for longer than 23.3 hours (one Bluetooth day).
- *Secure simple pairing*: radically improves the pairing experience for Bluetooth devices, while increasing the use and strength of security. It is expected that this feature will significantly increase the use of Bluetooth.
- *Near field communication (NFC) cooperation*: automatic creation of secure Bluetooth connections when NFC radio interface is also available. This functionality is part of the Secure Simple Pairing where NFC is one way of exchanging pairing information. For example, a headset should be paired with a Bluetooth 2.1 phone including NFC Just by bringing the two devices close to each other (a few centimeters). Another example is automatic uploading of photos from a mobile phone or camera to a digital picture frame just by bringing the phone or camera close to the frame.

Future of Bluetooth

- *Broadcast channel*: enables Bluetooth information points. This will drive the adoption of Bluetooth into mobile phones, and enable advertising models based around users pulling information from the information points, and not based around the object push model that is used in a limited way today.
- *Topology management*: enables the automatic configuration of the piconet topologies especially in scatternet situations that are becoming more common today. This should all be invisible to the users of the technology, while also making the technology just work.
- *Alternate MAC PHY*: enables the use of alternative MAC and PHY's for transporting Bluetooth profile data. The Bluetooth Radio will still be used for device discovery, initial connection and profile configuration, however

when lots of data needs to be sent, the high speed alternate MAC PHY's will be used to transport the data. This means that the proven low power connection models of Bluetooth are used when the system is idle, and the low power per bit radios are used when lots of data needs to be sent.

- *QoS improvements*: enable audio and video data to be transmitted at a higher quality, especially when best effort traffic is being transmitted in the same piconet.

High-Speed Bluetooth

On March 28, 2006, the Bluetooth Special Interest Group announced its selection of the WiMedia Alliance Multi-Band Orthogonal Frequency Division Multiplexing (MB-OFDM) version of UWB for integration with current Bluetooth wireless technology.

UWB integration will create a version of Bluetooth wireless technology with a high-speed/high-data-rate option. This new version of Bluetooth technology will meet the high-speed demands of synchronizing and transferring large amounts of data, as well as enabling high-quality video and audio applications for portable devices, multi-media projectors and television sets, and wireless VOIP.

At the same time, Bluetooth technology will continue catering to the needs of very low power applications such as mouse, keyboards, and mono headsets, enabling devices to select the most appropriate physical radio for the application requirements, thereby offering the best of both worlds.

Bluetooth 3.0

The next version of Bluetooth after v2.1, code-named Seattle (the version number of which is TBD) has many of the same features, but is most notable for plans to adopt ultra-wideband (UWB) radio technology. This will allow Bluetooth use over UWB radio, enabling very fast data transfers of up to 480 Mbit/s, while building on the very low-power idle modes of Bluetooth.

Bluetooth Low Energy

On June 12, 2007, Nokia and Bluetooth SIG announced that Wibree will be a part of the Bluetooth specification, being an ultra-low power Bluetooth technology. Expected use cases include watches displaying Caller ID information, sports sensors monitoring your heart rate during exercise, plus medical devices. The Medical Devices Working Group is also creating a medical devices profile and associated protocols to enable this market. Battery life for devices using Bluetooth low energy technology is designed to last up to one year.

Technical Information

Bluetooth Protocol Stack

"Bluetooth is defined as a layer protocol architecture consisting of core protocols, cable replacement protocols, telephony control protocols, and adopted protocols."

Core Protocols

Bluetooth's core protocols form a five-layer stack, consisting of the following:

- *Bluetooth Radio*—specifics details of the air interface, including frequency, frequency hopping, modulation scheme, and transmission power.
- *Baseband*—concerned with connection establishment within a piconet, addressing, packet format, timing, and power control.
- *Link Manager Protocol* (LMP)—establishes the link setup between Bluetooth devices and manages ongoing links, including security aspects (e.g. authentication and encryption), and control and negotiation of baseband packet size.
- *Logical Link Control and Adaptation Protocol* (L2CAP)—adapts the upper-layer protocols to the baseband layer, providing both connectionless and connection-oriented services.
- *Service Discovery Protocol* (SDP)—handles device information, services, and queries for service characteristics between two or more Bluetooth devices.

Cable Replacement Protocol

Radio frequency communications (RFCOMM) is the cable

replacement protocol used to create a virtual serial port used to make replacement of cable technologies transparent through minimal modification of existing devices. RFCOMM provides for binary data transport and emulates EIA-232 (formerly RS-232) control signals over the Bluetooth baseband layer.

Telephony Control Protocol

Telephony control protocol-binary (TCS BIN) is the bit-oriented protocol that defines the call control signaling for the establishment of voice and data calls between Bluetooth devices. Additionally, "TCS BIN defines mobility management procedures for handling groups of Bluetooth TCS devices".

Adopted Protocols

Adopted protocols are defined by other standards-making organizations and incorporated into Bluetooth's protocol stack, allowing Bluetooth to create protocols only when necessary. The adopted protocols include:

- *Point-to-Point Protocol* (PPP)—Internet standard protocol for transporting IP datagrams over a point-to-point link.
- *TCP/IP/UDP*—Foundation Protocols for TCP/IP protocol suite.
- *Object Exchange Protocol* (OBEX)—Session-layer protocol for the exchange of objects, providing a model for object and operation representation.
- *Wireless Application Environment/Wireless Application Protocol* (WAE/WAP)—WAE specifies an application framework for wireless devices and WAP is an open standard to provide mobile users access to telephony and information services.

Communication and Connection

A master Bluetooth device can communicate with up to seven devices. This network group of up to eight devices is called a piconet.

A piconet is an ad-hoc computer network, using Bluetooth technology protocols to allow one master device to interconnect with up to seven active devices. Up to 255 further devices can be inactive, or parked, which the master device can bring into active status at any time.

At any given time, data can be transferred between the master and one other device, however, the devices can switch roles and the slave can become the master at any time. The master switches rapidly from one device to another in a round-robin fashion. (Simultaneous transmission from the master to multiple other devices is possible, but not used much.)

Bluetooth specification allows connecting two or more piconets together to form a scatternet, with some devices acting as a bridge by simultaneously playing the master role and the slave role in one piconet.

Many USB Bluetooth adapters are available, some of which also include an IrDA adapter. Older (pre-2003) Bluetooth adapters, however, have limited services, offering only the Bluetooth Enumerator and a less-powerful Bluetooth Radio incarnation. Such devices can link computers with Bluetooth, but they do not offer much in the way of services that modern adapters do.

Setting up Connections

Any Bluetooth device will transmit the follcwing information on demand:

- Device name.
- Device class.
- List of services.
- Technical information, for example, device features, manufacturer, Bluetooth specification used, clock offset.

Any device may perform an inquiry to find other devices to connect to, and any device can be configured to respond to such inquiries. However, if the device trying to connect knows the address of the device, it always responds to direct connection requests and transmits the information shown in the list above if requested. Use of device services may require pairing or acceptance by its owner, but the connection itself can be initiated by any device and held until it goes out of range. Some devices can be connected to only one device at a time, and connecting to them prevents them from connecting to other devices and appearing in inquiries until they disconnect from the other device.

Every device has a unique 48-bit address. However these addresses are generally not shown in inquiries. Instead, friendly Bluetooth names are used, which can be set by the user. This name appears when another user scans for devices and in lists of paired devices.

Most phones have the Bluetooth name set to the manufacturer and model of the phone by default. Most phones and laptops show only the Bluetooth names and special programmes that are required to get additional information about remote devices. This can be confusing as, for example, there could be several phones in range named T610.

Pairing

Pairs of devices may establish a trusted relationship by learning (by user input) a shared secret known as a *passkey*. A device that wants to communicate only with a trusted device can cryptographically authenticate the identity of the other device. Trusted devices may also encrypt the data that they exchange over the airwaves so that no one can listen in. The encryption can, however, be turned off, and passkeys are stored on the device file system, not on the Bluetooth chip itself. Since the Bluetooth address is permanent, a pairing is preserved, even if the Bluetooth name is changed. Pairs can be deleted at any time by either device. Devices generally require pairing or prompt the owner before they allow a remote device to use any or most of their services. Some devices, such as mobile phones, usually accept OBEX business cards and notes without any pairing or prompts.

Certain printers and access points allow any device to use its services by default, much like unsecured Wi-Fi networks. Pairing algorithms are sometimes manufacturer-specific for transmitters and receivers used in applications such as music and entertainment. Bluetooth 2.1 has an optional "touch-to-pair" feature based on NFC. By simply bringing two devices into close range (around 10 cm), pairing can securely take place without entering a passkey or manual configuration.

Air Interface

The protocol operates in the license-free ISM band at 2.4-2.4835 GHz. To avoid interfering with other protocols that use the

2.45 GHz band, the Bluetooth protocol divides the band into 79 channels (each 1 MHz wide) and changes channels up to 1600 times per second. Implementations with versions 1.1 and 1.2 reach speeds of 723.1 kbit/s. Version 2.0 implementations feature Bluetooth Enhanced Data Rate (EDR) and reach 2.1 Mbit/s. Technically, version 2.0 devices have a higher power consumption, but the three times faster rate reduces the transmission times, effectively reducing power consumption to half that of 1.x devices (assuming equal traffic load).

Security

Overview

Bluetooth implements confidentiality, authentication and key derivation with custom algorithms based on the SAFER+ block cipher. In Bluetooth, key generation is generally based on a Bluetooth PIN, which must be entered into both devices. This procedure might be modified if one of the devices has a fixed PIN, e.g. for headsets or similar devices with a restricted user interface. During pairing, an initialization key or master key is generated, using the E22 algorithm. The E0 stream cipher is used for encrypting packets, granting confidentiality and is based on a shared cryptographic secret, namely a previously generated link key or master key. Those keys, used for subsequent encryption of data sent via the air interface, rely on the Bluetooth PIN, which has been entered into one or both devices. An overview of Bluetooth vulnerabilities exploits has been published by Andreas Becker.

Bluejacking

Bluejacking is the sending of either a picture or a message from one user to an unsuspecting user through Bluetooth wireless technology. Common applications are short messages (e.g. "You've just been bluejacked!"), advertisements (e.g. "Eat at Joe's") and business information. Bluejacking does not involve the removal or alteration of any data from the device.

History of Security Concerns

2003

In November 2003, Ben and Adam Laurie from A.L. Digital Ltd. discovered that serious flaws in Bluetooth security may lead to disclosure of personal data. It should be noted, however, that the reported security problems concerned some poor implementations of Bluetooth, rather than the protocol itself.

In a subsequent experiment, Martin Herfurt from the trifinite group was able to do a field-trial at the CeBIT fairgrounds, showing the importance of the problem to the world. A new attack called BlueBug was used for this experiment. This is one of a number of concerns that have been raised over the security of Bluetooth communications.

2004

In 2004 the first purported virus using Bluetooth to spread itself among mobile phones appeared on the Symbian OS. The virus was first described by Kaspersky Lab and requires users to confirm the installation of unknown software before it can propagate. The virus was written as a proof-of-concept by a group of virus writers known as "29A" and sent to anti-virus groups. Thus, it should be regarded as a potential (but not real) security threat to Bluetooth or Symbian OS since the virus has never spread in the wild.

In August 2004, a world-record-setting experiment showed that the range of Class 2 Bluetooth radios could be extended to 1.78 km (1.08 mile) with directional antennas and signal amplifiers. This poses a potential security threat because it enables attackers to access vulnerable Bluetooth-devices from a distance beyond expectation. The attacker must also be able to receive information from the victim to set up a connection. No attack can be made against a Bluetooth device unless the attacker knows its Bluetooth address and which channels to transmit on.

2005

In January 2005, a mobile malware worm known as Lasco. Targeting mobile phones using Symbian OS (Series 60 platform) using Bluetooth-enabled devices to replicate itself and spread to other devices. The worm is self-installing and begins once the mobile user approves the transfer of the file (velasco.sis) from another device. Once installed, the worm begins looking for other Bluetooth-enabled devices to infect. Additionally, the worm infects other. SIS files on the device, allowing replication to another device through use of removable media (Secure Digital, Compact Flash, etc.). The worm can render the mobile device unstable.

In April 2005, Cambridge University security researchers published results of their actual implementation of passive attacks against the PIN-based pairing between commercial Bluetooth devices, confirming the attacks to be practicably fast and the Bluetooth symmetric key establishment method to be vulnerable. To rectify this vulnerability, they carried out an implementation which showed that stronger, asymmetric key establishment is feasible for certain classes of devices, such as mobile phones.

In June 2005, Yaniv Shaked and Avishai Wool published a paper describing both passive and active methods for obtaining the PIN for a Bluetooth link. The passive attack allows a suitably equipped attacker to eavesdrop on communications and spoof, if the attacker was present at the time of initial pairing. The active method makes use of a specially constructed message that must be inserted at a specific point in the protocol, to make the master and slave repeat the pairing process. After that, the first method can be used to crack the PIN. This attack's major weakness is that it requires the user of the devices under attack to re-enter the PIN during the attack when the device prompts them to. Also, this active attack probably requires custom hardware, since most commercially available Bluetooth devices are not capable of the timing necessary.

In August 2005, police in Cambridgeshire, England, issued warnings about thieves using Bluetooth-enabled phones to track other devices left in cars. Police are advising users to ensure that any mobile networking connections are de-activated if laptops and other devices are left in this way.

2006

In April 2006, researchers from Secure Network and F-Secure published a report that warns of the large number of devices left in a visible state, and issued statistics on the spread of various Bluetooth services and the ease of spread of an eventual Bluetooth worm.

In October 2007, at the Luxemburgish Hack.lu Security Conference, Kevin Finistere and Thierry Zoller demonstrated and released a remote root shell via Bluetooth on Mac OS X v10.3.9 and v10.4. They also demonstrated the first Bluetooth PIN and Linkkeys cracker, which is based on the research of Wool and Shaked.

Health Concerns

Bluetooth uses the microwave radio frequency spectrum in the 2.4 GHz to 2.4835 GHz range. Maximum power output from a Bluetooth radio is 100 mW, 2.5 mW, and 1 mW for Class 1, Class 2, and Class 3 devices respectively, which puts Class 1 at roughly the same level as mobile phones, and the other two classes much lower. Accordingly, Class 2 and Class 3 Bluetooth devices are considered less of a potential hazard than mobile phones, and Class 1 may be comparable to that of mobile phones.

Origin of the Name and the Logo

Bluetooth was named after a tenth-century king, Harald Bluetooth, King of Denmark and Norway. Bluetooth is an anglicized version of Harald Blaatand, who was known for his unification of previously warring tribes from Denmark (including now Swedish Scania, where the Bluetooth technology was invented), and Norway. Bluetooth likewise was intended to unify different technologies, such as personal computers and mobile phones.

The name may have been inspired less by the historical Harald than the loose interpretation of him in *The Long Ships* by Frans Gunnar Bengtsson, a Swedish Viking-inspired novel.

The Bluetooth logo merges the Germanic runes analogous to the modern Latin letters H and B: (for *H*arald *B*luetooth) (Hagall) and (Berkanan) merged together, forming a bind rune.

Bluetooth Special Interest Group

The technology later known as Bluetooth began as an Ericsson project named *multi-communicator link*, or *MC link*. In 1997, Intel began collaborating on the project. A year later, Ericsson, IBM, Intel, Toshiba, and Nokia formed a consortium and adopted the code name Bluetooth for their proposed open specification. In December 1999, 3Com, Lucent Technologies, Microsoft, and Motorola joined the founders as the promoters of the Bluetooth Special Interest Group (SIG). Since that time, Lucent Technologies has transferred their membership to spinoff Agere Systems, IBM has transferred their promoter status to Lenovo, and 3Com has left the promoter group. Agere Systems was later merged with LSI Corporation and left the Bluetooth promoters group in August 2007.

The Bluetooth Special Interest Group (SIG) is a privately held, not-for-profit trade association with headquarters in Bellevue, Washington. As of January 2008, the SIG is composed of over 10,000 member companies in the telecommunications, computing, automotive, music, apparel, industrial automation, and network industries, and a small staff in Hong Kong, Sweden, and the USA. SIG members develop Bluetooth technology and implement and market the technology in their products. The Bluetooth SIG itself does not make, manufacture, or sell Bluetooth-enabled products. The executive director of the Bluetooth SIG is Michael W. Foley.

GSM INTERWORKING PROFILE

The GSM Interworking Profile, usually abbreviated to GIP and sometimes to IWP, is a profile for DECT that allows a DECT base station to form part of a GSM network, given suitable handsets. While proposed and tested, notably in Switzerland in 1995, the system has never been commercially deployed. Infrastructure issues make it less practical and useful to implement than the more recent GAN/UMA system, which can make use of usually unmetered and neutral Internet service to provide the connection back to the network operator.

Description

Like the later GAN/UMA standard, GIP makes use of a technology that does not require licensed spectrum to expand capacity and allow end users, in theory, to improve coverage in areas difficult to reach via large, external, cell towers.

GIP is a DECT *profile,* meaning a set of protocols that runs over the base DECT system. The most popular profile for DECT is GAP, which is used to provide cordless phone service, but this is not used for GIP.

In GIP, several of the GSM lower level protocols are replaced by DECT-friendly equivalents. Voice channels make use of 32 kbit/s ADPCM channels rather than 13 kbit/s FR/EFR/AMR channels, for example.

The system supports handoff, and authentication is done via the GSM SIM card as normal. However, DECT terminals need to authenticate themselves against the base station, and this added layer is implementation dependent.

The base station is usually connected back to the GSM network via an ISDN line. An "A interface" is implemented over the ISDN line just as it would be for a BSC. This allows multiple GSM calls and GSM control data to be multiplexed over the 64 kbit/s ISDN B channels.

Deployments

While GIP was deployed to some success at Telecom '95 in Geneva, the system has not been commercially deployed since. Hybrid DECT/GSM devices have appeared, but these have essentially been "Two phones in a box" systems that combine the functionality of a standard GAP phone with a GSM phone, so that a person can receive and make calls on either their home phone line or a mobile network without having to use two phones. An example of this approach is BT's/Ericsson's OnePhone service.

Most probably, the fact that the system requires an ISDN connection, which in most countries where ISDN is popular is priced by time used, has made GIP a difficult sell. In practice, the system appears to be oriented towards carriers instead of individuals, and carriers can more easily create microcells using their own spectrum, running ordinary GSM and not requiring the use of special handsets.

With the advent of the Internet and widespread availability of high speed Internet connections, GIP could be redesigned to make use of Internet instead of ISDN connections. However, the industry has gone in the direction of using GAN/UMA, which substitutes an 802.11 or Bluetooth air interface for GSM/UMTS's and as such can use unmodified commodity infrastructure.

HEALTH IMPACTS OF WIRELESS ELECTRONIC DEVICES

The World Health Organization has acknowledged that electromagnetic fields (EMFs) are influencing the environment (but not people), and that some people are worried about possible effects. In response to public concern, the World Health Organization established the *International EMF Project* in 1996 to assess the scientific evidence of possible health effects of EMF in the frequency range from 0 to 300 GHz. They have stated that although extensive research has been conducted into possible health effects of exposure to many parts of the frequency spectrum, all reviews conducted so far have indicated that exposures are below the limits recommended in the ICNIRP (1998) EMF guidelines, covering the full frequency range from 0-300 GHz, and do not produce any known adverse health effect.

International guidelines on exposure levels to microwave frequency EMFs such as ICNIRP limit the power levels of wireless devices and it is uncommon for wireless devices to exceed the guidelines. These guidelines only take into account thermal effects, as nonthermal effects have not been conclusively demonstrated. The official stance of the Health Protection Agency is that "[T]here is no consistent evidence to date that WiFi and WLANs adversely affect the health of the general population." And also that "... it is a sensible precautionary approach... to keep the situation under ongoing review...". Sir William has resisted any calls to further explain his comments.

Exposure Difference to Mobile Phones

While users of wireless devices are typically exposed for much longer periods than for mobile phones, the range of wireless devices (and hence their strength) is significantly less. As well, the devices are located significantly farther away from users' heads, resulting in far less exposure overall: The Health Protection Agency claims that if a person spends one year in a Wi-Fi hotspot, they will receive the same dose of radio waves as if they had made a 20-minute call on a mobile phone.

Wireless LAN

EMF levels for WiFi devices are much lower than mobile phones, and there is less public concern about any suggested health issues for wireless LAN devices. Most wireless LAN equipment is designed to work within pre-defined standards. Wireless access points are also often in close proximity to humans, but the drop off in the already low power is fast, following the inverse-square law.

WiFi has been anecdotally linked to the Electrical Sensitivity, but no studies have researched this association to date. Please read the Electromagnetic hypersensitivity article for information on the research so far into the possible association with exposure to mobile phones and other sources of radiofrequency electromagnetic fields.

The HPA's position is that "... radio frequency (RF) exposures from WiFi are likely to be lower than those from mobile phones." It also saw "... no reason why schools and others should not use WiFi equipment." In October 2007, the HPA launched a new "systematic" study into the effects of WiFi networks on behalf of the UK Government, in order to calm fears that had appeared in the media in a recent period up to that time." Dr. Michael Clark, of the HPA, says published research on mobile phones and masts does not add up to an indictment of WiFi.

Bluetooth

Bluetooth also uses the microwave frequency spectrum in the range of 2.4 GHz to 2.4835 GHz. The radiated output power of Bluetooth devices varies between 1 and 100 mW, and can operate continuously or sporadically (on demand), so total exposure to EMF radiation is quite variable. Bluetooth devices have not been linked with any health issues.

Other Devices

Radio frequency in the microwave and radio spectrum is used in a number of practical devices for professional and home use, such as:

- DECT and other cordless phones operating at a wide range of frequencies
- Remote control devices for opening gates, etc.
- Portable two-way radio communication devices, such as walkie-talkies
- Wireless security (alarm) systems
- Wireless security video cameras
- Radio links between buildings for data communication
- Baby monitors.

In addition, electrical and electronic devices of all kinds emit EM fields around their working circuits, generated by oscillating currents. Humans are in daily contact with computers, video display monitors, TV screens, microwave ovens, fluorescent lamps, electric motors of several kinds (such as washing machines, water pumps, etc.) and many others. The typical background power of electromagnetic fields in the home can vary from zero to 5 milliwatts per meter squared. Long-time effects of these electromagnetic fields on human and animal health are still unknown, and most of the studies available have shown no effect. However, the powerful fields produced by radio (and then TV) transmitters have been present for more than 100 years now with no established effects on people's health.

7

Sound Recording, Reproduction and Broadcasting: An Overview

SOUND RECORDING AND REPRODUCTION

Sound recording and reproduction is the electrical or mechanical inscription and re-creation of sound waves, usually used for the voice or for music.

Technology

The two main classes of sound recording technology are analogue recording and digital recording.

Analogue recording is achieved by a small microphone diaphragm that can detect changes in atmospheric pressure (acoustic sound waves) and record them as graphic sound waves on a medium. The first of these recordings were called sonograms and had no playback mechanism available. With an exclusively mechanical phonograph, the analogue conversion is in the form of sonogram grooves carved by a stylus. Newer phonographs use electronics in the process. With magnetic tape, the analogue conversion is first in the form of electrical current waves from the microphones conversion of diaphragm movement to electromagnetic fluctuation (flux) that modulate an electric signal, and second of magnetic particles drawn into sonogram-shaped clusters by flux from a tape head sensing the electrical current changes. Analogue sound reproduction is the reverse process with a bigger loudspeaker diaphragm causing changes to atmospheric pressure to form acoustic sound waves.

Digital recording and reproduction uses the same analogue technologies, with digitization of the sonographic data and signal, allowing it to be stored and transmitted on a wider variety of media. The digital binary numeric data is a representation of the periodic vector points in the raw analogue acoustic data at a sample rate most often too frequent for the human ear to distinguish differences in quality. Digital recordings are not necessarily at a higher sample rate, but are often considered higher quality because of less interference from dust or electromagnetic interference in playback and less mechanical deterioration from corrosion or mishandling the storage medium.

Early Developments

The automatic reproduction of music can be traced back as far as the 9th century, when the Banū Mūsā brothers invented "the earliest known mechanical musical instrument", in this case a hydropowered organ which played interchangeable cylinders automatically. According to Charles B. Fowler, this "cylinder with raised pins on the surface remained the basic device to produce and reproduce music mechanically until the second half of the nineteenth century." The Banu Musa also invented an automatic flute player which appears to have been the first programmable machine.

In the 14th century, Flanders introduced a mechanical bell-ringer controlled by a rotating cylinder. Similar designs appeared in barrel organs (15th century), musical clocks (1598), barrel pianos (1805), and musical boxes (1815). All of these machines could play stored music, but they could not play arbitrary sounds, could not record a live performance, and were limited by the physical size of the medium. The first device that could record sound mechanically (but could not play it back) was the phonautograph, developed in 1857 by Edouard-Leon Scott. One of his paper recordings of *Au Clair de la Lune*, a French folk song, was digitally converted to sound in 2008. It is believed to be the oldest existing recording of a recognisable human voice. Since the above recording was recovered the same team have since recovered a recording of a 435 Hz tuning fork (at that time the French standard concert pitch for A'—now 440 Hz). The tuning fork is barely audible. This second recording has thus become the oldest known recording of a recognisable sound.

The player piano, first demonstrated in 1876, used a punched paper scroll that could store an arbitrarily long piece of music. This piano roll moved over a device known as the 'tracker bar', which first had 58 holes, was expanded to 65 and then was upgraded to 88 holes (generally, one for each piano key). When a perforation passed over the hole, they noted sounded. Piano rolls were the first stored music medium that could be mass-produced, although the hardware to play them was much too expensive for personal use. Technology to record a live performance onto a piano roll was not developed until 1904. Piano rolls have been in continuous mass production since around 1898. A 1908 U.S. Supreme Court copyright case noted that, in 1902 alone, there were between 70,000 and 75,000 player pianos manufactured, and between 1,000,000 and 1,500,000 piano rolls produced. The use of piano rolls began to decline in the 1920s although one type is still being made today. The fairground organ, developed in 1892, used a similar system of accordion-folded punched cardboard books.

Phonograph Cylinder

The first practical sound recording and reproduction device was the mechanical phonograph cylinder, invented by Thomas Edison in 1877 and patented in 1878. The invention soon spread across the globe and over the next two decades the commercial recording, distribution and sale of sound recordings became a growing new international industry, with the most popular titles selling millions of units by the early 1900s. The development of mass-production techniques enabled cylinder recordings to become a major new consumer item in industrial countries and the cylinder was the main consumer format from the late 1880s until around 1910.

Disc Phonograph

The next major technical development was the invention of the gramophone disc, generally credited to Emile Berliner and commercially introduced in the United States in 1889.

Discs were easier to manufacture, transport and store, and they had the additional benefit of being louder (marginally) than cylinders, which by necessity, were single-sided. Sales of the gramophone record overtook the cylinder ca.1910, and by the end of World War I, the disc had become the dominant commercial recording format. In various permutations, the audio disc format became the primary medium for consumer sound recordings until the end of the 20th century, and the double-sided 78 rpm shellac disc was the standard consumer music format from the early 1910s to the late 1950s.

Although there was no universally accepted speed, and various companies offered discs that played at several different speeds, the major recording companies eventually settled on a *de facto* industry standard of nominally 78 revolutions per minute, though the actual speed differed between America and the rest of the world. The specified speed was 78.26 rpm in America and 77.92 rpm throughout the rest of the world (this was related to the speed of a mains-driven synchronous motor). The nominal speed of the disc format gave rise to its common nickname, the "seventy-eight" (though not until other speeds had become available).

Discs were made of shellac or similar brittle plastic like materials, played with needles made from a variety of materials including mild steel, thorn and even sapphire. Discs had a distinctly limited playing life which was heavily dependent on how they were reproduced.

The earlier, purely acoustic methods of recording had limited sensitivity and frequency range. Mid-frequency range notes could be recorded but very low and very high frequencies could not. Instruments such as the violin transferred poorly to disc; however, this was partially solved by retrofitting a conical horn to the sound box of the violin. The horn was no longer required once electrical recording was developed. The vinyl microgroove record was introduced in the late 1940s, and the two main vinyl formats—the 7-inch single turning at 45 rpm and the 12-inch LP (long-playing) record turning at 33 1/3 rpm— had totally replaced the 78 rpm shellac (sometimes vinyl) disc by the end of the 1950s. Vinyl offered improved performance, both in stamping and in playback, and came to be generally played with polished diamond styli, and when played properly (precise tracking weight, etc.) offered longer life. Vinyl records were, over-optimistically, advertised as "unbreakable." They were not, but were much less brittle and breakable than shellac. Nearly all were tinted black, but some were coloured, as red, swirled, translucent, etc.

Electrical Recording

Sound recording began as a mechanical process and remained so until the early 1920s (with the exception of the 1899 Telegraphone) when a string of groundbreaking inventions in the field of electronics revolutionized sound recording and the young recording industry. These included sound transducers such as microphones and loudspeakers, and various electronic devices such as the mixing desk, designed for the amplification and modification of electrical sound signals.

After the Edison phonograph itself, arguably the most significant advances in sound recording were the electronic systems invented by two American scientists between 1900 and 1924.

In 1906 Lee De Forest invented the "Audion" triode vacuum-tube, electronic valve, which could greatly amplify weak electrical signals (one early use was to amplify long distance telephone in 1915) which became the basis of all subsequent electrical sound systems until the invention of the transistor. The valve was quickly followed by the invention of the Regenerative circuit, Super-Regenerative circuit and the Superheterodyne receiver circuit, all of which were invented and patented by the young electronics genius Edwin Armstrong between 1914 and 1922. Armstrong's inventions made higher fidelity electrical sound recording and reproduction a practical reality, facilitating the development of the electronic amplifier and many other devices; after 1925 these systems had become standard in the recording and radio industry.

While E.H. Armstrong published studies about the fundamental operation of the triode vacuum tube before World War I, scientists at Bell Telephone Laboratories achieved their own understanding about the triode and were utilizing the audion as a repeater in weak telephone circuits. By 1925 it was possible to place a long distance telephone call with these repeaters between New York and San Francisco in 20 minutes, both parties being clearly heard.

With this technical prowess, Joseph P. Maxfield and Henry C. Harrison from Bell Telephone Laboratories were skilled in using mechanical analogues of electrical circuits and applied these principles to sound recording and reproduction. They were ready to demonstrate their results by 1924 using the Wente condenser microphone and the vacuum tube amplifier to drive the "rubber line" wax recorder to cut a master audio disc.

Meanwhile, radio continued to develop. Armstrong's groundbreaking inventions (including FM radio) also made possible the broadcasting of long-range, high-quality radio transmissions of voice and music. The importance of Armstong's Superheterodyne circuit cannot be over estimated—it is the central component of almost all analogue amplification and both analogue and digital radio-frequency transmitter and receiver devices to this day.

Beginning during World War I, experiments were undertaken in the United States and Great Britain to reprc duce among other things, the sound of a Submarine (u-boat) for training purposes. The acoustical recordings of that time proved entirely unable to reproduce the sounds, and other methods were actively sought. Radio had developed independently to this point, and now Bell Laboritories sought a marriage of the two disparate technologies, greater than the two separately. The first experiments were not very promising, but by 1920 greater sound fidelity was achieved using the electrical system than had ever been realized acoustically. One early recording made without fanfare or announcement was the dedication of the Tomb of the Unknown Soldier at Arlington Cemetery.

By early 1924 such dramatic progress had been made, that Bell Laboratories arranged a demonstration for the leading recording companies, Victor Talking Machine, and Columbia Phonograph Co's.

Columbia, always in financial straits, could not afford it, and Victor, essentially leaderless since the mental collapse of founder Eldridge Johnson, left the demonstration without comment. English Columbia, by then a separate company, got hold of a test pressing made by Pathe' from these sessions, and realized the immediate and urgent need to have the new system. Bell was only offering its method to United States Companies, and to circumvent this, Managing Director Louis Sterling of English Columbia, bought his once parent company, and signed up for electrical recording. When Victor Talking Machine was apprised of the Columbia deal, they too quickly signed. Columbia made its first electrical recordings on February 25, 1925 with Victor following a few weeks later. The two then agreed privately to "be quiet" until November 1925, by which time enough electrical repertory would be available.

Other Recording Formats

This period also saw several other historic developments including the introduction of the first practical magnetic sound recording system, the magnetic wire recorder, which was based on the work of Danish inventor Valdemar Poulsen. Magnetic wire recorders were effective, but the sound quality was poor, so between the wars they were primarily used for voice recording and marketed as business dictating machines.

In the 1930s radio pioneer Guglielmo Marconi developed a system of magnetic sound recording using steel tape. This was the same material used to make razor blades, and not surprisingly the fearsome Marconi-Stille recorders were considered so dangerous that technicians had to operate them from another room for safety. Because of the high recording speeds required, they used enormous reels about one metre in diameter, and the thin tape frequently broke, sending jagged lengths of razor steel flying around the studio. The K1 Magnetophon was the first practical tape recorder, developed by AEG in Germany in 1935.

The other major invention in sound recording in this period was the optical sound-on-film system, also generally credited to Lee De Forest. Although famous early "Talkies" like *The Jazz Singer* used a sound-on-disc system, the film industry eventually adopted the optical sound-on-film system and it revolutionized the movie industry in the 1930s, ushering in the era of 'talking pictures.' Optical sound-on-film, based on the photoelectric cell, became the standard film audio system throughout the world until it was superseded in the 1960s.

Magnetic Tape

Other important inventions of this period were magnetic tape and the tape recorder (Telegraphone). Paper-based tape was first used but was soon superseded by polyester and acetate backing due to dust drop and hiss. Acetate was more brittle than polyester and snapped easily. This technology, the basis for almost all commercial recording from the 1950s to the 1980s, was invented by German audio engineers in the 1930s, who also discovered the technique of AC biasing, which dramatically improved the frequency response of tape recordings. Tape recording was perfected just after the war by American audio engineer John T. Mullin with the help of Crosby Enterprises (Bing Crosby), whose pioneering recorders were based on captured German recorders, and the Ampex company produced the first commercially available tape recorders in the late 1940s.

Magnetic tape brought about sweeping changes in both radio and the recording industry. Sound could be recorded, erased and re-recorded on the same tape many times, sounds could be duplicated from tape to tape with only minor loss of quality, and recordings could now be very precisely edited by physically cutting the tape and rejoining it.

Within a few years of the introduction of the first commercial tape recorder, the Ampex 200 model, launched in 1948, American musician-inventor Les Paul had invented the first multitrack tape recorder, bringing about another technical revolution in the recording industry. Tape made possible the first sound recordings totally created by electronic means, opening the way for the bold sonic experiments of the Musique Concrète school and avant garde composers like Karlheinz Stockhausen, which in turn led to the innovative pop music recordings of artists such as Frank Zappa, The Beatles and The Beach Boys.

Tape enabled the radio industry for the first time to pre-record many sections of programme content such as advertising, which formerly had to be presented live, and it also enabled the creation and duplication of complex, high-fidelity, long-duration recordings of entire programmes. It also, for the first time, allowed broadcasters, regulators and other interested parties to undertake comprehensive logging of radio broadcasts. Innovations like multitracking and tape echo enabled radio programmes and advertisements to be pre-produced to a level of complexity and sophistication that was previously unattainable and tape also led to significant changes to the pacing of programme content, thanks to the introduction of the endless-loop tape cartridge.

Stereo and Hi-Fi

Magnetic tape also enabled the development of the first practical commercial sound systems that could record and reproduce high-fidelity stereophonic sound. Experiments with stereo dated back to the 1880s and during the 1930s and 1940s there were many attempts to record in stereo using discs, but these were hampered by problems with synchronization.

The first major breakthrough in practical stereo sound was made by Bell Laboratories, who in 1937 demonstrated a practical system of two-channel stereo, using dual optical sound tracks on film. Major movie studios quickly developed three-track and four-track sound systems, and the first stereo sound recording in a commercial film was made by Judy Garland for the MGM movie

Listen, Darling in 1938. The first commercially-released movie with a full surround soundtrack was Walt Disney's *Fantasia*, released in 1940. The sound for this production was originally recorded on a completely separate magnetic film, but because of the complex equipment required to present it, it was shown as a road show, but only in the United States. Regular releases of the film were on standard mono optical 35 mm stock until the film was transferred to multichannel 70 mm stock in the 1970s.

German audio engineers working on magnetic tape are reported to have developed stereo recording by 1943, but it was not until the introduction of the first commercial two-track tape recorders by Ampex in the late 1940s that stereo tape recording became commercially feasible. However, despite the availability of multitrack tape, stereo did not become the standard system for commercial music recording for some years and it remained a specialist market during the 1950s. This changed after the late 1957 introduction of the "Westrex stereo phonograph disc."

Decca Records in England came out with FFRR (Full Frequency Range Recording) in the 1940s which became internationally accepted and a worldwide standard for higher quality recordings on vinyl records. The Ernest Ansermet recording of Igor Stravinsky's Petrushka was key in the development of full frequency range records and alterting the listening public to high fidelity in 1946.

Most pop singles were mixed into monophonic sound until the mid-1960s, it was common for major pop releases to be issued in both mono and stereo until the early 1970s. Many Sixties pop albums now available only in stereo were originally intended to be released only in mono, and the so-called "stereo" version of these albums were created by simply separating the two tracks of the master tape. In the mid-Sixties, as stereo became more popular, many mono recordings (such as The Beach Boys' *Pet Sounds*) were remastered using the so-called "fake stereo" method, which spread the sound across the stereo field by directing higher-frequency sound into one channel and lower-frequency sounds into the other.

1950s and Beyond

Magnetic tape transformed the recording industry, and by the late-1950s the vast majority of commercial recordings were being mastered on tape. The electronics revolution that followed the invention of the transistor brought other radical changes, the most important of which was the introduction of the world's first "personal music device", the miniaturized transistor radio, which became a major consumer luxury item in the 1960s, transforming radio broadcasting from a static group experience into a mobile, personal listening activity.

The first multitrack recording made using magnetic tape was "How High the Moon" by Les Paul, on which Paul played eight overdubbed guitar tracks. In the 1960s Brian Wilson of The Beach Boys, Frank Zappa and The Beatles (with producer George Martin) were among the first popular artists to explore the possibilities of multitrack techniques and effects on their landmark albums *Pet Sounds, Freak Out!* and *Sgt. Pepper's Lonely Hearts Club Band.*

The next important innovation was small cartridge based tape systems of which the compact cassette, introduced by the Philips electronics company in 1964 is the best known. It eventually entirely replaced the competing formats, the larger 8-track tape (used primarily in cars) and the fairly similar 'Deutsche Cassette' developed by the German company Grundig. This latter system was not particularly common in Europe and practically unheard of in America. The compact cassette became a major consumer audio format and advances in microelectronics eventually allowed the development of the Sony Walkman, introduced in the 1970s, which was the first personal music player and gave a major boost to the mass distribution of music recordings. Cassettes became the first successful consumer recording/re-recording medium. The gramophone record was a pre-recorded playback only medium, and reel-to-reel tape was too difficult for most consumers and far less portable.

A key advance in audio fidelity came with the Dolby A noise reduction system, invented by Ray Dolby and introduced in 1966. A competing system dbx, invented by David Blackmer, found most success in professional audio. A simpler variant of Dolby's noise reduction system, known as Dolby B greatly improved the sound of cassette tape recordings by reducing the practical effect of the recorded hiss inherent in the narrow tape used. It, and variants, also eventually found wide application in the recording and film industries. Dolby B was crucial to the popularization and commercial success of the compact cassette as a domestic recording and playback medium, and became a part of the booming "hi-fi" market of the 1970s and beyond. The compact cassette also benefited enormously from developments in the tape material itself as materials with wider frequency responses and lower inherent noise were developed, often based on cobalt and/or chrome oxides as the magnetic material instead of the more usual iron oxide.

The multitrack audio cartridge had been in wide use in the radio industry, from the late 1950s to the 1980s, but in the 1960s the pre-recorded 8-track cartridge was launched as a consumer audio format by Bill Lear of the Lear Jet aircraft company (and although its correct name was the 'Lear Jet Cartridge', it was seldom referred to as such). Aimed particularly at the automotive market, they were the first practical, affordable car hi-fi systems, and could produce superior sound quality to the compact cassette. However, the smaller size and greater durability augmented by the ability to create home-recorded music "compilations" since 8-track recorders were rare saw the cassette become the dominant consumer format for portable audio devices in the 1970s and 1980s.

There had been experiments with multi-channel sound for many years—usually for special musical or cultural events—but the first commercial application of the concept came in the early 1970s with the introduction of Quadraphonic sound. This spin-off development from multitrack recording used four tracks (instead of the two used in stereo) and four speakers to create a 360-degree audio field around the listener. Following the release of the first consumer 4-channel hi-fi systems, a number of popular albums were released in one of the competing four-channel formats; among the best known are Mike Oldfield's *Tubular Bells* and Pink Floyd's *The Dark Side of the Moon*. Quadraphonic sound was not a commercial success, partly because of competing and somewhat incompatible four-channel sound systems (e.g., CBS, JVC, Dynaco and others all had systems) and generally poor quality, even when played as intended on the correct equipment, of the released music. It eventually faded out in the late 1970s, although this early venture paved the way for the eventual introduction of domestic Surround Sound systems in home theatre use, which have gained enormous popularity since the introduction of the DVD. This widespread adoption has occurred despite the confusion introduced by the multitude of available surround sound standards.

The replacement of the thermionic valve (vacuum tube) by the smaller, cooler and less power-hungry transistor also accelerated the sale of consumer high-fidelity "hi-fi" sound systems from the 1960s onward. In the 1950s most record players were monophonic and had relatively low sound quality; few consumers could afford high-quality stereophonic sound systems. In the 1960s, American manufacturers introduced a new generation of "modular" hi-fi components—separate turntables, pre-amplifiers, amplifiers, both combined as integrated amplifiers, tape recorders, and other ancillary equipment (like the graphic equalizer), which could be connected together to create a complete home sound system. These developments were rapidly taken up by Japanese electronics companies, which soon flooded the world market with relatively cheap, high-quality components. By the 1980s, corporations like Sony had become world leaders in the music recording and playback industry.

Digital Recording

The invention of digital sound recording and the compact disc in 1982 brought significant improvements in the durability of consumer recordings. The CD initiated another massive wave of change in the consumer music industry, with vinyl records effectively relegated to a small niche market by the mid-1990s. However, the introduction of digital systems was initially fiercely resisted by the record industry which feared wholesale piracy on a medium which was able to produce perfect copies of original released recordings. However, various protection system (principally SCMS) persuaded the industry to bow to the inevitable.

The most recent and revolutionary developments have been in digital recording, with the invention of purely electronic consumer recording formats such as the WAV digital music file and the compressed file type, the MP3. This generated a new type of portable solid-state computerized digital audio player, the MP3 player. Another invention, by Sony, was the minidisc player, using ATRAC compression on small, cheap, re-writeable discs. This was in vogue in the 1990s, and is still popular, especially in a newer, longer playing and higher fidelity version. New technologies such as Super Audio CD, DVD-A, Blu-ray Disc and HD DVD continue to set a very high rate of change in digital audio storage.

This technology spreads across various associated fields, from hi-fi to professional audio, internet radio and podcasting.

Technological developments in recording and editing have transformed the record, movie and television industries in recent decades. Audio editing became practicable with the invention of magnetic tape recording, but the use of computers has made editing operations faster and easier to execute with software, and the use of hard-drives for storage has made recording cheaper. Today, the process of making a recording is separated into tracking, mixing and mastering. Multitrack recording makes it possible to capture signals from several microphones, or from different 'takes' to tape or disc, with maximized headroom and quality, allowing previously unavailable flexibility in the mixing and mastering stages for editing, level balancing, compressing and limiting, adding effects such as reverberation, equalization, flanging, and much more.

In the 1920s, the early talkies featured the new sound-on-film technology which used photoelectric cells to record and reproduce sound signals that were optically recorded directly onto the movie film. The introduction of talking movies, spearheaded by *The Jazz Singer* in 1927 (though it used a sound on disk technique, not a photoelectric one), saw the rapid demise of live cinema musicians and orchestras. They were replaced with pre-recorded soundtracks, causing the loss of many jobs. The American Federation of Musicians took out advertisements in newspapers, protesting the replacement of real musicians with mechanical playing devices, especially in theatres.

Voice to Note

Voice-to-note refers to the capability of personal computers to be able to recognize notes that are sung, hummed, or whistled into a microphone. The pitch and duration of the notes are then calculated and converted into MIDI music files.

Legal Status

UK

Since 1934, sound recordings are treated differently from musical works under copyright law. *Copyright, Designs and Patents Act 1988* defines a sound recording to mean *(a) a recording of sounds, from which the sounds may be reproduced, or (b) a recording of the whole or any part of a literary, dramatic or musical work, from which sounds reproducing the work or part may be produced, regardless of the medium on which the recording is made or the method by which the sounds are reproduced or produced.* It thus covers vinyl records, tapes, compact discs, digital audiotapes, and MP3s which embody recordings.

DIGITAL AUDIO BROADCASTING

Digital Audio Broadcasting (DAB), also known as Eureka 147, is a digital radio technology for broadcasting radio stations, used in several countries, particularly in Europe. As of 2006, approximately 1,000 stations worldwide broadcast in the DAB format.

The DAB standard was designed in the 1980s, and receivers have been available in many countries for several years. Proponents claim the standard offers several benefits over existing analogue FM radio, such as higher fidelity audio, more stations in the same broadcast spectrum, and increased resistance to noise, multipath, fading, and co-channel interference. However, listening tests carried out by experts in the field of audio have shown that the audio quality on DAB is lower than on FM in the UK, which with 7 m sales, is the country that accounts for the vast majority of global DAB sales-to-date, due to 98 per cent of stereo stations using a bit rate of 128 kbit/s with the MP2 audio codec, which is unable to match the audio quality provided by FM.

An upgraded version of the system was released in February 2007, which is called DAB+. DAB+ is not backward-compatible with DAB, which means that only receivers that support the new standard will be able to receive DAB+ broadcasts. DAB+ is 2-3 times more efficient than DAB due to the adoption of the AAC+ audio codec, which means that DAB+ can provide higher audio quality and more radio stations than DAB allows. Reception quality will also be more robust on DAB+ than on DAB due to the addition of Reed-Solomon error correction coding.

Italy has started transmitting DAB+ stations, Malta, Switzerland and Hungary are due to launch DAB+ stations in 2008, and Australia and Germany planning on launching DAB+ in 2009. The radio industry in the UK is expecting DAB+ stations to launch between 2010-2013, and podcast services using the DAB+ format will be launched in the UK in 2009.

History

DAB has been under development since 1981 at the Institut für Rundfunktechnik (IRT). In 1985 the first DAB demonstrations were held at the WARC-ORB in Geneva and in 1988 the first DAB transmissions were made in Germany. Later DAB (or Eureka-147) was developed as a research project for the European Union (Eureka project number EU147), which started in 1987 on initiative by a consortium formed in 1986. The MPEG-1 Audio Layer II ("MP2") codec was created as part of the EU147 project. DAB was the first standard based on orthogonal frequency division multiplexing (OFDM) modulation technique, which since then has become one of the most popular transmission schemes for modern wideband digital communication systems.

A choice of audio codec, modulation and error-correction coding schemes and first trial broadcasts were made in 1990. Public demonstrations were made in 1993 in the United Kingdom. The protocol specification was finalized in 1993 and adopted by the ITU-R standardization body in 1994, the European community in 1995 and by ETSI in 1997. Pilot broadcasts were launched in several countries in 1995. The UK was the first country to receive a wide range of radio stations via DAB. Commercial DAB receivers began to be sold in 1999 and over 50 commercial and BBC services were available in London by 2001. By 2006, 500 million people worldwide were in the coverage area of DAB broadcasts, although by this time sales had only taken off in the UK and in 2006 there are approximately 1,000 DAB stations in operation world wide.

The standard was coordinated by the European DAB forum, formed in 1995 and reconstituted to the World DAB Forum in 1997, which represents more than 30 countries. In 2006 the World DAB Forum became the World DMB Forum which now presides over both the DAB and DMB standard.

In October 2005, the World DMB Forum instructed its Technical Committee to carry out the work needed to adopt the AAC+ audio codec and stronger error correction coding. This work led to the launch of the new DAB+ system.

DAB and FM/AM Compared

Traditionally radio programmes were broadcast on different frequencies via FM and AM, and the radio had to be tuned into each frequency. This used up a comparatively large amount of spectrum for a relatively small number of stations, limiting listening choice. DAB is a digital radio broadcasting system that through the application of multiplexing and compression combines multiple audio streams onto a single broadcast frequency called a DAB ensemble.

Within an overall target bit rate for the DAB ensemble, individual stations can be allocated different bit rates. The number of channels within a DAB ensemble can be increased by lowering average bit rates, but at the expense of the quality of streams. Error correction under the DAB standard makes the signal more robust but reduces the total bit rate available for streams.

Use of Frequency Spectrum and Transmitter Sites

DAB gives substantially higher spectral efficiency, measured in programmes per MHz and per transmitter site, than analogue communication. This has led to a vast increase in the number of stations available to listeners, especially outside of the major urban conurbations.

> *Numerical example*: FM requires 0.3 MHz per programme. The frequency reuse factor is approximately 15, meaning that only one out of 15 transmitters can use the same channel frequency without problems with co-channel interference, i.e. cross-talk. This results in 1/15/(0.3 MHz) = 0.22 programmes/transmitter/MHz. DAB with 192 kbit/s codec requires 1.536 MHz * 192 kbit/s/1136 kbit/s = 0.26 MHz per audio programme. The frequency reuse factor for local programmes and multi-frequency broadcasting networks (MFS) is typically 4, resulting in 1/4/(0.26 MHz) = 0.96 programmes/transmitter/MHz. This is 4.3 times as efficient. For single frequency networks (SFN), for example of national programmes, the channel re-use factor is 1, resulting in 1/1/0.25 MHz = 3.85 programmes/transmitter/MHz, which is 17.3 times as efficient as FM.

Note the above capacity improvement may not always be achieved at the L-band frequencies, since these are more sensitive to obstacles than the FM band frequencies, and may cause shadow fading for hilly terrain and for indoor communication. The number of transmitter sites or the transmission power required for full coverage of a country may be rather high at these frequencies, to avoid that the system becomes noise limited rather than limited by co-channel interference.

Sound Quality

The original objectives of converting to digital transmission were to enable higher fidelity, more stations and more resistance to noise, co-channel interference and multipath than in analogue FM radio. However, in the UK, Denmark, Norway and Switzerland, which are the leading countries with regard to implementing DAB, 98 per cent of stereo radio stations on DAB have a lower sound quality than FM due to the bit rate levels they use being too low for the inefficient MPEG Layer 2 audio codec to provide good audio quality.

The following paragraph about bit rate levels to be used on DAB was written by an engineer in the BBC Research and Development department and highlights why bit rates as low as 128 kbit/s should not be used on DAB:

> "A value of 256 kbit/s has been judged to provide a high quality stereo broadcast signal. However, a small reduction, to 224 kbit/s is often adequate, and in some cases it may be possible to accept a further reduction to 192 kbit/s, especially if redundancy in the stereo signal is exploited by a process of 'joint stereo' encoding (i.e. some sounds appearing at the centre of the stereo image need not be sent twice). At 192 kbit/s, it is relatively easy to hear imperfections in critical audio material."
>
> — BBC R&D White Paper WHP 061 June 2003

On 6 July 2006 the BBC reduced the bit-rate of transmission of Radio 3 from 192 kbit/s to 160 kbit/s. The resulting degradation of audio quality prompted a number of complaints to the Corporation. The BBC later announced that following this testing of new equipment, it would resume the previous practice of transmitting Radio 3 at 192 kbit/s whenever there were no other demands on bandwidth.

The UK Government seeks to maximize licence-revenue from the available spectrum. Therefore it 'squeezes in' as many stations as possible.

'Squeezing in' techniques include:

- Minimizing the bit-rate, to the lowest level of sound-quality that listeners are willing to tolerate. This is generally 128 kbit/s for stereo and 80 kbit/s or even 64 kbit/s for mono, although with these mono low rates acceptable quality is only achieved with speech only.
- Heavy compression—compressing the dynamic range of a signal (reducing sound-quality).
- Having few digital channels broadcasting in stereo.

These factors reduce sound-quality to the point where it is technically inferior to FM.

Maximizing Government license-revenue is not such an issue with TV, so BBC TV audio streams use a bit-rate of 256 kbit/s MP2.

Despite some criticism of sound quality, a recent survey among radio listeners in the UK, a territory where the low bit-rates are often criticized, revealed that 94 per cent experience a sound quality that is "much better", "better" or "the same" as FM.

Benefits of DAB

Current AM and FM terrestrial broadcast technology is well established, compatible, and cheap to manufacture. Benefits of DAB over analogue systems are explained below.

Improved End-User Features

DAB radios automatically tune to all the available stations, offering a list of all stations. DAB can carry "radiotext" (in DAB terminology, *Dynamic Label Segment*, or DLS) from the station giving real-time information such as song titles, music type and news or traffic updates. Advance programme guides can also be transmitted. A similar feature also exists on FM in the form of the RDS. (However, not all FM receivers allow radio stations to be stored by name.) Some radios offer a pause facility on live broadcasts, caching the broadcast stream on local flash memory, although this function is limited.

More Stations

DAB is more bandwidth efficient than analogue for national radio stations due to the use of SFNs, enabling more stations to be placed into a smaller section of the spectrum, although it is only marginally more efficient than FM for local radio stations.

In certain areas—particularly rural areas—the introduction of DAB gives radio listeners a greater choice of radio stations. For instance, in South Norway, radio listeners experienced an increase in available stations from 6 to 21 when DAB was introduced in November 2006.

Reception Quality

The DAB standard integrates features to reduce the negative consequences of multipath fading and signal noise, which afflict existing analogue systems.

Also, as DAB transmits digital audio, there is no hiss with a weak signal, which can happen on FM. However, radios in the fringe of a DAB signal, can experience a "bubbling mud" sound interrupting the audio and/or the audio cutting out altogether.

Less Pirate Interference

The specialized nature and cost of DAB broadcasting equipment provide barriers to pirate radio stations broadcasting on DAB. In cities such as London with large numbers of pirate radio stations broadcasting on FM, this means that some stations can be reliably received via DAB in areas where they are regularly difficult or impossible to receive on FM due to pirate radio interference.

Variable Bandwidth

Mono talk radio, news and weather channels and other non-music programmes need significantly less bandwidth than a typical music radio station, which allows DAB to carry these programmes at lower bit rates, leaving more bandwidth to be used for other programmes. However, this had led to the situation where some stations are being broadcast in mono.

Criticisms of DAB

Music Radio Stations Broadcasting in Mono

A number of music radio stations and stations that carry drama on DAB in the UK are being broadcast in mono when some argue that they should be in stereo. These stations are often available in stereo on other digital platforms, where capacity is not as constrainted, and on FM where applicable.

Reception Quality

The reception quality on DAB can be poor even for people that live well within the coverage area. The reason for this is that the old version of DAB uses weak error correction coding so that when there are a lot of errors with the received data not enough of the errors can be corrected and a "bubbling mud" sound occurs. In some cases a complete loss of signal can happen. This situation will be improved upon in the new DAB standard (DAB+, discussed below) that uses stronger error correction coding and as additional transmitters are built.

Signal Delay

The nature of a SFN is such that the transmitters in a network must broadcast the same signal at the same time. To achieve synchronization, the broadcaster must counter any differences in propagation time incurred by the different methods and distances involved in carrying the signal from the multiplexer to the different transmitters. This is done by applying a delay to the incoming signal at the transmitter based on a timestamp generated at the multiplexer, created taking into account the maximum likely propagation time, with a generous added margin for safety. Also delays in the receiver due to digital processing (e.g. deinterleaving) add to the overall delay to the listener. This delays the signal to the listener by about 2 seconds (depending on the decoding circuitry used). This has two disadvantages: (*i*) DAB radios are out of step with live events so time signals are not accurate and the experience of listening to live commentaries on events being watched is impaired, and (*ii*) listeners using a combination of FM and DAB radios (e.g. in different rooms of a house) will not hear an intelligible signal when both receivers are within earshot.

Coverage

As DAB is at a relatively early stage of deployment, DAB coverage is poor in nearly all countries in comparison to the high population coverage provided by FM.

Transmission Cost

Transmission on DAB is far more expensive than on FM, and measures taken by broadcasters to limit their costs have resulted in some DAB ensembles having to carry too many channels, forcing bit rates to be reduced to levels that deliver sound quality inferior to traditional FM.

Compatibility

In 2006 tests finally began using the much improved HE-AAC codec for DAB+. Virtually none of the current receivers in the field support the new codec, however, thus making them partially obsolete once DAB+ broadcasts begin and completely obsolete once the old MPEG-1 Layer 2 stations are switched off.

Power Requirements

As DAB requires digital signal processing techniques to convert from the received digitally encoded signal to the analogue audio content, the complexity of the electronic circuitry required to do this is high. This translates into needing more power to effect this conversion than compared to an analogue FM to audio conversion, meaning that portable receiving equipment will tend to have a shorter battery life, or require higher power (and hence more bulk).

As an indicator of this increased power consumption, dual FM/DAB radios quote the length of time they can play on a single charge. For DAB, this is often between one-sixth and one-twelfth of the time they can play when in FM mode.

Other Criticism

If the signal reception becomes marginal the audio will first start to burble or cut out rapidly and if the signal continues to degrade the audio will cut out more often. There is also less chance of long distance reception that hobbyists enjoy because each frequency/multiplex is used more often.

Technology

Bands and Modes

Eureka 147 DAB uses a wide-bandwidth broadcast technology and typically spectra have been allocated for it in Band III (174–

240 MHz) and L band (1452–1492 MHz), although the scheme allows for operation almost anywhere above 30 MHz. The US military has reserved L-Band in the USA only, blocking its use for other purposes in America, and the United States has reached an agreement with Canada that the latter will restrict L-Band DAB to terrestrial broadcast to avoid interference.

DAB has a number of country specific transmission modes (I, II, III and IV). For worldwide operation a receiver must support all four modes:

- Mode I for Band III, Earth,
- Mode II for L-Band, Earth and satellite,
- Mode III for frequencies below 3 GHz, Earth and satellite, and
- Mode IV for L-Band, Earth and satellite.

Protocol Stack

From a protocol stack viewpoint, the technologies used on DAB inhabit the following layers: the audio codec inhabits the application layer. Below that is the physical layer, which contains the error-correction coding and OFDM modulation, dealing with the over-the-air transmission and reception of data. Some aspects of these are described below.

Audio Codec

The older version of DAB that is being used in the UK, Ireland, Denmark, Norway and Switzerland, uses the MPEG-1 Audio Layer 2 audio codec, which is also known as *MP2* due to computer files using those characters for their file extension.

The new DAB+ standard has adopted the HE-AAC version 2 audio codec, commonly known as *AAC+* or *aacPlus*. AAC+ is approximately three-times more efficient than MP2, which means that broadcasters using DAB+ will be able to provide far higher audio quality or far more stations than they can on DAB, or, as is most likely, a combination of both higher audio quality and more stations will be provided.

One of the most important decisions regarding the design of a digital radio system is the choice of which audio codec to use, because the efficiency of the audio codec determines how many radio stations can be carried on a multiplex at a given level of audio quality. The capacity of a DAB multiplex is fixed, so the more efficient the audio codec is, the more stations can be carried, and vice versa. Similarly, for a fixed bit-rate level, the more efficient the audio codec is the higher the audio quality will be.

Error-Correction Coding

Error-correction coding (ECC) is an important technology for a digital communication system because it determines how robust the reception will be for a given signal strength stronger ECC will provide more robust reception than a weaker form.

The old version of DAB uses punctured convolutional coding for its ECC. The coding scheme uses unequal error protection (UEP), which means that parts of the audio bit-stream that are more susceptible to errors causing audible disturbances are provided with more protection (i.e. a lower code rate) and vice versa. However, the UEP scheme used on DAB results in there being a grey area in between the user experiencing good reception quality and no reception at all, as opposed to the situation with most other wireless digital communication systems that have a sharp "digital cliff", where the signal rapidly becomes unusable if the signal strength drops below a certain threshold. When DAB listeners receive a signal in this intermediate strength area they experience a "burbling" sound which interrupts the playback of the audio, and listeners find this to be more unpleasant to listen to than hiss on FM.

The new DAB+ standard has incorporated Reed-Solomon ECC as an "outer layer" of coding that is placed around the "inner layer" of convolutional coding used by the older DAB system, although on DAB+ the convolutional coding uses equal error protection (EEP) rather than UEP. This combination of convolutional coding as the inner layer of coding, followed by a byte interleaver then an outer layer of Reed-Solomon coding—so-called "concatenated coding" became a popular ECC scheme in the 1990s, and NASA adopted it for its deep-space missions. One slight difference between the concatenated coding used by the DAB+ system and that used on most other systems is that it uses a rectangular byte interleaver rather than Forney interleaving in order to provide a greater interleaver depth, which increases the distance over which error bursts will be spread out in the bitstream, which in turn will allow the Reed-Solomon error decoder to correct a higher proportion of errors.

The ECC used on DAB+ is far stronger than is used on DAB, which, with all else being equal (i.e. if the transmission powers remained the same), would translate into people who currently experience reception difficulties on DAB receiving a much more robust signal with DAB+ transmissions. It also has a far steeper "digital cliff", and listening tests have shown that people prefer this when the signal strength is low compared to the shallower digital cliff on DAB.

Modulation

Immunity to fading and inter-symbol interference (caused by multipath propagation) is achieved without equalization by means of the OFDM and DQPSK modulation techniques.

Using values for the most commonly used transmission mode on DAB, Transmission Mode I (TM I), the OFDM modulation consists of 1,536 subcarriers that are transmitted in parallel. The useful part of the OFDM symbol period is 1 millisecond, which results in the OFDM subcarriers each having a bandwidth of 1 kHz due to the inverse relationship between these two parameters, and the overall OFDM channel bandwidth is 1,537 kHz. The OFDM guard interval for TM I is 246 microseconds, which means that the overall OFDM symbol duration is 1.246 milliseconds. The guard interval duration also determines the maximum separation between transmitters that are part of the same single-frequency network (SFN), which is approximately 74 km for TM I.

Single-Frequency Networks

OFDM allows the use of single-frequency networks (SFN), which means that a network of transmitters can provide coverage to a large area up to the size of a country—where all transmitters use the same transmission frequency. Transmitters that are part of an SFN need to be very accurately synchronized with other transmitters in the network, which requires the transmitters to use very accurate clocks.

When a receiver receives a signal that has been transmitted from the different transmitters that are part of an SFN, the signals from the different transmitters will typically have different delays, but to OFDM they will appear to simply be different multipaths of the same signal. Reception difficulties can arise, however, when the relative delay of multipaths exceeds the OFDM guard interval duration, and there are frequent reports of reception difficulties due to this issue when there is a *lift*, such as when there is high pressure, due to signals travelling farther than usual, and thus the signals are likely to arrive with a relative delay that is greater than the OFDM guard interval.

Low power *gap-filler* transmitters can be added to an SFN as and when desired in order to improve reception quality, although the way SFNs have been implemented in the UK up to now they have tended to consist of higher power transmitters being installed at main transmitter sites in order to keep costs down.

Bit Rates

An ensemble has a maximum bit rate that can be carried, but this depends on which error protection level is used. However, all DAB multiplexes can carry a total of 864 "capacity units." The number of capacity units, or CU, that a certain bit-rate level requires depends on the amount of error correction added to the transmission, as described above. In the UK, most services transmit using 'protection level three', which provides an average ECC code rate of approximately ½, equating to a maximum bit-rate per multiplex of 1184 kbit/s.

Services and Ensembles

Various different services are embedded into one ensemble (which is also typically called a multiplex). These services can include:

- Primary services, like main radio stations
- Secondary services, like additional sports commentaries
- Data services
- Electronic programmeme Guide (EPG)
  - Collections of HTML pages and digital images (Known as 'Broadcast Web Sites')
  - Slideshows, which may be synchronized with audio broadcasts
  - Video
  - Java Platform Applications

- IP tunnelling
- Other raw data

DAB and DMB

Eureka 147 provides the infrastructure for several DAB versions.

DAB+

World DMB, the organization in charge of the DAB standards, announced a major non-backwardly compatible upgrade to the Eureka 147 system in 2006 when the HE-AAC v2 audio codec (also known as AAC+) was adopted. The new standard, which is called DAB+, has also adopted the MPEG Surround audio format and stronger error correction coding in the form of Reed-Solomon coding. DAB+ has been standardized as ETSI TS 102 563.

As DAB+ is not backwards-compatible ordinary DAB receivers cannot receive DAB+ broadcasts. However, DAB receivers that will be able to receive the new DAB+ standard via a firmware upgrade went on sale in July 2007. If a receiver is DAB+-upgradeable there will be a sign on the product itself or in the literature for the product, but the vast majority of receivers on sale do not support DAB+ yet.

DAB+ broadcasts have already launched in Italy, and several other countries are also expected to launch DAB+ broadcasts over the next few years, such as Switzerland, Malta and Hungary in 2008, Australia on 1 January 2009, Germany in 2009. When DAB+ stations launch in the UK, Norway and Denmark, they will transmit alongside existing DAB stations that use the old MPEG-1 Audio Layer II audio format, and most existing DAB stations are expected to continue broadcasting until the vast majority of receivers support DAB+, at which point stations using the old DAB format will be switched off. There is also a great deal of interest in using DAB+ in Asian countries, such as China. Read Regional implementations of DAB for details.

DMB

DAB-related standards Digital Multimedia Broadcasting (DMB) and DAB-IP are suitable for mobile radio and TV both because they support MPEG 4 AVC and WMV9 respectively as video codecs. However, a DMB video subchannel can easily be added to any DAB transmission—as DMB was designed from the outset to be carried on a DAB subchannel. DMB broadcasts in Korea carry conventional MPEG 1 Layer II DAB audio services alongside their DMB video services.

Regional Implementations of DAB

More than 20 countries provide DAB broadcasts, either as a permanent technology or as test transmissions. The UK, along with Denmark, Norway, Belgium, Switzerland and South-Korea maintain a growing base of DAB listeners.

Bibliography

(2006-05). "*Going Around with Bluetooth in Full Safety*" (PDF). F-Secure. Retrieved on 2008-02-04.

(2006-08-03). "*Simple Pairing Whitepaper*" (PDF). Version V10r00. Bluetooth SIG. Retrieved on 2007-02-01.

"802.11 X Wireless Network in a Business Environment—Pros and Cons.". NetworkBits.net. Retrieved on 2008-04-08.

"802.11n Delivers Better Range." *Wi-Fi Planet* (2007-05-31).

"About the Bluetooth SIG." *Bluetooth SIG*. Retrieved on 2008-02-01.

"ARRLWeb: Part 97—*Amateur Radio Service*." American Radio Relay League.

"As DVD Sales Fast-Forward, Retailers Reduce VHS Stock."

"*Authorization of Spread Spectrum Systems Under Parts* 15 and 90 of the FCC Rules and Regulations" (TXT). Federal Communications Commission (June 18, 1985). Retrieved on 2007-08-31.

"*BBC R&D White Paper WHP* 061 June 2003, DAB:An introduction to the EUREKA DAB System and a guide to how it works." Retrieved on 2007-05-08.

"Bezdrátové pøipojení k internetu." bezdratovepripojeni.cz. Retrieved on 2008-05-18.

"Big Easy Gets Free Wi-Fi Network." crn.com. Retrieved on 2008-04-14.

"BlueBug." Trifinite.org. Retrieved on 2007-02-01.

"Bluetooth." The Bunker. Retrieved on 2007-02-01.

"Canon to Stop Making Single-Lens Camera" Associated Press, 25 May 2006. Retrieved 2 September 2006.

"Channel Deployment Issues for 2.4 GHz 802.11 WLANs." Cisco Systems, Inc. Retrieved on 2007-02-07.

"CIE article on embedded WiFi for M2M applications." Retrieved on 2008-08-27.

"Cuadro nacional de Atribución de Frecuencias CNAF." Secretaría de Estado de Telecomunicaciones. Retrieved on 2008-03-05.

"DCI Cinema Specification v1.2."

"Death of video recorder in sight."

"Decca Developed FFRR Frequency Series"—History of Vinyl.

"Digital movie in Malayalam released", The Hindu (2006-08-19). Retrieved on 2006-08-23.

"DOWN THE LINE; LIGHT RAIL'S FIRST DAY; Getting off on the right track"; Star Tribune, June 27, 2004.

"EarthLink What a Disapointment." ccwifinews.com. Retrieved on 2008-04-14.

"Electromagnetic fields (EMF)." World Health Organization. Retrieved on 2008-01-22. "Electromagnetic fields of all frequencies represent one of the most common and fastest growing environmental influences, about which anxiety and speculation are spreading. All populations are now exposed to varying degrees of EMF, and the levels will continue to increase as technology advances."

"Enabling the Future of Wi-Fi® Public Access." Wi-Fi.org. Retrieved on 2007-08-31.

"Ermanno Pietrosemoli has set a new record for the longest communication Wi-Fi link." Retrieved on 2008-03-10.

"Estimated number of wi-fi spots globally." Retrieved on 2005-05-28.

"Europe's Broadcast Flag." Electronic Frontier Foundation (2005-09-29). Retrieved on 2007-08-15.

"F-Secure Malware Information Pages: Lasco. A." F-Secure.com. Retrieved on 2008-05-05.

"Health Protection Agency announces further research into use of WiFi." Health Protection Agency. Retrieved on 2008-08-28.

"How Bluetooth Technology Works." Bluetooth SIG. Retrieved on 2008-02-01.

"HTC TyTN Specification" (PDF). HTC. Retrieved on 2008-02-04.

"Image Clarity—High Resolution Photography" by John B. Williams, Focal Press 1990.

"Long Distance Snarf." Trifinite.org. Retrieved on 2007-02-01.

"Long Distance WiFi Trial." Retrieved on 2008-03-10.

"Magnetic Tape Used by RCA to Photograph Television Programme," The Wall Street Journal, Dec. 2, 1953, p. 1.

"MuniWireless » City Initiatives Directory." www.muniwireless.com. Retrieved on 2008-03-12.

"NATO Digital Cinema Requirements v2.0."

"Network Protection Technologies." Changes to Functionality in Microsoft Windows XP Service Pack 2. Microsoft Technet. Retrieved on 2008-02-01.

"New Deal on TV Seen at Parley," New York Times, May 1, 1953, p. 30.

"Official IEEE 802.11 working group project timelines" (2007-11-15). Retrieved on 2007-11-18.

"Phone pirates in seek and steal mission", Cambridge Evening News. Retrieved on 2008-02-04. Archived from the original on 2007-07-17.

"Quatech Rolls Out Airborne Embedded 802.11 Radio for M2M Market." Retrieved on 2008-04-29.

"Rechnernetze—The DECT Standard." (a summary of the DECT standard)

"Så ska Bluetooth överleva 10 år till." Ny Teknik. Retrieved on 2008-02-27.

"Securing Wi-Fi Networks with Today's Technologies." Wi-Fi.org. Retrieved on 2007-08-31.

"Specification Documents." Bluetooth SIG. Retrieved on 2008-02-04.

"Sunnyvale Uses MetroFi." unstrung.com. Retrieved on 2008-07-16.

"Switch on for Square Mile wi-fi." news.bbc.co.uk. Retrieved on 2007-11-08.

"Tape Recording Used by Filmless 'Camera'," New York Times, Nov. 12, 1951, p. 21. Eric D. Daniel, C. Denis Mee, and Mark H. Clark (eds.), Magnetic Recording: The First 100 Years, IEEE Press, 1998, p. 141.

"Tape-Recorded TV Nears Perfection," New York Times, Dec. 31, 1952, p. 10.

"The Bluetooth Blues", Information Age (2001-05-24). Retrieved on 2008-02-01.

"The Genesis of Unlicensed Wireless Policy." George Mason University (April 4, 2008). Retrieved on 2008-04-20.

"Update: EarthLink selected for Philadelphia Wi-Fi network." InfoWorld. Retrieved on 2008-04-14.

"Wal-Mart said to stop selling VHS."

"What is bluejacking?". Helsinki University of Technology. Retrieved on 2008-05-01.

"What is the True Meaning of Wi-Fi?". Teleclick. Retrieved on 2007-08-31.

"Wi-Fi Alliance—Certified Products." certifications.wi-fi.org. Retrieved on 2007-11-08.

"Wi-Fi Alliance—Get to Know the Alliance." www.wi-fi.org. Retrieved on 2007-11-08.

"Wi-Fi Finder." jiwire.com. Retrieved on 2008-04-20.

"Wi-fi health fears are 'unproven'", BBC News, BBC (2007-05-21). Retrieved on 2008-01-22.

"WiFi isn't short for Wireless Fidelity." boingboing.net. Retrieved on 2007-08-31.

"WiFi Summary". Health Protection Agency. Retrieved on 2008-01-22.

"Wi-Fi: Poskytovatelé bezdrátového pøipojení." internetprovsechny.cz. Retrieved on 2008-03-17.

"Wi-fi: should we be worried?", The Times. Retrieved on 2007-09-16. "All the expert reviews done here and abroad indicate that there is unlikely to be a health risk from wireless networks. ... When we have conducted measurements in schools, typical exposures from WiFi are around 20 millionths of the international guideline levels of exposure to radiation. As a comparison, a child on a mobile phone receives up to 50 per cent of guideline levels. So a year sitting in a classroom near a wireless network is roughly equivalent to 20 minutes on a mobile. If WiFi should be taken out of schools, then the mobile phone network should be shut down, too—and FM radio and TV, as the strength of their signals is similar to that from WiFi in classrooms."

"Wii Controller." Bluetooth SIG. Retrieved on 2008-02-01.

"Wireless Fidelity' Debunked." Wi-Fi Planet. Retrieved on 2007-08-31.

"Wireless technology is irreplaceable for providing access in remote and scarcely populated regions." Retrieved on 2008-03-10.

"Wireless Vulnerabilities & Exploits." wirelessve.org. Retrieved on 2008-04-15.

A New History of Photography" Könemann Verlagsgesellschaft/Michel Frizot 1998.

Alan Taylor. We, the media...", The Hollywood Representation of News Broadcasting, 1976-1999, Peter Lang, 2005, pp. 418.

American Cinema Editors—"2004 Oscar Nominees Discuss their Craft at the Egyptian Theater."

American Federation of Musicians. Cf. History—1927, 1928.

Ampex Corporation, Ampex Chronology.

Andreas Becker (2007-08-16). "Bluetooth Security & Hacks" (PDF). Ruhr-Universität Bochum. Retrieved on 2007-10-10.

Apple (2002-07-17). "Apple Introduces "Jaguar," the Next Major Release of Mac OS X." Press release. Retrieved on 2008-02-04.

Baker, Burton H. (2000), The Gray Matter: The Forgotten Story of the Telephone, Telepress, St. Joseph, MI, 2000.

Barnouw Erik. The Golden Web (Oxford University Press, 1968); The Sponsor (1978); A Tower in Babel (1966).

BlueZ—Official Linux Bluetooth protocol stack.

Bob Atkins. Size Matters. Photo.Net Equipment Article, 2003.

Bollywood Trade News Network (2007-10-15). "DG2L and UFO digitalize cinemas in Europe!", Yahoo! India Movies. Retrieved on 2007-10-15.

Book: Cordless Telecommunications Worldwide, pub Springer 1996, ed WHW Tuttlebee.

Book: Personal Wireless Communication with DECT and PWT, pub Artech 1998, J Philips & G MacNamee.

Briggs Asa. The BBC—the First Fifty Years (Oxford University Press, 1984).

Briggs Asa. The History of Broadcasting in the United Kingdom (Oxford University Press, 1961).

Broadcasting—News—Ofcom reveals DAB sound quality opinions—Digital Spy.

Bruce, Robert V. (1990), Alexander Graham Bell and the Conquest of Solitude, Cornell University Press, Ithaca, 1990.

City-wide wi-fi rolls out in UK.

Clive Bell. http://www.csulb.edu/~jvancamp/361r13.html "Art"], 1914. Retrieved 2 September 2006.

Coe, Lewis (1995), The Telephone and Its Several Inventors: A History, McFarland, North Carolina, 1995.

Covert Cathy, and Stevens John L. Mass Media Between the Wars (Syracuse University Press, 1984).

Current.org Popcorn available with this Ira Glass show, 2008.

DAB Around the World.

Daniel *et al.*, p. 148. BCE was acquired by 3M Company in 1956.

David Trottier (1998). The Screenwriter's Bible: A Complete Guide to Writing, Formatting, and Selling Your Script. Silman-James Press.

Dean M. Chriss. RAW Facts: The short life of today's RAW files: Demystifying the Debacle. DMCPhoto online article, April 29, 2005.

DECT Web: DECT/GSM DUAL MODE and the advent of the ONEPHONE SERVICE.

Digital Camera Sensor Sizes. Cambridge in Colour. Retrieved on 2007-10-14.

Digital Video Broadcasting (DVB); A Guideline for the Use of DVB Specifications and Standards" (PDF). Retrieved on 2008-08-30.

Dmytryk, Edward. On Film Editing: An Introduction to the Art of Film Construction, Boston: Focal Press, 1984.

Douglas B. Craig. Fireside Politics: Radio and Political Culture in the United States, 1920-1940 (2005).

DUO—Digital utgivelse ved Universitetet i Oslo—Lydkvalitetet i DAB digitalradio.

Ed Reitan, RCA-NBC Firsts in Colour Television (commented).

ETSI: ETR 341: Radio Equipment and Systems (RES) DECT/GSM Internetworking Overview.

Evenson, A. Edward (2000), The Telephone Patent Conspiracy of 1876: The Elisha Gray—Alexander Bell Controversy, McFarland, North Carolina, 2000.

Ewbank Henry and Lawton Sherman P. Broadcasting: Radio and Television (Harper & Brothers, 1952).

F. Leslie Smith, John W. Wright II, David H. Ostroff; Perspectives on Radio and Television: Telecommunication in the United States Lawrence Erlbaum Associates, 1998.

Ford-Long Wong, Frank Stajano, Jolyon Clulow (2005-04). "Repairing the Bluetooth pairing protocol" (PDF). University of Cambridge Computer Laboratory. Retrieved on 2007-02-01.

Fowler, Charles B. (October 1967), "The Museum of Music: A History of Mechanical Instruments," Music Educators Journal 54(2): 45-49.

Frazer, Bryant. Animating a Personal Flash Epic. Studio Daily. May 22 2008. Accessed on: May 22, 2008.

Freeman Patterson, Photography and The Art of Seeing, 1989, Key Porter Books.

Friends of Radio 3 (FoR3) BBC & R3 News.

Friends of Radio 3 (FoR3) Campaign Update.

Gaisberg, Frederick W., "The Music Goes Round", [Andrew Farkas, editor.], New Haven, Ayer, 1977.

Garcia Villegas, E. *et al.* (2007), "Effect of adjacent-channel interference in IEEE 802.11 WLANs", CrownCom 2007, ICST & IEEE.

Gibson George H. Public Broadcasting; The Role of the Federal Government, 1919-1976 (Praeger Publishers, 1977).

Gronow, Pekka, "The Record Industry: The Growth of a Mass Medium", Popular Music, Vol. 3, Producers and Markets (1983), pp. 53-75, Cambridge University Press.

Gronow, Pekka, and Saunio, Ilpo, "An International History of the Recording Industry", [translated from the Finnish by Christopher Moseley], London ; New York : Cassell, 1998.

Guy Kewney (2004-11-16). "High speed Bluetooth comes a step closer: enhanced data rate approved." Newswireless.net. Retrieved on 2008-02-04.

Gwenyth L. Jackaway; Media at War: Radio's Challenge to the Newspapers, 1924-1939 Praeger Publishers, 1995.

Hong Kong is entering a new era of digital broadcasting.

How Bluetooth got its name.

http://cr.yp.to/djbdns/forgery.html (first sentence).

http://worlddab.org/pdf/DAB+brochure.pdf

http://www.digitalradiotech.co.uk/documents/DRDB_UK_DAB+_policy.pdf

http://www.ofcom.org.uk/radio/ifi/rbl/dcr/applications/app_national/4digital.pdf

http://www.worlddab.org/upload/uploaddocs/WorldDMBPress%20 Release_November.pdf

Huurdeman, Anton A. (2003), The Worldwide History of Telecommunications, IEEE Press and J. Wiley & Sons, 2003.

Introduction to Bluetooth.

Jami Bernard (1995). Quentin Tarantino: The Man and His Movies. HarperCollins Publishers.

Jody Rosen (March 27, 2008). "Researchers Play Tune Recorded Before Edison", New York Times.

John Bellamy. Digital Telephony (3rd Edition, 2000).

John Dunning; On the Air: The Encyclopedia of Old-Time Radio, Oxford University Press, 1998.

John Oates (2004-06-15). "Virus attacks mobiles via Bluetooth," The Register. Retrieved on 2007-02-01.

Josephson, Matthew (1992), Edison: A Biography, Wiley, 1992.

Judith H. Haag, Hillis R. Cole (1980). The Complete Guide to Standard Script Formats: The Screenplay. CMC Publishing.

Juha T. Vainio (2000-05-25). "Bluetooth Security." Helsinki University of Technology. Archived from the original on 2006-05-19. Retrieved on 2008-02-04.

JVC (March 22, 1998). "Great Success for JVC ILA Projector in West End." Press release. Retrieved on 2007-08-30.

Kahn Frank J., ed. Documents of American Broadcasting, fourth edition (Prentice-Hall, Inc., 1984).

Kewney, Guy (2006-11-25). "Mast debaters strike again, ban Wi-Fi in UK schools." The Register. Retrieved on 2008-01-23.

Lazarsfeld Paul F. The People Look at Radio (University of North Carolina Press, 1946).

Levitt, B. Blake (1995). Electromagnetic Fields. San Diego: Harcourt Brace & Company, 29-38.

Lichty Lawrence W. and Topping Malachi C. eds. American Broadcasting: A Source Book on the History of Radio and Television (Hastings House, 1975).

Lipman, Samuel,"The House of Music: Art in an Era of Institutions", 1984. See the chapter on "Getting on Record", pp. 62-75, about the early record industry and Fred Gaisberg and Walter Legge and FFRR (Full Frequency Range Recording).

Looking for 802.11g Wireless Internet Access information, definitions and technology descriptions?

M. Hietanen, T. Alanko (2005-10). "Occupational Exposure Related to Radiofrequency Fields from Wireless Communication Systems" (PDF). XXVIIIth General Assembly of URSI—Proceedings. Union Radio-Scientifique Internationale. Retrieved on 2007-04-19.

Maclaurin W. Rupert. Invention and Innovation in the Radio Industry (The Macmillan Company, 1949).

Maxfield, J. P. and H. C. Harrison. Methods of high quality recording and reproduction of speech based on telephone research. Bell System Technical Journal, July 1926, 493-523.

Michael Oryl (2007-03-15). "Bluetooth 2.1 Offers Touch Based Pairing, Reduced Power Consumption", MobileBurn. Retrieved on 2008-02-04.

Millard, Andre J., "From Edison to the iPod", UAB Reporter, 2005, University of Alabama at Birmingham.

Millard, Andre J., "America on record : a history of recorded sound", Cambridge; New York: Cambridge University Press, 1995.

Murch, Walter. In the Blink of an Eye: a Perspective on Film Editing, Silman-James Press, 2nd rev. ed., 2001.

Newton, Harold (2007). Newton's telecom dictionary. New York: Flatiron Publishing.

Nicholas J. Wade, Stanley Finger (2001), "The eye as an optical instrument: from camera obscura to Helmholtz's perspective", Perception 30 (10), p. 1157-1177.

NoCat's goal is to bring you Infinite Bandwidth Everywhere for Free

Nokia (2007-06-12). "Wibree forum merges with Bluetooth SIG" (PDF). Press release. Retrieved on 2008-02-04.

OFCOM: Regulation in digital broadcasting: DAB digital radio bitrates and audio quality; Dynamic range compression and loudness.

Peers Frank W. The Politics of Canadian Broadcasting, 1920—1951 (University of Toronto Press, 1969).

Powell, James R., Jr. The Audiophile's Guide to 78 rpm, Transcription, and Microgroove Recordings. Gramophone Adventures, Portage, MI.

PRI.ORG. This American Life—Live!

Ray William B. FCC: The Ups and Downs of Radio-TV Regulation (Iowa State University Press, 1990).

Release: New High Efficiency Audio Option Added for DAB Digital Radio.

Robert W. McChesney; Telecommunications, Mass Media, and Democracy: The Battle for the Control of U.S. Broadcasting, 1928-1935 Oxford University Press, 1994.

Rosen Philip T. The Modern Stentors; Radio Broadcasting and the Federal Government 1920-1934 (Greenwood Press, 1980).

Scannell, Paddy, Cardiff, and David. *A Social History of British Broadcasting,* Volume One, 1922-1939 (Basil Blackwell, 1991).

Schramm Wilbur, ed. Mass Communications (University of Illinois Press, 1960).

Schwoch James. The American Radio Industry and Its Latin American Activities, 1900-1939 (University of Illinois Press, 1990).

Seashore, Carl Emil, "Psychology of Music", New York, London, McGraw-Hill Book Company, Inc., 1938.

See the wikinews article mentioned in this section.

Sprint, Clearwire Near WiMax Deal—TheStreet.com.

Stallings, William. (2005). Wireless communications and networks. Upper Saddle River, NJ: Pearson Prentice Hall.

Sterling Christopher H. Electronic Media, A Guide to Trends in Broadcasting and Newer Technologies 1920-1983 (Praeger, 1984).

Sterling Christopher, and Kittross John M. Stay Tuned: A Concise History of American Broadcasting (Wadsworth, 1978).

Stewart Brand. Escaping the Digital Dark Age. Library Journal Vol. 124. Issue 2, pp. 46-49, June 20, 2003.

Stewart Wolpin, The Race to Video, Invention and Technology, Fall 1994.

Taoufik Ghanname (2007-02-14), Wireless Net DesignLine. Retrieved on 2008-02-04.

Teun Koetsier (2001). "On the prehistory of programmable machines: musical automata, looms, calculators", Mechanism and Machine Theory 36, p. 590-591.

The Digital Dilemma. Strategic issues in archiving and accessing digital motion picture materials, Academy of Motion Picture Arts and Sciences, 2007.

The Oxford Companion to the Photograph, ed. by Robin Lenman, Oxford University Press 2005.

TI (2007-10-19). "DLP Cinema® Technology Surpasses 5,000 Screen Milestone", DCinematoday.com. Retrieved on 2007-10-19.

Tim Crook, International Radio Journalism: History, Theory and Practice Routledge, 1998.

Tom Ang (2002). Dictionary of Photography and Digital Imaging: The Essential Reference for the Modern Photographer. Watson-Guptill.

Tom McCourt; Conflicting Communication Interests in America: The Case of National Public Radio Praeger Publishers, 1999.

White Llewellyn. The American Radio (University of Chicago Press, 1947).

White-Smith Music Pub. Co. v. Apollo Co., 209 U.S. 1 (1908).

William A. Rugh; Arab Mass Media: Newspapers, Radio, and Television in Arab Politics Praeger, 2004.

Wilson, Tracy V. "How Municipal WiFi Works." computer.howstuff works.com. Retrieved on 2008-03-12.

World DMB forums list of benefits.

Yaniv Shaked, Avishai Wool (2005-05-02). "Cracking the Bluetooth PIN." School of Electrical Engineering Systems, Tel Aviv University. Retrieved on 2007-02-01.

Yves Lavandier (2005). Writing Drama, A Comprehensive Guide for Playwrights and Scritpwriters. Le Clown & l'Enfant.

Website Links

"http://en.wikibooks.org/wiki/Movie_Making_Manual/Production_Overview"

"http://en.wikibooks.org/wiki/Movie_Making_Manual-Currently_Untitled_Studio_(Pre-production)"

"http://en.wikipedia.org/wiki/Broadcasting"

"http://en.wikipedia.org/wiki/Digital_cinema"

"http://en.wikipedia.org/wiki/Digital_cinematography"

"http://en.wikipedia.org/wiki/Digital_telephony"

"http://en.wikipedia.org/wiki/Digital_versus_film_photography"

"http://en.wikipedia.org/wiki/Documentary_photography"

"http://en.wikipedia.org/wiki/IEEE_802.11"
"http://en.wikipedia.org/wiki/Post-production"
"http://en.wikipedia.org/wiki/Sound_recording_and_reproduction"
"http://en.wikipedia.org/wiki/Telephony"
"http://en.wikipedia.org/wiki/Wireless_electronic_devices_and_health"
"http://en.wikipedia.org/wiki/Wireless"
"http://en.wikiversity.org/wiki/LessonPage:Film_scoring:Introduction"
"http://en.wikibooks.org/wiki/Movie_Making_Manual/Blocking"

Index